Race and Reconciliation
in South Africa

Border Crossings: Toward a Comparative Political Theory, edited by Fred Dallmayr

Race and Reconciliation in South Africa: A Multicultural Dialogue in Comparative Perspective, edited by William E. Van Vugt and G. Daan Cloete

Gandhi, Freedom, and Self-Rule, edited by Anthony J. Parel

Race and Reconciliation in South Africa

A Multicultural Dialogue in Comparative Perspective

Edited by William E. Van Vugt
and G. Daan Cloete

LEXINGTON BOOKS
Lanham • Boulder • New York • Oxford

LEXINGTON BOOKS

Published in the United States of America
by Lexington Books
4720 Boston Way, Lanham, Maryland 20706

12 Hid's Copse Road, Cumnor Hill, Oxford OX2 9JJ, England

British Library Cataloging in Publication Information Available

Library of Congress Cataloging-in-Publication Data

Race and reconciliation in South Africa : a multicultural dialogue in comparative perspective / edited by William E. Van Vugt and G. Daan Cloete.
    p. cm. — (Global encounters)
  Includes bibliographical references and index.
    ISBN 0-7391-0142-0 (cloth : alk. paper)—ISBN 0-7391-0157-9 (pbk : alk. paper)
    1. South Africa—Race relations. 2. Race relations—Religious aspects—
  Christianity. 3. South Africa—Church history. I. Van Vugt, William E., 1957- II.
  Cloete, G. Daan. III. Series.
DT1756 .R33 2000
261.8'348'00968—dc21
                                                  00-028743
Printed in the United States of America

For the members of the Truth and Reconciliation Commission

Contents

Foreword

I AM PLEASED to write the foreword for this book, which resulted from a conference at the University of the Western Cape of which I have been chancellor for ten years. The essays in this book reflect a wide range of topics, all of which elucidate our understanding of race and reconciliation in South Africa.

My experiences as chairperson of the Truth and Reconciliation Commission were both painful and hopeful. Even though we have a long way to go to achieve justice and true reconciliation, it is my belief that through a better understanding of racism and injustice in South Africa—and a better understanding of what South Africans have achieved in the past several years—we can approach the future with hope and the determination that all our people will live in peace and harmony.

This book makes a contribution to that understanding, and I thank William Van Vugt, Daan Cloete, and the other contributors for their work.

Desmond Tutu
Archbishop Emeritus

Acknowledgments

THIS PROJECT WAS funded by a grant from the Calvin Center for Christian Scholarship. We thank the Governing Board for its advice and support and Ronald A. Wells, who with this project completes nine distinguished years as director, for his vision and encouragement. Program coordinator Donna Romanowski assisted with organizing the project and, with staff assistants Amy Bergsma and Lynn Vander Wal, helped prepare the manuscript for publication. Mike Buma assisted with proofreading and preparing endnotes. We also thank the University of the Western Cape, in Bellville, South Africa, for providing its facilities and resources to make this project possible.

William E. Van Vugt
G. Daan Cloete

Introduction

IN JANUARY 1999 scholars from Europe, North America, and Africa assembled at the University of the Western Cape (UWC) for a conference on race and reconciliation in South Africa. The conference was inspired by the collapse of apartheid in 1994, Nelson Mandela's rise to the presidency, and the formation of the Truth and Reconciliation Commission (TRC), which has now revealed to the world some of the awful reality of the apartheid era. While the TRC sought truth as a basis for racial reconciliation in South Africa, the conference at the UWC sought to create a multicultural, scholarly dialogue on the history, theology, philosophy, and politics of race and reconciliation in South Africa. Our aim was to enhance our understanding of South Africa's past and the important issues that the new South Africa faces in the future. This book is the product of that conference.

The authors have used a comparative perspective, using examples from other nations and cultures to explore what is distinctive about South Africa. Such an approach is especially fruitful for the study of South Africa, as a number of important books have demonstrated.[1] Daan Cloete begins by analyzing St. Paul's letter to the Galatians to examine how ethnic differences divided Jews from Gentiles and how Paul's call for racial reconciliation has as much application for modern South Africa as it did for the ancient Mediterranean world. It is a sobering fact that Scripture was used to justify apartheid in South Africa. Cloete reviews how apartheid contradicts the Scriptures and reminds us that all South Africans must keep the true spirit of the Gospel in mind as the nation proceeds with reconciliation.

For over one hundred years much of South Africa was part of the British Empire, so it is not surprising that British people, institutions, and exploitation left a lasting impact on the country that deserves attention in any study of race and reconciliation in South Africa. William Van Vugt presents a history of British migration to South Africa within the comparative context of British migration to the United States to explore how British people and culture shaped the two nations in similar and yet different ways. Though far more Britons came to America than to South Africa, British immigrants still had a great impact on South Africa's economy, society, and racial attitudes and policies. Nevertheless, Van Vugt finds that the African environment and the Afrikaner population had their own effect on the immigrants and that their interaction explains much about nineteenth-century racial attitudes and subsequent policies. John De Gruchy continues the exploration of the British impact on South Africa by presenting a comparative history of the so-called English-speaking churches in

South Africa. In this insightful chapter De Gruchy outlines three phases of the churches' "chastening process": their loss of political power, their loss of ethnic domination, and their loss of moral innocence. Through both a recognition of the churches' loss of innocence in the history of race in South Africa and a spirit of penitence, De Gruchy sees much hope for renewal and reconciliation.

The United States and South Africa unfortunately share a long history of black oppression under systems that were similar in some ways, different in others. In his comparative study of the historical development of evangelical churches in the United States and South Africa, Drew Smith recounts how the churches in both nations dealt with racial separation in their practices and confessions and sees some striking parallels and differences. Smith also traces the limited move toward progressive racial politics and integration in the United States, the increase of segregation under apartheid in South Africa, and how South African liberals responded. Finally, Smith suggests how South Africa can learn from the American experience.

Tracy Kuperus, in her examination of religious associations in South Africa and Zimbabwe, shows that South Africa can also be better understood by comparing it to other African countries and how they relate to civil society and democracy. Though the two African nations share many similarities in their history and progression toward democratization, Kuperus points to the differences in their outcomes, the relative strength of South Africa's constitution and civil society, and how South Africa should be cautious and yet hopeful for the future.

Of course, any book on race and reconciliation in South Africa must consider the Afrikaners, their culture, and how they have shaped the nation. Being the first white settlers in southern Africa, most Afrikaners lived under British authority more or less from 1806 until the Union of South Africa was formed in 1910 and then took complete control when the National Party formed a government in 1948 and established apartheid. The Dutch Reformed Church (DRC) was instrumental in shaping South African social policy in the twentieth century, and Russel Botman provides a black perspective on the DRC's historical relationship with apartheid. By reviewing the main theological statements that condemned apartheid—including the Cotteslow Statement of 1960, the Belhar Confession of 1982, and the Kairos Document of 1985—and the DRC's response, Botman sheds new light on the DRC's responsibility for apartheid. Botman then calls for the DRC to commit itself fully to a reconciling history, to support the Africanization of the church, and to commit itself to complete racial equality and integration.

The analysis of Afrikaner history and culture continues with Elaine Botha's comparison of the Free University of Amsterdam and the Potchefstroom University for Christian Higher Education. It is remarkable that both of these important institutions were based on a Reformed and Calvinist legacy, and yet developed very different positions on the issues of racial integration. Botha explains how and why Potchefstroom University defended apartheid for so long and addresses the issues about what a university's role ought to be in the process of reconciliation.

In 1996 South Africa replaced the interim constitution of 1993 with a new, liberal constitution that is understandably very "rights conscious" and supported by a constitutional court. Lourens du Plessis analyzes the constitution's bill of rights, which "preaches reconciliation," and addresses some of the important legal and moral questions that lie behind South Africa's quest for reconciliation. Du Plessis also explains what the constitution provides to enable South Africa to achieve "the optimally just society."

The term *multiculturalism* is being used more and more in the world these days, and too often without a clear understanding of its meaning and implications for society. In fact, there are disparate forms of multiculturalism. Distinguished philosopher Johan Degenaar takes us through the maze of different forms and understandings of multiculturalism, and presents "critical multiculturalism" as an effective way of coping with the challenges that South Africa and other nations face in this increasingly pluralistic world. By reflecting on the Zulu concept of *ubuntu*, Degenaar sees the multicultural situation in South Africa as "a wonderful opportunity to discover our humanness."

It is frequently said that, now that South Africa has performed the "political miracle" of democracy, it must also perform an "economic miracle" of greater prosperity and material equality. The truth of this statement is abundantly clear to any visitor to the country. With one of the most unequal income distributions in the world, South Africa still in effect suffers apartheid, as black poverty grinds against white riches. Lizo Jafta offers an African perspective on the impact that globalism and economic development are having on South African culture. He then calls for a program of economic empowerment that respects both economic freedom and African culture and that would bring about greater social justice.

It is fitting that this book ends with a moving account by the Reverend Pieter Meiring, member of the Truth and Reconciliation Commission. He shares what he and other commissioners experienced as persons confessed horrible crimes—often while the victims' families looked on—and received amnesty. Meiring also reminds us that the victims rightly continue to seek a restoration of human and civil dignity—what the Archbishop Desmond Tutu calls "restorative justice."

We hope that this book offers some better understanding of the depth of injustice in South Africa's past, but also a deeper appreciation for the achievement of the present and the promise of the future. Notwithstanding the very real problems and challenges that remain, South Africa could become a paradigm for the rest of the world where people must still learn to live in multiethnic peace and harmony. We pray that this may be so.

G. Daan Cloete
William Van Vugt
August 1999

Note

1. See, for example, George M. Fredrickson, *White Supremacy: A Comparative Study in American and South African History* (Oxford: Oxford University Press, 1981); Fredrickson, *Black Liberation: A Comparative History of Black Ideologies in the United States and South Africa* (Oxford University Press, 1995); Heribert Adam, Frederik Van Zyl Slabbert, and Koglia Moodley, *Comrades in Business: Post-Liberation Politics in South Africa* (Cape Town: Tafelberg, 1997).

Chapter One

South Africa and Paul's Letter to the Galatians: A Struggle with Ethnicity and Race

G. Daan Cloete

A DOMINANT FEATURE of South African history has been the problems of race and ethnicity and the repeated attempts to find solutions that would bring lasting peace and reconciliation. While the problem may have been present in the unrecorded history of this subcontinent, it was complicated and intensified by the arrival of western influence in the seventeenth century. Basic to the issue are two sociocultural and religious realities: (1) the reality of our cultural diversity in one country and (2) the reality of the religious disposition of the South African people. Since we now have embarked on the process of reconciliation in the post-Truth and Reconciliation Commission (post-TRC) period, it is clear that these two realities will continue to affect the future development of the country.

As far as sociocultural diversity is concerned, nobody can deny that this is a reality in South Africa. On the one hand, previous models for political solutions have absolutized this diversity to the extent of racial separation. Such models failed because of a number of misjudgments, such as not taking into consideration the measure of social integration that has already taken place, or the socioeconomic impact of such a policy, or the racial prejudice that inspired the approach. On the other hand, present models focus on nation-building and unity, but they may underestimate the tenacity of the diversity.

Within the broader context of the social world, the religious reality needs to be highlighted. When it is said that Africa is incurably religious, then it is true of South Africa too. The great majority of people are prepared to acknowledge their allegiance to one or another religion of which Christianity may have the strongest support. It is significant that in the history of seeking solutions for social problems, religious leadership has played a dominant role in both emphasizing diversity and promoting national unity.

In this chapter, I wish to revisit New Testament Christianity with a special focus on Paul's letter to the Galatians, which seems to reflect a crisis around similar issues in early Christianity. Although it was of a complex nature, the crisis reveals the tensions around race and ethnicity as the New Testament

Church struggled to integrate persons from multicultural backgrounds into one faith community. This and other similar struggles in early Christianity were perhaps insignificant events in their contexts, but their impact would eventually affect society in the centuries that followed and to a large extent influence the course of history. In focusing on that particular period, it is hoped that we may discover some common ground and develop some insights that will allow dialogue between early Christianity and our own situation in the post-TRC period in South Africa.

Of course, we have to realize that commensurability between ancient and modern cultures cannot readily be assumed. For example, questions are rightly being asked to what extent one can apply the theories and models developed by modern sociologists and anthropologists to ancient situations. Walters's comment in this respect is still very relevant, namely: "there are no social laws yet known which apply trans-historically to all society."[1] It seems that at this stage, one can go no further than to use some findings from the social sciences to assist in asking some meaningful questions about New Testament times. The problem may, however, also be rephrased more positively: Given that there may be some analogies between the situation in the New Testament era and our own context, perhaps the way that Paul dealt with a particular situation may present some directives to the understanding of our own situation. An additional problem is that in spite of exciting archaeological discoveries, there remains a paucity of evidence and limited sources of information that make it difficult to obtain proper access to an understanding of the ancient world. What is available should, therefore, be interpreted in a discrete manner in the hope of getting a glimpse of the dynamics at work during those times and in those contexts. It is with these premises in mind and with the consciousness of these constraints that I wish to cautiously read Paul's letter to the Galatians.

While it may be so that the primary focus of the New Testament documents is theological, it is also true that the sociocultural and ethnic circumstances within the Christian communities played a significant role in shaping these communities and in determining their nature. The sociocultural reality of the broader world behind the New Testament is complex and characterized by many contradictions and inequalities. In terms of human relationships, Leon Morris pictures the first-century society as one in which "the Jews despised the Gentiles (even proselytes were often not fully accepted), the Greeks looked down on uncultured people outside of their race, the Romans felt themselves superior to those they had conquered, and so on."[2] This suggests an underlying tempestuous atmosphere that prevailed during the period. Ethnic tensions seemed to have been characteristic even of that society in spite of the process of hellenization and the Pax Romana.[3] Both the tensions and the process of universal peace affected the development of Christianity. It is, therefore, not surprising also that the tense relationship between Jewish and Gentile Christians is a common underlying theme in most of the New Testament documents. Against the background of this relatively stable society, the new community, called the church, eventually emerged.

The nature of the conflicts among the different Christian groups in the congregations that Paul addresses in his different letters was usually very complicated, with tensions not only among the various communities, but also within the communities themselves. There obviously were many factors involved, but close scrutiny reveals that a major underlying factor was of an ethnic or racial nature. By ethnic is meant the cultural, religious, and other boundaries that define a particular group, the community's self-understanding, which is its beliefs, its cherished norms and values, its behavioral patterns, and its institutional structures. Racism is when these ethnic characteristics are used to boast, as well as to discriminate, to exploit, and to exclude those who do not necessarily share the same characteristics.[4] The complexity of the New Testament situation is illustrated in the documents of the New Testament itself. As F. F. Bruce puts it: "It is clear both from Paul's letters and from the record of Acts that the gospel principle of complete equality of Jew and Gentile before God was not accepted in the early church without a struggle."[5]

Raymond Brown identified four different developments in New Testament times as Christianity extended its influence beyond the borders of Palestine and into the Gentile world.[6] These were:

1. Gentile Christians who joined Jewish Christians in the same manner that Gentiles became Jews, namely, through proselytizing, which meant they observed the full law, including circumcision. This seems to have been the position of the so-called Judaistic Christians. Paul was particularly opposed to this.

2. Gentile Christians who joined Jewish Christians by adopting certain aspects of the law in the same manner that Gentiles took up a position of "god fearer" to Judaism. James and Peter probably took this position.

3. Jews and Gentiles who entered the new faith community on an equal basis, accepting that both were sinners and that, therefore, both received righteousness through faith without the law to enter the community. This was primarily the Pauline position.

4. Judaism was replaced by Jesus. This means that all the cultic practices and other particular characteristics of Judaism fell away totally, and a new religion started to emerge. This was probably the Johannine position.

Paul's letter to the Galatians reflects a complex situation in which it seems that the primary issue was the basic demand of the gospel in terms of its understanding in the particular sociocultural background. In what appears to be a predominantly Gentile setting, these Galatians became believers through the ministry of the apostle Paul along the lines of position three, that is, through faith in Jesus Christ with an ignorance about the law of Moses. A subsequent development that apparently happened under the pressures of Jewish Christians and in the absence of Paul, resulted in their switching to position one, that is, they allowed themselves to be subjected to the observance of the full Jewish law, including circumcision.

In his letter, written in a very dramatic style, Paul now attempts to persuade them to revert to the original position three. In his argument, Paul rejects the apparent claim of his opponents that position one guarantees righteousness, and he also suggests to the congregation that their submission to the false teachers is equal to returning to their pre-Christian life.

Various interesting questions emerge out of these developments behind and in the letter. First, what were the motifs by which the Jewish Christians insisted that the Gentile Christians observe the full law? Could any political or cultural sentiments have played a role? Bruce, in his commentary, remarks: "The cleavage between Jew and Gentile was for Judaism the most radical in the human race. It was indeed possible for a Gentile to become a Jewish proselyte: . . . But a Gentile who became a proselyte crossed over [to] the Jewish side of the gulf; the gulf remained."[7] Did the Jewish Christians, by insisting that these Gentile Christians become Jewish Christians, see in this an opportunity for Jews to "get back" at the oppressing political culture dominated by Gentiles?[8] Was Paul's "liberal" approach seen by Jewish Christians as an undermining of the solidarity that existed between the Jews and the Christians in the face of continued Roman repression? Or was it the sincere religious belief of Jewish Christians that this is the demand of the law and the prophets and that it cannot be ignored?

Second, what made the Galatians so compliant to the teachings of these false teachers (in the eyes of Paul)? Did it have anything to do with their own social position in the greater Roman Empire, in which they were not really accepted because of their particular history and background? Dieter Lührmann concludes that the Galatians were Gentiles to the Jews, and barbarians to the Romans.[9] Was this an action of solidarity with the Jews because of their own experiences of humiliation by the Romans? Or were they simply impressed by the discipline and ethical codes of Judaism since this was a paucity in their religion and culture and a vacuum in the gospel message of Paul? Another possibility could be that the Gentile Christians suffered persecution at the local level after embracing the gospel brought to them by Paul. The imperial cult seems to have prevailed in that area, which could have led to persecution of those who did not submit to it. But Judaism was a permitted religion. Therefore, it would have been a way out for Gentile Christians to become Jewish proselytes in order to escape persecution. In this way they could still keep their Christian identity. If this was the situation, it was nevertheless unacceptable for Paul.[10]

Third, why was Paul so outraged by this development? Being of Jewish background himself, Paul might be expected to be more complacent to these Gentile Christians becoming "Jewish" Christians. Was this to him simply an undermining of his authority as an apostle?[11] Or was it his sincere belief that the only lasting solution was to be found in a new religious direction, given his experiences in Jerusalem and Antioch?[12]

In reading the text, it is very interesting to follow Paul's understanding and interpretation of specific Old Testament themes like: What is the meaning of the law and how far does it extend? Was circumcision purely a religious ritual or does it also relate to ethnic identity? What does it mean to be a child of Abraham? What does oneness in Christ really mean (3:28)? Or what does being a new creation (6:15) mean?

A debate has been going on for a long time about which Galatians we are reading about in Paul's letter. This is the issue about the north and south Galatian theories, about the geographical location of the congregation(s). Usually the north Galatian hypothesis concerns the so-called ethnic Galatians. Bruce gives a historical and geographical overview of these people from their origin in the Danube Valley to their dispersion all over Europe in the first three centuries B.C.[13] From his analysis, it becomes evident that a core of these people settled in the region known as North Galatia; but one can readily accept that even the south included, and was perhaps dominated by, ethnic Galatians. One has to accept that most of the nations that made up the Roman Empire had a geographical base. For the Jews it was Judea or Palestine; for the Egyptians, Egypt; for the Syrians, Syria; for the Galatians it was Galatia. But it is also true that a significant component of each ethnic group lived in diaspora all over the empire. It means that the congregations that Paul addressed may not have been absolutely "pure" in the ethnic sense, even though his letter gives the general impression of a homogeneous group. For our purpose, we want to accept that whether one opts for the ethnic North Galatia or the provincial South Galatia, the dominant group in both positions were the ethnic Galatians.[14]

It is also clear that Paul was instrumental in establishing this congregation. In doing this, he had a particular style in evangelizing them, one that may have differed from the way that he approached Jews (1 Cor. 9:19-23). His approach seems to have been one in which he took into consideration their ignorance regarding the Old Testament history of salvation. Therefore, he did not put unnecessary demands on them about what the Law of Moses required. Faith in Jesus the Messiah sufficed to obtain righteousness. In this approach, Paul was confident that he was proclaiming to them the "true" gospel.

As has already been stated, one has to recognize that from the beginning of early Christianity, the issue of race and ethnicity was critical. The issues that Paul addresses in this letter have ethnic overtones and are brought about by ethnic tensions. Though the commission to the apostles was clear in terms of the extent to whom, or where, they should take the gospel (Matt. 28:16-20), there seems to have been an uncertainty on their part to execute it, as is clear from the example of Peter in Acts 10-11. Perhaps the apostles lacked an example since Jesus himself did not venture outside the boundaries of Palestine, but this can also be ascribed to some measure of inherent prejudice toward the non-Jews by these Jewish apostles. So the Jewish Christians, being the first bearers of the gospel, thought that perhaps it was the safest to follow the familiar approach, namely to invite those outside Judaism to accept Jesus as the Messiah and to bring them into Judaism. What apparently started off innocently became an obsession to some Jewish Christians and was strongly promoted in the congregations, such as Galatia in the absence of Paul. Although the promoters of this position could have come from Jewish members within the congregation, it appears to have been the result of a movement coming from outside. It is not impossible that there may have been a deliberate attempt to oppose Paul's liberal approach to the Gentiles. Cousar's view is that what was probably at stake was the standing these Jewish Christians sought to maintain within the Jewish community and the fear that in becoming Christians they would be ostracized from their own Jewish community. This is how he interprets "by compelling the circumcision of Gentile converts": They avoid persecution "for the cross of Christ." Being able to report progress in their work lessened the pressures and removed the harassment they would otherwise have experienced. One can only guess that the pressure on those Jewish Christian opponents came from militant, nationalistic Jews who resented the biracial character of the Christian community and thus promoted a missionary zeal for circumcision. If the Jewish Christians could show that they were making Jewish proselytes from among the Gentile converts to Christianity, then they no longer needed to fear their more ardent and exclusionistic compatriots.[15]

It is not impossible that the letter was the product of a very fundamental rethinking that Paul had done about the problems that Christianity had encountered, especially at the level of race, ethnicity, class, and gender. It is generally accepted that he continues this discussion in the letter to the Romans in a more rational manner. Although the letter is addressed to the Galatians, it is clear that he also had both the larger Jewish and the Christian audiences in view as is reflected in the choice of the concepts and topics.[16] Issues of race and ethnicity lie at a deeper structural level but are presented at the surface level in the theological concept of how to receive righteousness from God. The purpose of the letter is to take issue with the proponents of a homogeneous Judaistic Christianity on what the implications of the gospel are with regard to race, ethnicity, slavery, and gender.

It seems that Paul used the opportunity of the problems in the faith community of Galatia to put forward a well-structured argument to deal with this wider problem that Christianity has been struggling with from the moment that it extended its mission beyond the boundaries of Judaism.[17] Put in another way, the issue was how to deal with people from diverse sociocultural, economic, and religious backgrounds in order to integrate them into one community of faith, as the gospel seems to demand. It is not a new argument to say that the impact of this document together with others, like Paul's letter to the Romans, could have resulted in the change of direction of early Christianity away from Judaism toward the Gentiles.[18]

It seems that Paul made very significant statements at strategic places in the letter that persuaded his audience of the radical new direction the faith community had to take. These statements are contained in certain key texts that I now wish to concentrate on.

Levelling the Playing Fields between Jews and Gentiles

What is the basic demand for all people to receive righteousness from God? The answer is contained in the statement in Galatians 2:15-16. "We ourselves are Jews by birth, not Gentiles and sinners. But we know that no man is ever justified by doing what the law demands, but only through faith in Jesus Christ; so we too have put our faith in Jesus Christ so that we might be justified through this faith, and not through deeds dictated by law; for by such deeds, Scripture says, no mortal man shall be justified."

In these verses Paul interprets, in an almost cynical manner, the traditional relationships between Jews and Gentiles and suggests how that has changed in the light of the coming of Jesus Christ. Paul, himself a Jew, speaks here from the standpoint of a Jew's view about Gentiles, that is, all those who are outside Judaism. According to Paul's own perception, everybody not included in the covenant, are ipso facto (or by nature) sinners because the law was not entrusted to them, and circumcision was not demanded of them. Jews, however, are not sinners precisely because they are born directly into the unique covenantal relationship with God. Jews could become sinners through disobedience to the law and their unfaithfulness to God. This seems to be the main thrust of the statement: "Jews by birth and not sinners as Gentiles." Obviously Paul does not simply make a religious distinction between Jews and Gentiles here, but wants to address the basic perceptions, attitudes, and prejudices that exist. It is true that the statement in its religious sense indicates the exceptional privilege that Jews enjoyed over and against Gentiles through the covenantal relationship with God, but in this context of the tensions of Jewish and Gentile Christians' relationship, it exposes the self-boasting, self-righteousness, and superior attitude that Jews developed as a result of their privilege position.[19]

Paul interprets the Jewish attitude to mean that to obtain righteousness the law is absolutely essential. While Jesus can be recognized as the Messiah, faith in him does not take away the obligation to observe the law for righteousness. Similarly, while it is quite acceptable for Gentiles to believe in Jesus Christ, they also need the works of the law to receive righteousness. By reevaluating the situation, Paul wishes to deal simultaneously with these misconceptions and expose the hypocrisy behind it. He argues that the works of the law do not achieve righteousness for anybody (any flesh), which means not even for the Jews. In fact, these works, which are the requirements of the law, in effect become a curse because they do not achieve what they promise. The conclusion is that even Jews are not able to achieve righteousness through the law—they also need faith to obtain it. In this way Paul levels the playing fields between Jews and Gentiles in two ways: first, by stating that Jews in their inability to observe the law become equal to the Gentiles in their sinfulness and, second, because of this, Jews and Gentiles are now also equal in their need of faith for righteousness. In this way Paul also condemns the superior attitude that Jewish Christians showed toward the Gentile Christians.[20]

Rediscovering the Roots of Faith

Another possible argument of Paul's opponents could have been: What claim would Gentiles have to be called the children of Abraham if they do not honor the law? To respond to this question, it is important to focus on Galatians 3:6-9: "Look at Abraham: he put his faith in God and that faith was counted to him as righteousness. You may take it, then, that it is the men of faith who are Abraham's sons. And Scripture, foreseeing that God would justify the Gentiles through faith, declared the gospel to Abraham beforehand: 'In you all nations shall find blessing.' This is the men of faith who share blessing with faithful Abraham."

With these words Paul counters another false argument of the Jewish preachers—that their superiority was based on their genealogical and religious descent from Abraham. They probably argued that they were children of Abraham in two distinct manners, which cannot be separated. First, there is the genealogical aspect, which is not debated openly in the letter. Second, there is the covenantal aspect, which appears to be the primary issue here. Central to this is circumcision. But circumcision is included under the law by the false teachers even though circumcision dates back to the time of Abraham, 430 years before the law was given. This bringing of circumcision under the law by false teachers probably finds its ground in the fact that circumcision is reaffirmed in the law, especially during the time of Joshua (5:2 and further). Therefore, circumcision was necessary to qualify as a true child of Abraham. And by doing so, one is obedient to the law that is necessary for righteousness. The law was given as a distinguishing mark to the chosen nation, but they subsequently expanded it to include circumcision and made it a symbol of ethnic identity. They then claimed the circumcised Abraham as their father and themselves as his exclusive children.[21] In this way they reaffirmed their claim for biological descent from Abraham by their circumcision. To them the line between Jews and Gentiles was drawn when God called Abraham and made a promise to him and required that he be circumcised as a rite of that promise and covenant. Because circumcision was part of the law, it had to be upheld even in its symbolic meaning. Concretely, this meant that Gentiles who wished to have the status of children of Abraham had to become Jewish proselytes.

Abraham is an exceptionally authoritative person in the Bible, an example for the Jews and essential in their self-definition as the "seed" of Abraham and as the heirs of the promise made to him by God. Therefore, in order to counter this ethnic construction, Paul makes a very strong argument for what it really means to be a child of Abraham.[22] He does this by giving a particular interpretation of the history of salvation, of God's dealings with Abraham as narrated in the book of Genesis, the origin of Judaism. The chronology of events in Genesis is very important for Paul's argument, and, in his view, it developed as follows: The first step was when God called Abraham and made his promise to him that in him all the nations would be blessed (Gen. 12, 15). The second step followed after some time had elapsed when the promise was repeated and

Abraham was now only instructed to undergo circumcision (Gen. 17). The last step was 430 years later, when God gave the law to the people of Israel.

It is very interesting that Paul does not seem to oppose the false teachers with regard to their attachment of circumcision to the law, in spite of the long time span between them. Also interesting is that Paul seems to regard as very significant the fact that there appears to be a period of time between the first pronouncement of the promise and its later reaffirmation with the circumcision of Abraham. To him, this means that the promise was made to Abraham when he was still a "Gentile," when all nations were still "Gentiles," when there was no circumcision, and when they were not yet an elect people of God. This allows him to put the law, including circumcision, over and against the promise to Abraham.[23]

The promise without circumcision receives precedence with Paul because it is inclusive of all the nations. The fact that Abraham believed God is to Paul the significant aspect of the promise, not the circumcision. It means that Abraham trusted God's promise and this trust was already interpreted in the Old Testament as an act of faith.

Another essential aspect in Paul's argument is the fact that this promise found its fulfilment in Jesus Christ, who is the one seed of whom the promise actually spoke. What it means is that Abraham believed, in anticipation of Christ's coming as the fulfilment of the promise made to him. The promise is in fact a pre-preaching of the gospel. In this way, the believing Abraham becomes the father and prototype of all believers. This again underlines that faith and not circumcision is the determining feature of this promise. To become a child of Abraham is not in the first instance to have been circumcised but to have faith. By arguing that faith and not the law is the supreme characteristic of the people of God even in the Old Testament, Paul indicates that the basis to becoming a child of Abraham is the same in the old and the new covenants. He also interprets the covenant with Abraham to be inclusive of Jews and Gentiles since it is based on faith. Paul's opponents wish to draw the proclamation of the gospel into the racial framework of Judaism, and Paul wishes to argue for the transcendence of the gospel message beyond the racial sphere and categories in which his opponents want to keep it. Paul's conclusion is that the promises made to Abraham are the inclusive property of those who have faith in Jesus Christ, both Jew and Gentile.[24]

Daring to State the Truth about Equality

The further implications that Paul draws from this position are found in his statements in Galatians 3:26-29: "For through faith you are all sons of God in union with Christ Jesus. Baptized into union with him, you have put on Christ as a garment. There is no such thing as Jew and Greek, slave and freeman, male and female; for you are all one person in Christ Jesus. But if you thus belong to Christ, then you are the 'issue' of Abraham, and so heirs by promise."

Paul continues his argument that the Gentiles are children of Abraham and of God and that they are not demanded to observe the law. He wishes to expose the discriminatory motives, the deep-rooted prejudices, and the possible political agenda of his opponents. In this chapter he goes even further than just to prove their racial intentions by adding to it the social and sexual discriminatory attitudes of the society of his time and how these are upheld and entrenched in the position of his adversaries.

These verses represent some inferences from his whole argument of what it means to be a child of Abraham. He addresses the Galatians directly and again emphasizes that faith in Christ is fundamental. He now adds to his argument the symbolic act of baptism, most probably to counter the insistence of his opponents that circumcision is a sine qua non for righteousness. In baptism, people put on Christ, as Paul puts it. This means that through faith in Christ children of Abraham come to stand in radically new relationships to one another. The ethical, social, and sexual characteristics that used to be walls of separation, alienation, and discrimination now serve as mere distinctions. This relationship is described in the term *sonship*, which expresses the intimate relationship with God, in the first place of Christ, but also of those who believe and have been baptized in him. Sonship is no longer the exclusive privilege of Jews, free people, or males, as Paul's opponents believed.

Paul suggests that Christ broke the attitudes of national distinctiveness. Christ brings a new era of cultural revolution that becomes the cultural mandate to the church. This mandate, according to Paul, has three dimensions: (1) an ethnic or racial dimension that challenges the racism in the broader society; (2) a social dimension that challenged the institution of slavery of that time; and (3) a gender dimension that challenges the sexual abuses in the family and social structures. Paul dares to state the truth, but he also had to present it in a diplomatic manner, given the unprepared and sometimes hostile environment, as well as people's acceptance of their fate as victims of slavery, male chauvinism, and racial prejudice.

The argument to challenge these discriminatory social structures is based on the fact that in Christ the believers are one person. This comes about through the incorporation into the body of Christ through personal faith in him that is then sacramentally sealed in baptism.[25] This makes these differences irrelevant and exposes them to be sinful. Behind this argument is Paul's conviction that God is one and that, since he is one, he must be the God of all the culturally, socially, and sexually separated groups. He created one humanity, not many; thus there can no longer be barriers separating groups, disparate or otherwise. For example, circumcision implied division between Jew and non-Jew and between male and female. Baptism into Christ, however, means unity across all these distinctions.[26] The unity expressed in sonship that Paul declares is not one in which these distinctions vanish, in which the barriers of hostility, chauvinism, the sense of superiority, and the mentality of inferiority are destroyed.[27] These are the benefits of being sons, which also means being the heirs of Abraham.

Bruce comments: "Abraham's heritage is the heritage of faith and those who share this heritage are thereby manifested as the sons of Abraham."[28]

Freedom to Transform with a New Identity

Paul seems to realize that he has left much hanging in the air. Therefore, before closing his letter, he sums up with a concluding statement in Galatians 6:15: "Circumcision is nothing; uncircumcision is nothing; the only thing that counts is a new creation." To this must be added the problematic expression in verse 16 of the "whole Israel of God."

According to Paul's understanding, Jews exploited the law in two ways: First, they claimed it as the symbol of their ethnic identity and now wanted to enforce it on the Gentile Christians (6:13). Second, and related to the first, they emphasized the compelling works of the law as the way to righteousness. Both of these understandings of the law, its exclusivistic application and its legalistic use, are described by Paul in terms of enslavement.

Paul used the images of bondage and freedom to describe the two different positions, namely of those who accepted the gospel inclusive of the law over and against those who believed the gospel exclusive of it. It was a well-selected image for a number of reasons: First, slavery was a typical phenomenon and a common institution of ancient society and Paul could in this way subtly challenge the discriminatory institution of his time. Second, it was also a useful image to remind the Jewish component of their audience that the law was given to Israel after their liberation from slavery in Egypt. It was given to them to regulate freedom, especially the moral aspect of their lives. During this period of their history, Israel actually confirmed its identity as God's people. So both concepts, freedom and law, are closely associated with Israel's identity. It now seems that the order has been reversed during the course of history. Instead of being an instrument to structure and preserve freedom, the law has gradually become a symbol of enslavement, Paul seems to suggest. Third, if the majority of his immediate audience was a homogeneous Gentile group, they also were familiar with this concept in terms of their relationship to Rome or to the elements of the universe. Fourth, this freedom was already characteristic of God's dealings in the history of Abraham as Paul wants to illustrate in the Hagar-Sarah allegory.[29]

Against this background Paul now wishes to emphasize that Christ has come to liberate people from this degeneration of the law. To Paul the gospel is synonymous with freedom. And to him this primarily means freedom from the understanding of the law in the sense of bringing righteousness and defining identity. Put in another way, the freedom[30] received in Christ is a radical one that does bring a new identity and does also demand a new morality.[31] In terms of his rhetorical strategy, Paul in one argument seeks an alienation from the law, but then argues for a reidentification with it with the purpose of developing a new identity.

Concerning the new identity, the statement in 6:15 is of significance in terms of the concepts that Paul uses. First, he uses the categories of the creation. He contrasts the new creature with the issue of circumcision. In other words, Paul clearly relates it to the tension around identity between Jew and Gentile. He mentions, in 5:6, both circumcision and uncircumcision in order to level the playing fields between these two positions and to treat them on an equal basis.[32] It is significant that Paul speaks of a new creation. In doing so, he apparently wants to emphasize the importance of the total transformation, a replacement of the old order by the new. This new creation, in-as-much as creation refers to the human being, emphasizes the central position that humanity has in creation. But inasmuch as the new refers to the transformation, it also emphasizes the significance of the cross as separating the old from the new creation.[33] The crucified Christ is first and foremost the new creation. But Paul certainly wants to present himself also as an example of the new creation precisely because he regards himself as crucified with Christ. From this flows the idea of a new humanity by which he wishes to argue for the impartiality of God, the Creator, regarding ethnicity and race.

Second, and related to the concept of the new creation, is the expression "the whole Israel of God." In using it, Paul wishes to describe the new identity in the categories of the covenant of God with Israel and his original intentions with Israel in the covenant.[34] By this, Paul wants to show a continued loyalty to the Jewish community and its traditions. But at the same time the phrase contains a proposal for a new beginning, a third way between the circumcised and the uncircumcised, between the Jew and the Gentile, between the slave and the free man, between male and female. This is an identity that surpasses nationalistic interest and wishes to establish a new community based on the relationship with God. Unity, not uniformity, is the real issue in Paul's argument.

Freedom to Transform with a New Morality

The question may now be asked: What does the new identity mean for the normal life situation? This is best expressed in the words of Galatians 5:1: "Christ set us free to be free men. Stand firm, then, and refuse to be tied to the yoke of slavery again."

This brings us to the issue of whether the new identity requires a new morality. In this regard Paul states that this new creation is a canon, that is, a rule of conduct by which the Galatians must now live (6:16). It is the path along which they have to walk. Ridderbos remarks that "to walk by this rule means that in thought and action alike the Gelatinise are to be guided by their disposition towards that rule."[35] This suggests that the new creation be not only a state but also a command, not only an infinitive but also an imperative. An appropriate morality is a logical consequence and has to follow a new identity.

Paul endorses another expression that he used earlier, namely to "put on Christ," which means to be clothed by or in Christ (3:27). Symbolically this happens at baptism.[36] Different images are recalled in trying to understand this expression often used by Paul, but they all suggest that this asks for not only a fundamental change in identity, but also in behavior. The change in identity could mean the restoration of the person to the original bearer of the image of God as God intended it at creation, namely in righteousness and holiness (Eph. 4:24). Or it could also refer to the person in the eschatological sense, the new person of the future.

Against this background, it is noticeable that Paul does not reject the law outright but reinterprets it to serve much more as a moral code and not to obtain justification.[37] To him the law is the law of Christ, that is, the law of love. Faith in Christ finds expression in love to the neighbor. In this sense works—a demonstration of faith, love, and service—are valid.[38]

For this new morality, the relationship among the concepts of freedom, the law, and the Holy Spirit are crucial. First, there is the correlation between the law and freedom. Paul realizes that freedom can become a space for the operation of the evil nature, as most probably happened with the Galatians after Paul preached the gospel without the law to them. This could be a reason why they found the gospel with the law of Paul's opponents so attractive. The evil nature finds expression in a wide range of actions that serve the self and eventually threaten freedom again. Therefore, the need to hold on to the freedom in Christ is of paramount importance. The law can be allowed to operate and to serve as an ethical guide within the context of freedom, to actually regulate freedom. This is the law that serves the faith.

Paul also correlates the law and the Holy Spirit. The law, in the legalistic sense of the word, actually encourages the actions of the evil nature and bears the fruit of sin. Within the new creation it is the Holy Spirit who uses the law in its new sense, as the law of Christ to serve as a regulating mechanism. In the life of the person and the new community it bears the fruit of love.

The new morality is characteristic of the total transformation that Paul proposes. It attacks the social prejudices and racial attitudes that are inherent in the gospel of Paul's opponents and the social and moral world of his time. It is new in the sense that it wants to return to the origins of God's intentions with humanity in creation and his dealings with the people of Israel in history. It wishes to rediscover the norms and values that prevailed in the early beginnings and reappropriate them in the new situation. It seeks to find a different way of looking at the world around, to develop a new attitude toward fellow human beings in the manner that Christ taught and lived. That is why the new morality is called the law of Christ.

In summary, Paul's Letter to the Galatians is to my mind a unique document in the New Testament. As one of the oldest documents of the New Testament it seems to indicate a watershed in the development of early Christianity. The Jesus movement started off being a messianic sect within Judaism, constituted by Jews only. Those from outside Judaism who wanted to become part of it had to be incorporated into it in the same way as they normally would be proselytized into Judaism. This became an untenable situation as Paul experienced in Jerusalem, in Antioch with Peter and Barnabas, in other places, and in Galatia. Perhaps he discovered some ulterior motives of a racial kind in the manner in which some, primarily the Jewish Christians, approached the issues. He found the solution to lie in a radically new direction, in a new structure that appropriates both Jews and Gentiles. This means the development of a new community with its own ethos.[39]

It is unlikely that Paul foresaw the implications and ramifications of his views as expressed in Galatians and Romans. He was addressing contingent situations of a critical nature in these letters. But the letter to the Galatians has a revolutionary character.[40] It perhaps unintentionally wishes to change society radically when the thrust of its message is taken seriously in a universal setting. What Paul did was perhaps risky in the sociopolitical climate that prevailed at that time. If taken seriously, it was bound to undermine the racial overtones of his opponents' "gospel" and even challenge the discriminatory attitudes in a broad sense within the society of his time. It exposed the hypocrisies within the Roman society of both Jews and Gentiles, but at the same time it wanted to offer a direction to reconcile the broader society.[41]

The principles underlying the issues of civil, human, and women's and children's rights that receive our attention in South Africa today may have their roots in various developments in history. But it cannot be denied that Christianity has and will continue to play a significant role in establishing these principles and seeking the advancement of these issues.[42] And as for Christianity, its roots were nourished by the way that Paul interpreted and proclaimed the gospel. He helped us to understand that the gospel of reconciliation goes further back in history, in God's promise to Abraham, in creation itself.

In the foreword of the book *To Remember and to Heal*, Archbishop Desmond Tutu says: "The Truth and Reconciliation Commission [is] at its heart a deeply theological and ethical initiative. For people of faith, the experience of honesty and mercy, confession and forgiveness, justice and peace, repentance and reconciliation are what truth and reconciliation is all about."[43] What happened under apartheid was the result of deep-rooted racial prejudices, the kind of attitude that Paul also seems to have experienced and exposed in early Christianity. Fortunately, he also suggested a way to embark on a process of healing. Tutu is, therefore, also correct when he reminds us that "those of us who stand within the Christian tradition have, perhaps, a special responsibility in this regard because this nation has through the years employed Christian theological resources to promote apartheid—a system that is today accepted by people throughout the world as a crime against humanity."[44] In taking on this special responsibility, it is important to consider the message of Paul to the Galatians.

Notes

1. James C. Walters, *Ethnic Issues in Paul's Letter to the Romans: Changing Self-Definitions in Earliest Roman Christianity* (Valley Forge, Pa.: Trinity Press, 1993), 3.

2. Leon Morris, *Galatians: Paul's Charter of Christian Freedom* (Downers Grove, Ill.: InterVarsity Press, 1996), 121.

3. It is generally accepted that the process of hellenization and the Pax Romana helped the emergence of the church.

4. It is interesting that Paul refers to "boasting" in 6:14, apparently something that his opponents were guilty of.

5. F. F. Bruce, *The Epistle to the Galatians: A Commentary on the Greek Text* (Exeter: Paternoster Press, 1982), 188.

6. R. E. Brown and J. P. Meier, *Antioch and Rome: New Testament Cradles of Catholic Christianity* (London: G. Chapman, 1983), 1-9.

7. Bruce, *The Epistle to the Galatians*, 188.

8. Walters, *Ethnic Issues*, 47, refers to a fragment of Dio Cassius that mentions Tiberius's expulsion of the Jews also because they were converting any of the natives to their ways. Tiberius also used repressive measures to check the spread of the non-Roman cults that continued to make inroads into Roman society. He apparently did not make any distinction between Jews and Christians in doing this. The situation probably was not much different at the time when Gelatinise was written. Under Claudius there was the expulsion of the Jews from Rome with the reference to this "Chrestus" (probably meaning Christ).

9. Morris, *Galatians*, 121, quotes Dieter Lührmann, *Galatians* (Minneapolis: Fortress, 1992), who said: "Actually the Galatians were neither: to the Jews they were Gentiles, but to the Greeks, barbarians." Morris then adds: "But the Galatians would have known accordingly what it was to be despised by both!"

10. Bruce Winter, *Seek the Welfare of the City* (Grand Rapids, Mich.: Eerdmans, 1994), suggests that this could have been the case. However, one gets the impression that this switch by the Gentile Christians was more because of the initiative of the Jewish Christians than because of persecution.

11. Wayne Meeks, *The First Urban Christians: The Social World of the Apostle Paul* (New Haven, Conn.: Yale University Press, 1983), 115, is of such an opinion: "Paul sees this as a direct attack on his own authority as apostle and founder of the Galatian churches and as a perversion of the one gospel."

12. H. D. Betz, *Galatians: A Commentary on Paul's Letter to the Churches in Galatia* (Philadelphia: Fortress, 1979), 320.

13. Bruce, *The Epistle to the Galatians*, 3-18.

14. Meeks, *The First Urban Christians*, 73, agrees with Malherbe that there is an "emerging consensus" that "a Pauline congregation generally reflected a fair cross-section of urban society."

15. C. B. Cousar, *Galatians: Interpretation, a Bible Commentary for Teaching and Preaching* (Atlanta: John Knox, 1982), 149.

16. F. J. Matera, *Galatians: Sacra Pagina* (Collegeville, Minn.: Liturgical Press, 1992), 144, indicates that Paul uses a scheme of "we" meaning the Jews and including himself and "you" meaning the Galatians. Paul applies this scheme also in Romans (1:16).

17. There does not seem to be much difference of opinion about the basic structure of the document. Its beginning (1-2:14) is historical, the middle section (2:15-4:1) is

theological or doctrinal, and the rest (5:2-6: 18) is ethical. Betz, with his commentary on Galatians, has shown rather convincingly the rhetorical style that characterizes the letter.

18. The impact of these two Pauline documents with regard to the developments that led to the Reformation is usually acknowledged, but not their impact on developments in the early church.

19. J. D. G. Dunn, "The Theology of Galatians: The Issue of Covenantal Nomism," in *Pauline Theology*, vol. 1, ed. Jouette M. Bassler (Minneapolis: Fortress, 1990), 126, describes covenantal nomism as Jewish self-understanding in which the "typical mind-set . . . included a strong sense of special privilege and prerogative over and against other peoples. . . . But it also and inevitably meant a reinforcing of the sense of national identity and separateness from other nations." He borrows this concept from E. P. Sanders, who coined it.

20. Bruce, *The Epistle to the Galatians*, 188, remarks: "Paul's position was clear-cut: had the law shown itself able to impart life, this would have given the Jews an overwhelming advantage; but since the law's inability to do any such thing had been demonstrated, there was now no distinction between Jews and Gentiles before God in respect either of their moral bankruptcy or of their need to receive his pardoning grace."

21. Dunn, "The Theology of Galatians," 128, describes the function of the law to mean that "however universal the claims made for the law might have been, it never ceased to be the Jewish law; its religious appeal . . . was never such as could be divorced from its national function as the civil and criminal code of the Jews as a distinct ethnic entity. This 'social function of the law' I believe to be important for our fuller understanding of the mind-set with which Paul is engaging in Gelatinise."

22. Bruce, *The Epistle to the Galatians*, 153, emphasizes that for Paul's distinctive understanding of the history of salvation Gen. 15:6 is a key text.

23. Morris, *Galatians*, 101, quotes Lenski in a footnote: "While Abraham is the forefather of the Jews, when he received this promise he was as much a Gentile as the Gentile Gelatinise themselves. He was still uncircumcised." Morris then adds: "This was important for the apostle; his Gentile converts were just as surely accepted by God as was Abraham."

24. F. Watson, *Paul, Judaism, and the Gentiles: A Sociological Approach* (Cambridge: Cambridge University Press, 1986), 48, seems to suggest "that Paul's attitude towards Judaism exactly fitted the structure of an ideology legitimating separation" and that "he seeks to reinforce the barrier separating the church from the Jewish community," 47. This is perhaps overstating Paul's intentions. It is true that his approach eventually led to this separation.

25. Bruce, *The Epistle to the Galatians*, 184. Also D. Wenham, *Paul, Follower of Jesus or Founder of Christianity?* (Grand Rapids, Mich.: Eerdmans, 1995), 67, who argues that for Paul, faith has two dimensions, namely an element of intellectual belief, but it also involves a commitment of life. These correspond with the ideas of identity and morality.

26. Cousar, *Galatians*, 85, states: "Circumcision implied division between Jew and non-Jew and between male and female. Baptism into Christ means unity."

27. Cousar, *Galatians*, 86, remarks: "the new unity given in Christ has tremendous social implications. The very fact that the differences no longer matter means that Christians must treat people and groups in this light not only in church on Sunday but in the total affairs of life, in the so-called secular arena as well as the sacred. . . . In 2:11-14 he defends the right of Gentiles to be present with Jews on a common basis at a social

gathering. It is not just at worship services that the Jew-Gentile distinction is rendered irrelevant."

28. Bruce, *The Epistle to the Galatians*, 155.

29. Martin McNamara, *Palestinian Judaism and the New Testament*, Good News Studies, vol. 4 (Wilmington: Michael Glazier, Inc., 1983), 258, remarks: "In the early Church Christian freedom and the identity of the true heirs of the promises became real issues. In his effort to clarify his teaching on the point Paul invoked the persons of Hagar and Sarah and their children Ishmael and Isaac. In his treatment of the subject he probably used both the biblical narrative and a current Jewish midrashic elaboration of this. In this we see both the theological edifice being erected and the scaffolding used for the construction (Galatians 4:21-31)."

30. Betz, *Galatians*, 255, states that: "As a result, ('freedom') is the central theological concept which sums up the Christian's situation before God as well as in this world. It is the basic concept underlying Paul's argument throughout the letter."

31. Betz, *Galatians*, 256, interprets 5:1 as follows: "The whole sentence states in a very concise form both the 'indicative' and the 'imperative' of Christian salvation in the Pauline sense. Christian freedom is the result of Christ's act of having liberated those who believe in him (the 'indicative'), but this result is stated as a goal, purpose, and direction for the life of the Christian (the 'imperative')."

32. Betz, *Galatians*, 320, comments: "It is also significant that both Judaism and paganism are viewed on the same level as part of the 'old world.'"

33. R. Scroggs, "Salvation History," in *Pauline Theology*, 212, points out the importance of crucifixion language in Gelatinise: "The cross marks the separation between this world and the new world of the church. In Gelatinise, at least, this is the basic function of cross language. It shows the radical distinction between church and world, and the principle upon which that distinction is created and sustained."

34. Watson, *Paul, Judaism, and the Gentiles*, 72, in dealing with crisis in Gelatinise argues that Paul is busy to transform a (Jewish) reform movement into a (Gentile) sect and continues "that Jewish tradition, truly interpreted, was the exclusive possession of his sectarian Gentile communities."

35. H. N. Ridderbos, *The Epistle of Paul to the Churches of Galatia* (Grand Rapids, Mich.: Eerdmans, 1953), 226.

36. Wenham, *Paul, Follower of Jesus or Founder of Christianity*, 284-286, discusses Gal. 3:28 and baptism. He comments: "For him no male and female has to do with relationship to Christ and will lead to mutual care and respect . . . , but does not mean the removal of created differences or created sexuality."

37. J. L. Martyn, "Events in Galatia," in *Pauline Theology*, 170, also makes the point that "the divorce between God and the Law is not absolute."

38. Wenham, *Paul, Follower of Jesus or Founder of Christianity*, 85-86, discusses Paul's frequent use of the triad: faith, hope, and love.

39. Betz, *Galatians*, 320.

40. Robert Banks, *Paul's Idea of Community*, rev. ed. (Peabody, Mass.: Hendrickson's, 1994), 1, comments as follows: "It is not merely the extent of Paul's contribution that sets it apart from others in the first century, but its quality. We find here the most clearly developed and profound understanding of community in all the early Christian writings. Not that he provides any systematic treatment of the idea. For the most part he worked out his views in response to the problems of particular communities. . . . But they do reveal an energetic and creative thinker who has the ability to engage in both theoretical reflection and the subtleties of argument."

41. B. R. Gaventa, "The Singularity of the Gospel: A Reading of Gelatinise," in *Pauline Theology*, 149, sums it up well: "The word 'christocentrism' is the right word, in that Paul presupposes from the beginning to the end that there is only one gospel (1:6-9), the singularity of which consists of the revelation of Jesus Christ as God's son whose crucifixion inaugurates the new age. This singular gospel results in a singular transformation for those called as believers, who are themselves moved into a new identity in Christ alone (2:19-21; 3:26-29) and new life in the Spirit (3:1-4; 5:16-25). The new creation results in the nullification of previous identifications, whether these come from within the law (1:11-17) or from outside (4:8-11)."

42. Banks, *Paul's Idea of Community*, 191, rightly states: "While in view of a changed cultural situation his [Paul's] actual practices are not always applicable today, the principles underlying them continue to attract the attention of those actively seeking community. His understanding of community raises serious questions both for established ecclesiastical structures that claim a historical link with Paul and for counterculture groups that ardently promise 'community' to those who join them."

43. H. R. Botman and R. M. Peterson, eds., *To Remember and to Heal* (Cape Town, South Africa: Human & Rousseau, 1996), 7.

44. Botman and Petersen, *To Remember and to Heal*, 8.

Chapter Two

British Immigration during the Nineteenth Century: The American and South African Experience

William E. Van Vugt

Introduction

SCHOLARS HAVE LONG recognized the significance of immigration in American history. Frederick Jackson Turner was accurate when in 1892 he claimed that "we shall not understand the contemporary United States without studying immigration historically."[1] The British were especially important in American immigration. Not only did they provide the greatest total numbers from 1607 to the present, but they also brought the language and the basic cultural, religious, and political heritage that America adopted—with some modifications—as its own.[2]

Scholars of South Africa seem less interested in immigration, even though it is so important to the nation's history. In terms of percentage of total immigrants and cultural impact the British were less important for South Africa than for the United States, but they were still very influential indeed. In our attempt to comprehend the history of race and reconciliation in South Africa we can gain some insight by comparing two different and yet similar streams of British immigrants—those to the United States and those to South Africa during the formative years of the nineteenth century. A thorough social-economic and demographic analysis is beyond the scope of this chapter. Our more general interest is the role of British immigration in the history of race in South Africa, within the comparative context of the United States. To begin, it is helpful to draw some social-economic and political comparisons and their racial implications.

Structural Comparisons

The end of the Napoleonic Wars was a catalyst for British migration to many parts of the world. Demobilized soldiers flooded back to Britain in search of employment, only to find it scarce, especially in the industrial towns that had relied on military contracts. In addition, the technological changes and urbanization associated with the industrial revolution were disrupting the traditional lives of many people and causing new hardships. Agriculture was also depressed in many counties, and farm workers faced competition from mechanization. With these new economic dislocations and the renewal of Britain's dominance of the high seas, it is no wonder that British migration to various parts of the world increased dramatically.

Throughout the century, most headed for the United States.[3] During the 1820s and 1830s most came from Britain's rural and less-developed regions, and roughly three-fourths traveled with family members, a proportion much higher than any other immigrant group arriving at the time. Though many were poor laborers, artisans, or industrial workers, the movement was not dominated by the casualties of the industrial revolution. Actually, by the 1830s many British immigrants to America were the beneficiaries of the expanding industrial economy, or they were farmers with some capital. They could afford to emigrate as families, and they were freely choosing the United States as their new nation. Probably most had friends or relatives who had preceded them to America and had informed them on what to expect in the new land. These "networks" of people and information eased the physical and psychological burdens of migration and directed it to the United States.[4] In contrast, comparatively few British immigrants came to South Africa, and those who did arrived with minimal knowledge and highly idealized images about the new country.[5] This was due to one of the essential differences between the two streams of British immigrants: Practically all of those to the United States were making free decisions and financing their migration with their own resources (or that of their relatives or friends), while most of those to South Africa during the first half of the century were assisted and directed there by government, business, or philanthropic leaders who had exaggerated South Africa's appeal in order to attract the immigrants.

Another structural difference between the two streams of immigrants pertains to their host culture and experience with assimilation. British immigrants to the United States were entering a society and culture predominantly of British origin. They were "invisible immigrants" in the sense that they could blend in more immediately with mainstream America than other immigrant groups.[6] Although they did have some difficulties with adjustment, they shared the same language and essential cultural traits and, as a result, did not need to form ethnic communities or enclaves. Of all immigrants, they had the highest rates of intermarriage with American-born people, and their children were usually indistinguishable from native white Americans. Generally they were seen not as foreigners, but as "cousins" who were in a sense already Americans. Contrarily, British immigrants to South Africa were entering an African and Afrikaner world that could hardly have seemed more different. Here most British immigrants felt a need to form enclaves. They never blended in and lost their ethnic cohesion to the extent that those entering the United States did, but eventually they did experience some assimilation that had racial implications.

The two streams of British immigrants did share some experiences that shaped their racial attitudes and eventually affected racial policy. Both encountered a frontier where real and imaginary dangers tended to harden their attitudes toward indigenous peoples. On the American frontier some Britons who had arrived with idealized images of Native Americans as "noble savages" came to see them as a threat to life and property. Many Britons in South Africa also adopted harsher racial attitudes because of the frontier, and as we shall see below, because of the influence of the British government and missionaries, and of the Afrikaner community.[7]

The racial attitudes of British immigrants were also shaped considerably by the respective governments of the two host countries. Being adjacent to western lands, the United States developed a sense of Manifest Destiny to extend its control and institutions from coast to coast, a mission that would serve to justify many occasions of land seizure and cruelty to indigenous peoples. The British government could never have such an urgent sense of mission in a colony as distant as South Africa, but they did invent what Rudyard Kipling called "the white man's burden" to "civilize" the empire. Cruelty and injustice were part of the formula here as well—but generally not on the American scale. As Native Americans were decimated by diseases, and then forced to relocate to reservations, whites became a large majority of the population with a monopoly on power. Native South Africans remained numerically superior to the European settlers, yet were stripped of their lands and denied political power. In spite of such oppression, both the American government and British government in South Africa insisted that their rule would bring indigenous peoples the benefits of higher civilization.

Though both streams of British immigrants were largely economically motivated, the American economy offered greater and more varied opportunities. This goes far in explaining the two different magnitudes of migration. Yet in both places, British immigrants enjoyed economic and racial superiority. The United States was in its agricultural "golden age," especially during the antebellum period, when farming opportunities were at their greatest for poor people. During much of the nineteenth century, the United States enabled more people to become farmers of their own land than at any other time or place in history. The nation was expanding westward and absorbing a land that was ideal for persons who wished to engage in independent, self-sufficient agriculture, or in commercial agriculture if they were connected to the multiplying town markets. British immigrants from every conceivable background took advantage of these opportunities to become American farmers. It was their shared cultural traits with the Americans, their contacts with Britons already in America, and the relatively short and cheap voyage that enabled them to come in such large and steady numbers. Such unprecedented opportunities, of course, were made at the expense of Native Americans, whose brutal removal to marginal western lands is seen by some historians as "the American Holocaust."[8]

South African agriculture was not nearly as attractive. Commercial farming was limited, often impossible without substantial capital, and thus immigrants of modest means found it hard to enter and prosper as independent farmers. With a huge oppressed black and coloured labor force available for exploitation, there were also fewer opportunities for poor Britons to begin as laborers and work their way up to farmers. South Africa could never attract as many British immigrants as America. America had much more to offer, and was a lot closer in terms of geography, culture, and agricultural life.

The two countries' different stages of economic development certainly affected the size and composition of British immigration. By the 1830s, the United States had a strong market economy that was rapidly industrializing and in need of skilled workers. Iron, textiles, mining, engineering, and virtually all other forms of industrial enterprises and crafts were practically begging for immigrants from Britain, the world's first industrial nation. South Africa's economy was still preindustrial by comparison, with a narrower range of opportunities; but industrial capitalism would grow there too, thanks in part to British labor, skills, and capital. Thus the social and economic rise of British immigrants in both the United States and South Africa was based on their skills and expertise in industrial and mechanical occupations. In South Africa their rise above the Afrikaners was boosted by the latter's lack of receptiveness to machines or modernizing industries.[9]

However, the racial and political advantages that came with being British in either the United States or South Africa were also essential to the immigrants' relatively high economic and social status. In both places, British immigrants immediately enjoyed a supremacy and higher social status over not only indigenous peoples (and persons of African descent in America), but people of European descent as well—the Irish in America, for example, and the Afrikaners in South Africa. It is interesting and very telling that in both America and South Africa British immigrants arrived near the top of the social system, while typically immigrants arrive near the bottom. This advantage, then, was based on their economic success and their shared racial and cultural heritage with members of the dominant economic and political elite.

An Overview of British Migration to South Africa

Early nineteenth-century migration from Britain to South Africa was largely promoted and financed by the government or charitable groups. After Britain assumed control of the Cape in 1806, British settlers began arriving as part of three small private colonizing projects. The most significant of these consisted of a group of 196 poor unemployed apprentices from Scotland, who left Leith in 1817 under the leadership of one Benjamin Moodie. The young men were mechanics and laborers who were assisted to the Cape under a contract that committed them to work in a manner similar to the many British indentured servants who came to America during the eighteenth century. Soon after their arrival, however, most broke their contracts, found work on their own terms, and prospered. Moodie became bankrupt and the project failed.

In 1819, the British government became seriously interested in promoting British migration to the Cape for strategic reasons. Having acquired what had been a Dutch colony that was populated mainly by indigenous peoples, the British were now determined to hang on to it, develop it, extend it, and civilize it by making it as "British" as possible. This required extensive British immigration. The result was a government grant of £50,000 in 1820 to move roughly five thousand British people, most of whom were in dire economic situations, to start over in the new Albany settlement on Algoa Bay, near today's Port Elizabeth. Because of the influence of evangelical humanitarianism, and what would develop into "Cape liberalism," there were important conditions for the new settlers: They could neither own slaves nor hire native labor, or they risked forfeiting their lands.

On the surface, the 1820 settlers appear to have had an occupational profile similar to those going to America at the time: About 40 percent claimed to have been involved in "farming and country pursuits" in Britain, a third were skilled artisans or mechanics, a tenth were in commerce, and most of the rest were professionals of some sort.[10] But these stated occupations disguise significant differences. On average, the 1820 settlers were poorer, more distressed, and in need of financial assistance to emigrate. They were "casualties of the Napoleonic Wars" and of the social dislocations associated with industrialization and urbanization of the period, and as such they came to South Africa mainly to get out of Britain. Many would have preferred to go to America, but lacked the funds.[11]

Additional evidence for the relative poverty of the English bound for South Africa during the 1820s comes from the data that we have on their county of origin. Whereas 85 percent of those to the United States with known counties of origin were from prosperous industrial high-wage counties (like Middlesex, Lancashire, and Northumberland), the figure for those to South Africa is 63 percent. Only 6 percent of the United States-bound migrants were from the severely distressed low-wage agricultural counties (like Surrey, Wiltshire, and Buckinghamshire), as compared to 24 percent of those bound for South Africa. Historian Charlotte Erickson concluded that the emigrants to the United States during this early period were "people who could afford to emigrate and who made positive choices about where they wanted to live," while E. Morse Jones concluded that the South Africa-bound immigrants "represented areas of considerable depression and distress."[12]

One reported difference between the two groups of British migrants was their character. As one observer remarked, about a third of the 1820 settlers were "persons of respectability of character, and possessed of some worldy [sic] substance." But the remaining two-thirds "were for the most part composed of individuals of a very unpromising description—persons who had hung loose upon society—low in morals or desperate in circumstances . . . too many appeared to be idle, insolent, and drunken, and mutinously disposed towards their masters and superiors." Other observers were even harsher.[13]

Such observations are inherently subjective and open to prejudice. But it is striking that British immigrants to America were usually described in very different terms. Of course some British immigrants to America were ill-suited or undesirable, but the great majority were viewed as sober, industrious, God-fearing persons who would make vital contributions to the development of the United States and the character of its people. Indeed, until 1824 the British government found it necessary to forbid the emigration of skilled Britons to America because of the perceived problem of the "highest quality" emigrants going to the United States instead of the colonies, and these concerns persisted through much of the century.

The questionable character and suitability of many of the early immigrants to South Africa is further revealed in the observations of the governor of the Cape, Sir Harry Smith. In 1849, he was relieved to find that the British settlers arriving in that year were "decidedly of a more respectable class, and more regular and orderly in their behaviour than those who arrived by former ships."[14] Smith attributed the better quality of British immigrants to an improved selection process and to a regulation that required a clergyman on board all emigrant ships; but again, his comments underscore the relative poverty and unsuitability of many of the earlier immigrants. Regardless of these reported shortcomings, the early British colonists are still considered by modern historians as "the most wealthy, active and intelligent class" in South Africa.[15] As a whole, British immigrants were the most literate members of South African society, and as such they contributed greatly to literacy, schools, and libraries in South Africa, as well as to the development of a free press, which would prove crucial for the development of independent thought and self-government. In the process they brought an urban and commercial culture that gradually filtered into the interior.[16]

The 1820 settlers failed to establish the agricultural settlement that was envisioned for them. The main problem was that too many were poor urban artisans without meaningful agricultural experience. Furthermore, little of the land around the Zuurveld was suitable for cultivation, and the one hundred-acre allotments were too small to support a family. Facing poverty in a new and strange land, the settlers soon abandoned the project. Some became frontiersmen; but most left the land, went to towns, and resumed their old trades, which enabled most of them to succeed. Eventually they contributed disproportionately to the economic development of the colony, introducing wool farming and other export enterprises. They also brought a distrust of autocratic government and a willingness to agitate for their rights, as did British immigrants in colonial America. When a British ship loaded with Irish convicts tried to land in 1848, British immigrants united with Afrikaners to force the ship back and the government to abandon the policy. Thus began the agitation for representative self-government that was granted under the new constitution of 1853.[17]

The Mid-Nineteenth Century

During the late 1820s, 1830s, and early 1840s British migration to South Africa was self-financed but very limited, with only a few hundred arriving per year.[18] Then, during the late "hungry forties," British migration surged to all destinations, including South Africa. The United States still took the vast majority. The Colonial Land and Emigration Commission Reports for 1851 reveal that for every Briton arriving in South Africa, four arrived in Australia and New Zealand, seven went to British North America, while nearly fifty (forty-nine) went to the United States.[19] There was much painful dislocation and plenty of social misery to go around in Britain during this time, and increased numbers of unemployed textiles workers, miners, and poor unskilled laborers did leave for America. But these alone do not explain the high numbers. Rather, it was people who may have felt threatened by future change, and had contact with Britons in America and some resources who swelled the ranks of the immigrants. It was still America's legendary cheap and fertile farmland, together with expanding agricultural markets that probably continued to attract most of these people. One important factor in the prosperity of American agriculture was the fact that in 1846 Britain repealed her Corn Laws, the protective tariffs on imported grain. This act of Parliament allowed American farmers to tap British markets, which prompted British farmers who could not adjust to the falling prices that repeal allowed, to farm in America instead. It was this integrated "Atlantic Economy" and the integrated Anglo-American culture that made the flow of Britons to America such a natural movement. It is no wonder that with such great and diverse opportunities and such well-established links in the transatlantic chain of migration that so many people were leaving Britain for America during this time.[20]

Mid-century British migration to South Africa was again very different. Like the 1820 settlers, most were assisted, either by the government (which was concerned with maintaining and extending the empire) or capitalists (who were hoping to make their fortunes by developing the colony, which also pleased the politicians in London). Between 1847 and 1866 alone, nearly 11,000 English, Scottish, and Welsh immigrants were assisted to the Cape or to Natal at the expense of the British government, while others came through private charitable schemes.[21] The immigrants who participated in these schemes were thus agents in the growing influence of the British Empire, helping to establish and maintain a British influence in South Africa. In a real sense they were "pawns" in the government's imperial and racial chess game. So, in spite of their limited numbers, British immigrants had a profound influence on South Africa.

The influence of mid-century immigration was especially pronounced in Natal. After Natal was declared a British colony in 1843, the authorities saw British immigration as a means of keeping Natal, as Governor Sir P. Maitland put it, from "degenerating into little more than a Colony of Natives." Another advocate put it this way: "nothing but immigration can save this splendid country."[22] Thus, a number of assisted emigration schemes were launched.

Between early 1849 and mid-1852, almost five thousand English and Scottish immigrants were assisted to Natal. Many were lured to the colony by the promise of free passages and land, and by deceptively attractive reports of how good life in Natal would be—one saying literally that Natal was "a land flowing with milk and honey."[23]

Roughly two-thirds of the five thousand to Natal arrived under the auspices of Joseph Charles Byrne, a son of an Irish cattle dealer who had emigrated temporarily to Australia and on his return trip to Britain stopped in Cape Town where he met merchants who were interested in developing Natal. After returning to England, Byrne made money in speculation and met people connected with shipping firms who showed a similar interest in Natal. He then presented his scheme to the Colonial Office, which supported it on a trial basis by providing land grants that of course had at some point been seized from native South Africans. Byrne had to pay for the immigrants' passages but would get the money refunded by the government after they were successfully settled on the land.

Byrne was hopeful of attracting farmers with capital, knowing that such persons were indispensable for a successful colony. He selected the immigrants through an application process designed to attract farmers, farm laborers, and artisans who could develop a rural economy; however, many unemployed factory workers, urban laborers, and clerks simply claimed to be agriculturists in order to qualify for the assistance. Perhaps as little as 1 percent were bona fide agriculturists. As was the case in Australia, assisted immigration tended not to attract the kind of people who were recruited to develop the colony.[24] Furthermore, the selected lands were not suitable for small farmers, especially those without farming experience. In the end Byrne lost about £14,000 and declared bankruptcy.[25]

For the settlers, the scheme was not necessarily a disaster. About a thousand left for Australia in 1852 after gold was discovered there. Most of the rest abandoned the scheme itself and drifted to the developing towns, especially Durban, where they either resumed their old trade or learned a new one. Like the 1820 settlers, they did eventually contribute to the economic development of the colony, though not in the way that was originally envisioned. Some also became early political leaders. Unfortunately, many immigrants in Natal also developed racist attitudes and eventually rejected the assimilative ideals of Cape liberalism in favor of segregation. Historians see this primarily as a consequence of their contact with Africans and especially Afrikaners, whose own racist attitudes were already deeply engrained.[26] However, it should be noted that some of the pressure for segregation and land seizure came from recent British immigrants who had become wool farmers or merchants in the eastern Cape and now demanded more grazing lands in the Ciskei region.[27]

Such colonization schemes seem to have been doomed to fail. This was also true of those attempts made in the United States. In several cases, British industrial workers banded together to form "emigration societies," in which subscribers pooled their meager savings to purchase land in America. Lotteries were then held to determine which members would be funded to emigrate to the colony, get a parcel of land, and take up farming. The goal was twofold: to reduce the supply of skilled labor in Britain in order to raise wages for those who stayed behind, and to enable artisans to pursue the dream of farming their own land. The most ambitious of these schemes was that of the British Emigration Temperance Society, which was organized in Liverpool in 1842 and actually assisted about seven hundred Britons to migrate to southwest Wisconsin by 1850. Another was the Iowa Emigration Society, which relocated smaller numbers to Clinton County in that state, as well as the Potters' Joint-Stock Emigration Society, which was organized in 1844 and bought land in Columbia County, Wisconsin. Many other smaller ventures were attempted, some of them with a vision based on the ideas of Charles Fourier and other socialists.

These projects failed because, as in the colonization efforts in South Africa, the organizers underestimated their costs and inherent difficulties. They also tended to purchase cheap land that was either infertile or too distant from markets to make agriculture pay, and they failed to attract the right type of immigrant—one with some capital and agricultural ability. Those who did participate soon left the settlements and mingled with the white American population. Most remained in America, either as local farmers or artisans in nearby towns; the colonies soon faded from the scene. The parallel with the government-assisted colonies to South Africa is striking and illustrates the inherent difficulties and weaknesses of such organized emigration—as opposed to the free, independent migration that characterized the great bulk of immigrants to the United States. In spite of continued government or charitable assistance, nineteenth-century British migration to South Africa would never achieve the scale and dynamism that the government hoped for in order to "Anglicize" the distant colony.[28]

There were a number of successful attempts at assisting young, poor British women, particularly domestic servants, to South Africa, in order to remedy a perceived "surplus" of females in Britain and a lack of them in South Africa. Other schemes, like the Female Middle Class Emigration Society, brought women of education and some refinement to the colony where they became teachers or missionaries and as such served to educate and minister to Africans and promote the cause of reform.[29]

Reform, Race, and Abolitionism

In both the United States and South Africa the movement for the abolition of slavery and greater racial equality was rooted in British and Anglo-American Protestantism, though the immigrants themselves would play rather different roles. Many British immigrants in America were influenced by the evangelical movement, particularly the Methodist secession movement, which started attacking slavery in the empire in the eighteenth century. This was part of a larger humanitarian reform movement that had originated as a response to the social dislocations that resulted from industrialization. Mainly a middle-class movement, it was linked with the liberal capitalist ideas of Adam Smith, and it also targeted political corruption and limitations on trade. It preached the virtues of economic liberalism, specifically free-labor capitalism, which argued that unfree labor degraded employers and workers alike.[30] Thus the chief results of liberal reform include agitation for parliamentary reform (which produced the Great Reform Bill of 1832), free trade (which produced the repeal of the Corn Laws in 1846), and the abolition of the slave trade throughout the empire and of slavery itself in 1833.

English evangelicals led the attack on slavery in both the empire and America. Frederick Douglass himself acknowledged that American abolitionism "was largely derived from England." The phenomenal success of his lecture tour in Britain in 1847, as well as Harriet Beecher Stowe's *Uncle Tom's Cabin,* which in its first year of publication (1852) sold seven times more copies in Britain than in the United States, were indications of the vitality of Britain's antislavery movement. Britain's working classes had a particularly deep revulsion for American slavery. They were the people most likely to immigrate to America or to have family members living there, but they also saw their own struggle for complete freedom and equality in Britain as part of a larger international movement that included emancipation for American slaves. Because Methodists were significantly overrepresented among British immigrants to the United States, the immigrants were generally strongly opposed to slavery. Virtually all British immigrants had an opinion on American slavery, and all but a small fraction deplored it as a violation of God's law and America's ideals.[31]

Thus, it was no surprise that British immigrants were prominent in America's abolition movement and that they fought for the Union in the American Civil War in disproportionately high numbers. Many arriving in the late 1850s, or even during the war itself, volunteered to fight. They served in every imaginable capacity, and in every campaign; at least two were colonels of black regiments. They fought to prove their loyalty to their new homeland, for the adventure, but for many also for the cause of black freedom.[32]

British immigrants, some government officials, and especially missionaries introduced liberal reform ideals to South Africa.[33] The immigrants to South Africa also included disproportionately high numbers of Methodists, but the issue of race and how the immigrants dealt with it were different than in America. In the United States in 1860 there were still nearly four million black slaves. Such an overt abomination could easily arouse passions and the sense of injustice. Of course, abolitionism was often mixed with less altruistic motives, such as a concern for competing with black labor in western lands. In South Africa, though black and coloured Africans remained oppressed, slavery itself had been abolished in 1833. Here British immigrants were no longer confronting an institution in which people legally owned, bought, and sold other people. As great as the racial injustices were, they did not register as deeply in the immigrant's mind as American slavery did.

Whatever their denomination, British immigrants in South Africa attended churches that were there to serve them and their colonial authorities, while missionaries ministered to indigenous peoples quite apart from the English-speaking churches. Thus the religious institutions of British immigrants in South Africa were forces of segregation that sanctioned and deepened the immigrants' sense of racial superiority and legitimized their favored position in society.[34]

Though the English-speaking churches contributed to the gulf between British immigrants and black South Africans, Britain's evangelical movement and missionaries do have a more positive role in the history of race and reconciliation in South Africa. The London Missionary Society (LMS), in Cape Town already in 1799, took the lead in fighting both slavery and serfdom. To be sure, the LMS and the larger evangelical and humanitarian movement of which it was a part had its shortcomings, not the least of which were a willingness to have segregated churches, a paternalistic attitude, and the belief that British culture was superior and the best avenue for conversion. Furthermore, humanitarianism and Cape liberalism were clearly adulterated by the fiscal concerns of administrating an empire. However, it is also true that the missionaries, with the support of British administrators, were "striving to be relevant to the conditions and struggles of the Coloureds and Africans,"[35] which angered and alarmed not only nationalist Afrikaners, but also many British immigrants as well as some Anglican and Presbyterian clergymen. Adulterated though it was, Cape liberalism did promote racial tolerance and equality before the law, and English-speaking churches were among the first to call for a multiracial society.[36]

Thus the British missionaries' witness marked the beginning of the church's fight against racial injustice in South Africa. But when the missionaries sided with the coloureds and Africans, as they sometimes did, some immigrants adopted the Afrikaners' point of view. Both groups of whites in South Africa were experiencing a colonial policy that was formed in London and often appeared to be against their interests. During the tensions that produced the Great Trek, some Britons were more sympathetic with the Afrikaners than with the liberals and missionaries.[37] This, along with the perceived dangers of the frontier, marked a step in their assimilation as white South Africans.[38]

It appears, then, that life in both South Africa and the United States hardened the racial attitudes of many British immigrants. Furthermore, in both places, sympathy for the oppressed was generally waning. After the Civil War had freed America's slaves, the gross inequality that remained was often overlooked, and concessions were made to southern white supremacists and their Jim Crow laws. Meanwhile, black leaders like Booker T. Washington essentially acquiesced and urged black Americans to raise themselves up through self-help, rather than by pushing for equal rights and antagonizing white America in the process. To top it off, Social Darwinism was providing a pseudoscientific basis for white supremacy. As immediate members of the dominant Anglo-American class, new British immigrants could readily accept an ideology that benefited them and sustained their privileges.

Meanwhile, British humanitarianism and Cape liberalism were fading in South Africa. One can see a shift already in 1854, when British immigrants united with Afrikaners to demand that the government consider the "Kafirs" in Natal as "foreigners" without land rights. The British government, mindful of a need to lighten the cost of its military and keep relations between whites harmonious, essentially acquiesced. After diamonds and gold were discovered, Social Darwinism contributed to the British authorities' decision to grant British immigrants and other white settlers their vast powers over Africans. In both places, then, the humanitarian component of liberalism faded, while the economic component (laissez-faire capitalism) persisted, though even this eventually succumbed to racism.[39]

The Late-Nineteenth Century

During the last third of the nineteenth century, British migration to America rose quite significantly, peaking to over eighty thousand annually in the 1880s. Most were young individuals from towns, either unskilled laborers or skilled in building trades or mining.[40] In both America and South Africa the extractive mining industries were significant inducements for British immigration. British immigration to South Africa increased to several thousand per year during the 1870s and 1880s, but assisted immigrants remained an important part of the migration. Between 1873 and 1883 alone, 22,300 were assisted to South Africa, at a cost to the colony of about a quarter-million pounds. Many were artisans and craftsmen threatened by economic depression and mechanization, or railway workers, unskilled laborers, and persons connected with mining and other extractive industries.[41] By 1891 there were 188,000 persons of English, Welsh, or Scottish birth living in South Africa, and among the "English" were a very significant number who were actually Cornish.[42]

The Cornish were notable among the British immigrants to both the United States and South Africa. They had the highest migration rate of all Britons to America, and probably to South Africa as well. This was due to a combination of factors. While tin and manganese mines were nearing exhaustion in many parts of Cornwall, America's lead, silver, iron, and gold deposits were being discovered and awaited development. Cornish miners also had a tradition of migration in search for the highest rewards for their work. Thus, during the mid-nineteenth century the Cornish were crucial for developing the rich lead regions of the Upper Mississippi River Valley of southwestern Wisconsin, northwestern Illinois, eastern Iowa, and parts of Missouri. They not only brought the earliest hearths and furnaces that could smelt the ore efficiently, but also the experience and skills necessary to develop the mines fully. By 1850, six thousand Cornish immigrants were living in the region, and they had established an unmistakably Cornish culture that still exists today in the form of architecture, foods, and even language idioms. At the same time, they turned their attention to the new iron mining regions of Upper Michigan, the gold fields of California, and then the many silver mining regions of the American West. In all of these places the

Cornish quickly rose to positions of mine captain or mine owner and enjoyed a higher status than other immigrant groups. They also showed a remarkable willingness to move in search of the greatest mining opportunities, and because many enjoyed the adventure of travel and seeing the world, many would inevitably find themselves in South Africa.[43]

The Cornish were also important in the development of South Africa's mining industry. Some had arrived with the 1820 settlers and quarried stone for some of the first permanent buildings. After the British had extended their hold to the southern boundary of the Orange River in 1847, Cornish immigrants arrived to develop the copper fields of Namaqualand. When in 1854-1855 there was a virtual copper mania in South Africa, the Cornish rushed in to fill the demand for advanced mining skills. British miners also brought the ideas and organizational structures of trade unionism to South Africa and America. By the turn of the century, roughly a quarter of the white mine workers on the Rand were Cornishmen.[44] Some mining villages still show the influence of the Cornish in the form of buildings and foods, like the Cornish pasty. To this day there are well over one hundred Cornish place names in South Africa.[45]

One significant difference was that the Cornish in America arrived as families, while those in South Africa were largely single males. This was due to the fact that most of the Cornish miners to America intended to remain in America, many of them using their earnings to buy a farm. In contrast, most of those to South Africa intended to make fast money and return to Britain, or go to America or Australia, though many ended up settling permanently. The comparative lack of Cornish women led to a high rate of intermarriage between Cornishmen and black Africans and to racial attitudes that were sometimes more enlightened than that of most whites.[46]

The Cornish also brought a religious tradition and outlook that influenced race relations in South Africa. Being mostly Wesleyan Methodists, the Cornish tended to be a devout and a moderating influence on the rough South African mining frontier, as they were in America. In both the United States and South Africa, the Cornish quickly established churches and temperance societies in an attempt to counter the lawlessness and moral decay that characterized settlements on the mining frontier. They were also known for being less rowdy and militant than other miners. Though probably most Cornish believed in the superiority of their own race, many also seem to have had comparatively progressive racial attitudes. This is illustrated by the fact that when they established cricket teams and led cricket tours in Namaqualand, black mine workers were invited to participate, and did.

South Africa's geology promoted an especially wide gap between highly skilled and unskilled labor. Because its ore deposits were so deep and not highly concentrated, South Africa's mining industry had special requirements for advanced engineering skills and extensive capital investment.[47] The British immigrants who filled these positions, as well as other skilled, financial, and mercantile positions, were an elite group of unskilled whites and nonwhites alike. The same was true in America, but the difference was even greater in

South Africa, especially as mining grew in dominance. Thus the large mining companies' aggressive expansion contributed significantly to South Africa's racially divided and discriminatory labor force.

But racism was the most potent force in creating social division in South Africa, especially when combined with the white monopoly on political power. It is perhaps not surprising that even in the age of laissez-faire, the government intervened in the labor market in order to preserve and extend white supremacy. In effect, the theoretically free-operating labor system that was championed by political economists and laissez-faire capitalists was trumped by racism. The government prevented greater economic and political equality by forcing low wages on black workers and preventing them from voting by raising the qualifications for the franchise—an oppressive intervention at least as severe as what occurred in the American South after the Civil War. White miners, for example, pressured the Cape government to restrict diggers' licenses to whites, and government taxation was sometimes designed specifically to restrict black labor's mobility.[48] As industrial capitalism spread, South Africa moved farther and farther from the early ideals embodied by Cape liberalism, and true economic liberalism was sacrificed to keep an oppressed nonwhite labor force available for exploitation. In this way, racism proved even more powerful than capitalist ideology. For South African society, racism and industrial capitalism were a particularly powerful and corrosive combination.

From this survey it appears that, as far as the history of race and reconciliation is concerned, the original social-economic and religious characteristics of British immigrants in South Africa were less important than the new environment they found themselves in and their experience with assimilation. Unfortunately, for many immigrants, assimilation created or intensified racism. This is not to say that liberal ideas and humanitarianism died within the English-speaking community in South Africa. English-speaking South Africans as a whole do have a more liberal record than other white South Africans. But ultimately, humanitarianism could not compete with racism and the powerful economic forces that ushered in South Africa's modern industrial era—a time that was indeed "baptized in blood and the subjugation of small nations."[49]

Immigration from Britain to South Africa declined in the late nineteenth century, as the second Anglo-Boer War unfolded and repulsed potential immigrants. Not surprisingly, concentration camps and guerrilla warfare alienated the Afrikaners from the British to such an extent that bitterness would remain throughout the twentieth century. But ironically, the war also caused the Colonial Office to be more conciliatory toward the Afrikaners, for the government considered white unity and the security it would supposedly bring to that part of the empire more important than the political and land rights of black and coloured South Africans. The threat of German expansion in southern Africa contributed to the sense of urgency for white unity. Therefore the government opened the way for more exploitation of the country's resources and granted the whites even more power to rule more or less absolutely over black

South Africans, as they had done before the arrival of Cape liberalism. After union in 1910 and the end of governmental interference from London, full segregation and the apartheid state were possible. [50]

Between the war and union, the government tried again to assist English immigration to South African farms. One goal was to break down the divisions between the two groups of whites. Another was to counterbalance the net outward flow of Britons from South Africa to Britain. Ultimately, the government was still hoping to use Anglicization as a means of reducing the threat of Afrikaner nationalism; but the attempt only exacerbated the tension and mistrust between the two white groups. The plan for assisted immigration failed in part because Afrikaner nationalism was growing and making South Africa less attractive to British migrants. But probably more important was the fact that Canada and Australia were offering generous land grants and assisted passages to British emigrants, making them far more attractive destinations.[51]

During the twentieth century, the British continued to be among the most migratory of Europeans, and increased numbers did go to South Africa after World War II. They were coming to a South Africa different from the one their predecessors had found, particularly after the rise of the National Party and the establishment of the apartheid state. It is true that the British immigrants in South Africa and their descendents were overrepresented among liberal whites who condemned the regime. It is also true that the modern capitalistic state that they had helped to create, and their government's policies toward Afrikaners, helped make apartheid a reality. In the history of South Africa and the United States, and indeed many other parts of the world, the influence of British people and institutions has been truly formative.

Notes

1. Everette E. Edwards, ed., *The Early Writings of Frederick Jackson Turner* (Madison: University of Wisconsin Press, 1938), 82.

2. David Hackett Fischer, *Albion's Seed: Four British Folkways in America* (Oxford: Oxford University Press, 1989); Kevin Phillips, *The Cousins' Wars: Religion, Politics, and the Triumph of Anglo-America* (New York: Basic Books, 1999); William E. Van Vugt, "British," in *A Nation of Peoples: A Sourcebook on America's Multicultural Heritage*, ed. Elliott R. Barkan (Westport, Conn.: Greenwood Press, 1999), 75-95.

3. Dudley Baines has calculated that 56 percent of the permanent English and Welsh emigrants from 1853-1900 chose the United States, though the percentage for earlier years was considerably higher. See *Migration in a Mature Economy: Emigration and Internal Migration in England and Wales, 1861-1900* (New York: Cambridge University Press, 1985), table 3.3, p. 63.

4. Charlotte Erickson, *Leaving England: Essays on British Emigration in the Nineteenth Century* (Ithaca: Cornell University Press, 1994), ch. 4.

5. John Stone, *Colonist or Uitlander?: A Study of the British Immigrant in South Africa* (Oxford: Oxford University Press, 1973), 96, 99-100.

6. Charlotte Erickson, *Invisible Immigrants: The Adaptation of English and Scottish Immigrants in Nineteenth-Century America* (Leicester: Leicester University Press, 1972).

7. William E. Van Vugt, *Britain to America: Mid-Nineteenth Century Immigrants to the United States* (Urbana: University of Illinois Press, 1999), ch. 9; Stone, *Colonist or Uitlander?* 103-104; Leonard Thompson, *A History of South Africa* (New Haven: Yale University Press, 1990), 56.

8. David E. Stannard, *American Holocaust: Columbus and the Conquest of the New World* (New York: Oxford University Press, 1992).

9. George M. Fredrickson, *White Supremacy: A Comparative Study in American and South African History* (Oxford: Oxford University Press, 1981), 210.

10. Stone, *Colonist or Uitlander?* 100-101; Thompson, *A History of South Africa*, 55.

11. John De Gruchy, *The Church Struggle in South Africa*, 2d ed. (Grand Rapids, Mich.: Eerdmans, 1986), 10; D. Hobart Houghton, *The South African Economy* (Cape Town: Oxford University Press, 1964), 10; M. H. De Kock, *Selected Subjects in the Economic History of South Africa* (Cape Town: Juta, 1924), 89-90; L. C. A. Knowles, *The Economic Development of the British Overseas Empire,* 2d ed. (London: Routledge, 1928), 92.

12. Erickson, *Leaving England*, 161; E. Morse Jones, *Role of the British Settlers in South Africa: Part I: Up to 1826* (Cape Town: Balkema, 1971), 5-6. I have compiled the percentage data as follows:

British Immigrants to the USA, 1827		British Immigrants to SA, 1820-1826
Agricultural Low-wage	6	24
Agricultural High-wage	7	6
Industrial Low-wage	2	7
Industrial High-wage	85	63
Total	**100**	**100**

Source: *Erickson and Jones*, as cited above.

13. Quoted in Stone, *Colonist or Uitlander?* 101-102, who cites T. Pringle, *Narrative of a Residence in South Africa* (1851; reprint, Cape Town: Struik, 1966), 12-13. Hockly also said that the 1820 settlers included a "considerable number of affluent emigrants," however he goes on to say that most were poor. See H. E. Hockly, *The Story of the British Settlers of 1820 in South Africa* (1948; reprint, Cape Town: Juta, 1957), 31.

14. Public Record Office, CO 48 294, 10 January 1849.

15. H. J. Simon and R. E. Simon, *Class and Colour in South Africa, 1850-1950* (London: Penguin, 1969), 21.

16. T. R. H. Davenport, *South Africa: A Modern History*, 2d ed. (Toronto: University of Toronto Press, 1978), 31; Monica Wilson and Leonard Thompson, eds., *Oxford History of South Africa*, vol. 1 (Oxford: Clarendon, 1969).

17. Hockly, *The Story of the British Settlers of 1820*, 70; M. S. Geen, *The Making of South Africa* (Cape Town: Maskew Miller, 1958), 81.

18. British migration statistics are notoriously problematic, in part because of the lack of differentiation between English, Scots, Welsh, and Irish. The best available are those compiled in N. H. Carrier and J. R. Jeffery, *External Migration: A Study of the Available Statistics, 1815-1950* (London: Her Majesty's Stationery Office, 1953). See table 2, pp. 99-100; table 3, p. 15. Between 1825 and 1845 (before assisted migration resumes) 5,354 English and Welsh were recorded as entering South Africa. A similar number was recorded for those from "Great Britain and Ireland." Most of those were probably Irish, but there is no way to determine how many.

19. Calculated from CLEC Report of 1851.

20. Van Vugt, *Britain to America*, chs. 2-3.

21. Fred Hitchens, *The Colonial Land and Emigration Commission* (Philadelphia: University of Pennsylvania Press, 1931), 321-22.

22. Maitland to Lord Stanley, 30 March 1846, *Parliamentary Papers*, 1849, vol. 2, 586. The second statement was made by J. S. Christopher, who applied to launch his own scheme of assisted immigration, in *Parliamentary Papers, 1850,* vol. 38, 524.

23. Alan Frederick Hattersley, *The Natal Settlers, 1849-1851* (Pietermaritzburg: Shuter and Shooter, 1949), 7. Many were led by James Erasmus Methley, son of a Wesleyan minister from Leeds.

24. Erickson, *Leaving England*, 172, 183.

25. "Reports of the Colonial Land and Emigration Commissioners," *Parliamentary Papers, 1949*, vol. 2, 586-95; 1850, vol. 38, 687, 704-709.

26. Hattersley, *The Natal Settlers*; Stone, *Colonist or Uitlander?* 114; Wilson and Thompson, *Oxford History of South Africa*, 383. Fredrickson, *White Supremacy*, 185.

27. Nigel Worden, *The Making of Modern South Africa: Conquest, Segregation, and Apartheid* (Cambridge, Mass.: Oxford University Press, 1994), 17.

28. In 1857 another £50,000 was voted to assist 12,000 settlers. During 1857-62, another 10,000 came, and few had paid their own passage. In 1861 alone, £25,000 was approved to assist British immigration for that year. See Esme Bull, *Aided Immigration from Britain to South Africa, 1857 to 1867*, ed. J. L. Basson (Pretoria: Human Sciences Research Council, 1991), 12. De Kock reports that in 1858-59, 6,343 British immigrants were introduced to meet the demand for laborers at the Cape, and that this was the last major organized scheme for European immigration. See *Selected Subjects in the Economic History of South Africa*, 138.

29. Cecillie Swaisland, *Servants and Gentlewomen to the Golden Land: The Emigration of Single Women from Britain to Southern Africa, 1820-1939* (Oxford: Berg Publishers, 1993).

30. David Turley, *The Culture of English Antislavery, 1780-1860* (London: Routledge, 1991); Fredrickson, *White Supremacy*, 162-63, 176, 180-81; Davenport, *South Africa*, 76; Elizabeth Elbourne and Robert Ross, "Combating Spiritual and Social Bondage: Early Missions in the Cape Colony," in *Christianity in South Africa: A Political, Social, and Cultural History*, ed. Richard Elphick and Rodney Davenport, (Berkeley: University of California Press, 1997), 31-50.

31. Van Vugt, *Britain to America*, ch. 9. Methodists and other nonconformists were overrepresented among British immigrants to both the United States and South Africa, and probably other destinations because nonconformists already felt detached from Britain, where they could still experience some forms of discrimination and where they found it difficult or impossible to rise within the political and educational establishment. At the same time, many knew they could feel quite at home in America, where they could enjoy the company and support of relatives and friends already there. Solid networks of communication were laid across the Atlantic by Methodists already in the eighteenth century, and these became effective conduits for many who were leaving Britain during the mid-nineteenth century.

32. Van Vugt, *Britain to America,* ch. 9.

33. George Kitson Clark, *The Making of Victorian England* (Cambridge, Mass.: Harvard University Press, 1962); Thompson, *A History of South Africa*, 56-57.

34. For more discussion of the role of the English-speaking churches in South African society, see the chapter by John De Gruchy in this volume, "The Chastening of the English-Speaking Churches in South Africa."

35. De Gruchy, *The Church Struggle in South Africa*, 12.

36. Thompson, *A History of South Africa*, 87; Fredrickson, *White Supremacy*, 138; De Gruchy, "Grappling with a Colonial Heritage: The English-Speaking Churches under Imperialism and Apartheid," in *Christianity in South Africa: A Political, Social, and Cultural History*, ed. Richard Elphick and Rodney Davenport (Berkeley: University of California Press, 1997), 157.

37. Davenport, *South Africa: A Modern History*, 31, 38, 53, 62; A. Theodore Wirgman, *The History of the English Church and People in South Africa* (1895; reprint, New York: Negro Universities Press, 1969), 90-92; Rodney Davenport, "Settlement, Conquest, and Theological Controversy: The Churches of Nineteenth-Century European Immigrants," in *Christianity in South Africa*, 62.

38. Thompson, *A History of South Africa*, 56; Stone, *Colonist or Uitlander?* 23, 30-32.

39. Davenport, "Settlement, Conquest, and Theological Controversy," 62; Wilson and Thompson, *Oxford History*, 383-84; Fredrickson, *White Supremacy*, 186, 195-96.

40. Erickson, *Leaving England*, ch. 3.

41. Stone, *Colonist or Uitlander?* 41, 114. For figures on numbers of immigrants during the 1880s, see F. G. Brownell, *British Immigration to South Africa, 1946-1970* (Pretoria: The Government Printer, 1985), 3.

42. Carrier and Jeffery, *External Migration*, table 3, p. 15. The data on British immigration to South Africa remained very problematical during the late nineteenth century because they do not always separate the British from the Irish, and the permanent from the temporary immigrants.

43. John Rowe, *The Hard-Rock Men: Cornish Immigration and the North American Mining Frontier* (Liverpool: Liverpool University Press, 1974); Arthur C. Todd, *The Cornish Miner in America: The Contribution to the Mining History of the United States by Emigrant Cornish Miners* (Cornwall: Barton, Clark, 1967); Van Vugt, *Britain to America*, ch. 5.

44. Gill Burke, "The Cornish Diaspora of the Nineteenth Century," in *International Labour Migration: Historical Perspectives*, ed. Shula Marks and Peter Richardson (London: Institute of Commonwealth Studies, 1984), 57-75.

45. Stone, *Colonist or Uitlander?* 117 n. 46.

46. G. B. Dickason, *Cornish Immigrants to South Africa: The Cousin Jacks' Contribution to the Development of Mining and Commerce, 1820-1920* (Cape Town: Balkema, 1978).

47. Thompson, *A History of South Africa*, 118-20; Fredrickson, *White Supremacy*, 217.

48. Fredrickson, *White Supremacy*, 201-203, 216-17.

49. *Apartheid and the History of the Struggle for Freedom in South Africa* (CD-ROM), Forum Technologies, IDC Publishers.

50. De Gruchy, "Grappling with a Colonial Heritage," 156; Worden, *The Making of Modern South Africa*, 32; Fredrickson, *White Supremacy*, 139, 239-40.

51. Carrier and Jeffery, *External Migration*, table 2, p. 100. In 1899, 1904, and 1906-8, there was a net migration from South Africa of people described as from "Great Britain and Ireland." On the failure of early-twentieth century assisted migration, see Kent Fedorowich, "Anglicization and Politicization of British Immigration to South Africa, 1899-1929," *The Journal of Imperial and Commonwealth History* 19 (1991): 222-46.

Chapter Three

The Chastening of the English-Speaking Churches in South Africa

John W. De Gruchy

THE STATUS OF Christianity in South Africa has never been under as much critical scrutiny as it is today. After more than three centuries of religious domination, Christianity no longer has the position it had come to expect and enjoy. The evidence is not hard to find and needs no elaboration here. While a significantly large proportion of the population remains Christian, and while churches continue to play an important role within society, this has to be undertaken in open contest with other religious and ideological constituencies and options. At least that it is how the new constitution declares it should be. Yet, there are other reasons for this loss of quasi-official status. Not least among these has been Christianity's association with European colonization and the ambiguous role played by most of the churches during the apartheid era. The extent to which the Dutch Reformed Church (DRC) helped give birth to the ideology of apartheid and supported its implementation has undoubtedly severely tarnished the image of Christianity.

Generalizations about Christianity are notoriously problematic. This is certainly true of Christianity in South Africa, which is an amalgam of many different streams that have flowed into the region from various sources during the past three and a half centuries. Foremost among them have been the different varieties of European Christianity. But there have been many other tributaries, and, perhaps most significantly of all, there has been the remarkable development of African initiated churches. Given the range of denominations as well as the multiplicity of theological positions, ecclesiastical structures, and spiritualities that they represent, it is more appropriate to speak of contesting Christianities rather than Christianity in South Africa. If any discussion of Christianity within South African society is to avoid the dangers of generalization, it has to focus quite specifically on particular instances. The need to do so has led to the development of various typologies such as that which distinguishes between the Afrikaans-speaking Dutch Reformed and the so-called English-speaking churches.[1] Even such basic typologies as these are problematic, but at least they provide a more meaningful way of trying to understand the place and role of Christianity in contemporary South Africa.

The So-Called English-Speaking Churches

The term *English-speaking churches* is problematic, something that is immediately apparent by the frequent use of the adjective *so-called*. For one thing, it has invariably excluded denominations who are equally English-speaking, such as the Baptist Union, the Church of England in South Africa, and the Roman Catholic Church. For another, it does not indicate that the ethnic composition of these churches has changed dramatically during the twentieth century, nor the fact that English is no longer the home language of the majority of their memberships. Whatever usefulness the term has served, its value in the new South Africa is in question. Indeed, the need to distinguish churches according to language is no longer particularly relevant. After all, English has become the dominant language of politics, education, and commerce, and within the ecclesiastical sphere it is as much the language of some Pentecostal and charismatic churches as it is of the Anglican or Methodist. So the term *English-speaking churches* has lost much of its historic specificity.

When it was originally coined earlier this century, however, the term *English-speaking churches* referred to a clearly identifiable group of churches (Anglican, Congregational, Methodist, Presbyterian).[2] These were mainline denominations as distinct from mission churches with similar names, such as the Bantu Presbyterian Church. They were led by white male English-speaking clergy. Financial power and control over policy was firmly entrenched in white male hands, and the dominant membership comprised English-speaking whites despite the fact that the majority was already black and coloured. During the apartheid era these so-called English-speaking churches found common cause in opposing Afrikaner nationalism and the ideology of apartheid, even though they were not always clear, unanimous, or active in their opposition. This ambiguity reflected the reality that their white members were as much beneficiaries of apartheid as other white members of society.

The English-speaking churches were also in the forefront of the ecumenical movement in South Africa, providing much of the leadership of the South African Council of Churches, even though their ecumenical commitment was not always as strong as it might have been. Their sense of somehow belonging together can be seen from the fact that in 1967 they embarked on an ambitious search for union. But what is probably as important as any of this is the fact that these churches were generally regarded as the English-speaking churches by the media, by the government, and by the Dutch Reformed churches. They were the churches "in opposition" as it were—white liberals at prayer—at least from the perspective of Afrikanerdom. One reason why other English-speaking churches, such as the Baptist or Church of England in South Africa, did not want to be included under this label was precisely their reluctance to be tarred with the same political or ecumenical brush.

Times have certainly changed since those difficult days. The ecumenical imperative that bound the English-speaking churches together no longer has quite the same power. Moreover, as demonstrated at the Faith Community Hearings of the Truth and Reconciliation Commission (TRC), churches such as the Baptist and Church of England in South Africa have begun to join the mainstream, at least as far as their confessions of guilt for the past and commitments for future reconciliation are concerned.[3] So quite apart from the fact that there is a black majority within the English-speaking churches and that English is not the majority home language, the term *English-speaking churches* is no longer appropriate or serviceable in the way it was previously. If the churches formerly referred to in this way need to be classified corporately, then a new term is necessary. Perhaps *churches of British origin* might be considered. For the purposes of this chapter, however, I want to stay with the term English-speaking churches because it is appropriate to the subject. But I intend to use it mindful of its historical significance. As such, it refers specifically to the group of churches I have indicated above as they related to each other and the broader ecumenical and social situation in South Africa from about the 1930s until the official end of the apartheid era.

But the term has another important connotation. It refers not just collectively to the churches, but specifically to the churches as they were under white leadership and at a time when their white membership was dominant even if not in the majority. The English-speaking churches represented the culture and interests of our equivalent of the WASPs in the United States. So when I speak of the chastening of the so-called English-speaking churches in South Africa, I speak specifically of this constituency. In other words, *English-speaking churches are primarily an ethnic description rather than a theological or ecclesiastical one, and one that refers especially to them during a specific historic period.* This does not mean that there were or are no theological or ecclesiastical commonalities among them. On the contrary, they share much in common due not least to their exposure to and participation in the ecumenical movement both locally and internationally. Nor does it mean that the term is no longer appropriate if used in the way indicated. The chastening of the English-speaking churches, then, has to do primarily with their white British or Anglo-Saxon membership and heritage, something that parallels more broadly the chastening of white South Africa in the transition to the new South Africa.

Chastening is a process of disciplining, purifying, or correcting. In biblical language it is best expressed by the word *judgment.* God's judgment of Israel, for example, is often described in the Old Testament as a process of disciplining and purifying. Perhaps the most appropriate text in the New Testament that relates to my theme is that in the first letter of Peter: "For the time has come for judgment to begin with the household of God" (4:17). The point here is that the chastening of the nation should begin with the chastening of the church. Or, to put it in another way, the church should lead the way in recognizing that the "hour of judgment," or *kairos,* has arrived with its demand for *metanoia,* or fundamental change without which transformation and reconciliation will remain elusive.

Just as the chastening of the Dutch Reformed churches is essential if Afrikanerdom is to enter fully into the new South Africa, so the chastening of the English-speaking churches is an essential element in enabling white English-speaking South Africans to do the same. That is, they must put their gripes aside and recognize that much of what has happened and what is happening in the country is not only a judgment on their failures, but also an invitation to them to participate in the just transformation of the country. However, the chastening of the English-speaking churches is somewhat different in character from that of the Dutch Reformed for reasons that, if not already obvious, should become so as we proceed to examine what I suggest are three phases or aspects of the chastening process. The first is the loss of political status, the second is the loss of ethnic dominance, and the third is the loss of moral innocence. Coming to terms with these losses is a necessary prelude to reconciliation and transformation.

The Loss of Political Status

The transplanting of British Christianity in South Africa can be traced to the first British occupation of the Cape in 1795, which heralded more than a century of colonial rule.[4] This resulted in the arrival of soldiers and civil servants as well as chaplains and then settlers, notably from 1820 onward, who brought with them their particular denominational brands. But British Christianity also came in two distinct forms, the one serving the interests of the colonial authorities and the increasing numbers of settlers, the other seeking to convert and culturally domesticate the indigenous peoples. Within a few decades, most of the major British missionary societies were hard at work establishing mission stations and harvesting converts. Both the settlers and the missionaries were committed to establishing British Christianity as a reproduction of what was familiar "back home," whether in liturgy and hymnody, theology and spirituality, or architecture and ecclesial structure.[5] In this they were remarkably successful.

Brought together by historical circumstances, these British churches were bonded by culture and language as a minority in a strange and threatening context. But they were also aware of their differences and very conscious of the reasons for them. There was not a great deal of love lost between colonial Anglican bishops and clergy and the ministers of other British churches (Baptists, Congregationalists, Methodists, and Presbyterians). Anglican leaders were more concerned to develop relationships with the dominant Dutch Reformed Church (DRC) than they were with the English Nonconformists or Scottish Presbyterians. Hence the first synod of the Church of the Province of South Africa (Anglican [CPSA]) in 1870 decided to explore the possibility of union with the Dutch Reformed Church. This soon came to naught. But the notion that Anglicans might seek union with the other branches of British Christianity was not really entertained until well into the twentieth century when the term *English-speaking churches* gradually came to describe them corporately.

What led Robert Gray, the first Anglican bishop of Cape Town, to propose union with the Dutch Reformed Church? It had to do with the perceived need for a state church that would unite Christians of European descent. The small Church of England, despite being the established church of the colonial authorities, could not function as a "national" church apart from the much larger and better established Dutch Reformed Church. The possibility of a union between the two established churches was remote, but the fact that the idea was contemplated by Gray and his fellow bishops is significant. It was almost inconceivable to both the Anglicans and the Dutch Reformed that they could properly fulfill their public role unless they had the necessary political status. The other British denominations could be left to their own devices and desires, even though these were not always to the liking of the Anglicans or the Dutch Reformed Church leadership. For, true to their conscience and after years of struggle, lay representatives of Nonconformity (notably the Congregationalists) were successful in bringing about an end to any formal establishment of Christianity in the colony through the Voluntary Act passed by the Cape parliament in 1875. In the end, both the CPSA and the Dutch Reformed Church reluctantly accepted the Voluntary Act because it enabled them to deal with internal problems without state interference. The fact that it would take many more years for this event to achieve its goals, namely in the recognition of South Africa as a secular state in the 1994 constitution, should not detract from its historical significance as the first step in that long process.

Despite this, the Anglicans continued to act as if they were the established church, as did the Dutch Reformed Church with perhaps more justification if size and influence were any measure. Certainly representatives of the crown were always present at CPSA synods and there was a great deal of contact between the bishops and senior colonial officials. As all the bishops were themselves expatriates and Oxbridge products, they also had a strong network of personal relations with political leadership back home. Symbols of the connections between the CPSA, the empire, and colonial authority abound in most Anglican cathedrals in South Africa. But it was not only an Anglican matter. When it came to support for the empire, there was virtual unanimity among all the British churches and missions. British Christianity as a whole (the Quakers being a significant but very small exception) provided the spiritual legitimation for colonial conquest and imperial adventure, as well as moral purpose for the economic advancement of British settlers. During the South African War (1899-1902), Anglicans, Nonconformists, and Presbyterians together provided the necessary moral and spiritual sanctions for the British war effort. It was, they argued, God's instrument of judgment on the recalcitrant Boer republics and, somewhat as a necessary afterthought, God's means of saving the black races from oppression.

After the war, the latter conviction was subordinated to their unqualified support for Lord Milner's attempt to impose British cultural and political hegemony on the Afrikaners in the interests of white unity and national reconciliation. Just as Bishop Gray had attempted to unite the CPSA and DRC in order to build a united (white) Christian nation, so now the English-speaking churches understood their mission as helping to foster a government of national unity within the empire. Racial segregation was regarded as preordained by virtually all whites, whether Afrikaans or English, so national unity and reconciliation certainly did not embrace more than those of European lineage. Even those English-speaking church leaders who warned that blacks could not be excluded in the long term, such as Archbishop Carter of Cape Town, accepted the new white Union of South Africa as a divine blessing and participated in its celebration.

English-speaking South Africans were demographically larger in the period following the Anglo-Boer war than at any period either before or since. It certainly looked then that South Africa would become a British dominion like Australia or Canada in which the white English-speaking population would take control of the future. The English-speaking churches were an integral part of this process. Church schools, modelled on the British public school system, provided an upper crust of white leadership in all walks of life. A constant inflow of British clergy, missionaries, public servants, and educators ensured that British Christianity was firmly entrenched, and the British control of the mining industry meant that however much Afrikaners were the majority within white South Africa, they could not compete economically. British Christianity went hand in glove with British and South African English economic interests.[6]

But the expectations and aspirations that Milner inspired within the English-speaking community were not to be realized. The English-speaking churches certainly continued to grow, but their growth in white membership did not keep pace with their growth in either African and coloured membership or national demography. They also began to lose their political influence as Afrikaner nationalism grew in strength and eventually came to power. This did not mean that they were without significance, but it was a significance that was being painfully redefined. Nonconformists were accustomed to being "against the government," even if this was not so much the case in South Africa where they were part of colonial hegemony. Now, however, all the English-speaking churches were forced to become nonconformist—churches which, by their very definition as English-speaking and increasingly black in membership, were in opposition to the government. It is true, of course, that they remained trapped to a large extent in their colonial past. Their white membership was among the privileged even if the churches no longer represented those in power, and their racial attitudes were often no better than those of the majority of Afrikaners who were far more maligned. But they could no longer claim to be the spiritual arm of colonial power. That power base was gone forever and any clinging to it was wishful thinking.

The loss of political influence became ever more apparent as the apartheid years passed. Although the synods of the English-speaking churches continued for some years to address letters of faithful and prayerful support to the governor general, even that time-honored tradition began to lapse and was eventually discontinued after South Africa left the Commonwealth in 1961. The English-speaking churches both individually and corporately continued to address social and political issues, but now their stance was more critical as apartheid policy began to be formulated and implemented. Whether they were sufficiently critical or faithful in the practical implementation of their resolutions is another matter. That aside, the fact is that their resolutions condemning apartheid were virtually ignored. Church leaders who went on delegations to the prime minister or members of the cabinet invariably returned empty-handed. If judged according to the effectiveness of such traditional ways of relating to the state, the English-speaking churches were politically powerless. Such power as they had did not reside in the role or influence of their white leadership or membership but with their black constituency. However, until the 1970s that power had not yet managed to influence the churches significantly, let alone strongly influence politics through the churches. This required that the white power base within the English-speaking churches would lose their dominance.

The Loss of Ethnic Dominance

We have already noted that the demographic size and political influence of the white English-speaking population in South Africa peaked during the years that followed the formation of the Union of South Africa. Yet, white English-speakers continued to dominate and control the English-speaking churches for many decades despite the growing number of black members within their ranks. This was so even though, in contrast to the Dutch Reformed Church, they accepted the need to become multiracial rather than segregated denominations. But this multiracial policy did not make much difference at the local parish or congregational level, nor did it lead to a change of control in the administration and policy making of the churches. Racism was rife throughout white South African society whether Afrikaans- or English-speaking. Segregation was almost as much a reality as it was within the Dutch Reformed Church, except for the difference that it was not formally sanctioned. Nonetheless, the fact that the English-speaking churches did not formally adopt segregationist policies had far-reaching consequences.

Black Christians have had three options as far as membership within church institutions is concerned. The first option meant that they could join one of the myriad African initiated churches that are unashamedly African and under African control. The second option has been membership within so-called mission churches, that is, the churches established by European missionary societies or white churches within South Africa. Although these churches have invariably been dependent upon the financial support of mission boards, they have generally gained their autonomy and are now under black control. The third option was membership in the so-called mainline churches that were, in principle, open to all races though practicing de facto segregation such as the English-speaking churches. That many did join these churches is perhaps remarkable for it meant accepting white domination within the church, even if there was considerable black control at the parish and congregational level. Blacks within the English-speaking churches were second-class citizens.

This second-class status remained the case until very recent times, though the beginnings of change can be traced back to the post-Second World War period. The first phase in the process I refer to as tokenism, that is, the recognition by white leaders of the need to include leading black representatives within the higher echelons of the churches, but in such a way that this did not really affect the balance of power. Having said this, among the black Christian elite who belonged to the English-speaking churches have been some of the most important black political and social leaders of the country. The participation of Dr. Z. K. Matthews, Chief Albert Luthuli, and Z. K. Mahabane at the Cottesloe Consultation in 1960 is indicative of this, but they are only three of many distinguished African leaders within these churches, both clergy and lay. They knew, of course, that they were being used as tokens, and on occasion they said so with considerable force. They were also remarkably patient and restrained, knowing that history was on their side. However, it was not until the late 1970s that there was a significant move to elect blacks to high office within the church, and even then it was not normally the case that they had any leadership role among the white constituency. Until that began to happen, no matter how significant the representative role of individual black leaders, until they could determine policy and exercise power, the charge of tokenism was entirely appropriate.

The second phase in the process was signalled by the advent of the Black Consciousness Movement (BCM) and black theology in the life of the English-speaking churches. The BCM within these churches was, as elsewhere, essentially a rejection of the white monopoly of power, privilege, and influence. It was a categorical repudiation of all forms of tokenism. As such it involved, in the first instance, a strategy of withdrawal from the domain of white hegemony. Hence the development of black caucuses within the English-speaking churches and the refusal to be co-opted in support of programs and policies that were neither designed by blacks nor in their interest. In this they were following the path chosen by a previous generation who founded the African initiated churches, but from within the mainline churches. Withdrawal was a clear strategy both to undermine tokenism and to exercise control. The role of the Federal Theological Seminary in the training of ministers and priests for the English-speaking churches was, during the 1970s and 1980s, a vital instrument in the development of a new generation of black clergy and leaders who adopted this position. That story need not be retold here. However, its significance was profound and far-reaching not only at the level of theological articulation and of consciousness, but also in terms of the practical effect it had on the life of the English-speaking churches.

First of all, it led to a new awareness that the English-speaking churches had become black majority churches and that this had implications for the leadership, structures, and policy of the churches. Increasing numbers of blacks were elected to representative leadership positions. Second, it had a decisive impact on the way in which the English-speaking churches related to the struggle against apartheid. For example, their response to the World Council of Churches' (WCC) Program to Combat Racism would have been far more cautious had it not been for the black pressure. Third, it led to the alienation of more conservative whites and various strategies of reaction. The most decisive of these was withdrawal from the churches and the joining of other denominations that were less "political." Another was through withdrawal of financial support, or simply withdrawal from the wider life of the denominations in favor of the white suburban local parish or congregation. Fourth, it led to the churches' being regarded by the government as black institutions supportive of revolution and therefore as churches that had to be actively opposed. Hence the rise of state-sponsored right-wing, antiecumenical, and anti-English-speaking church organizations aimed at influencing white opinion within the churches. This certainly had considerable success, as became apparent when churches such as the Church of England in South Africa, which had benefited from the strategy, made its submission to the TRC.

Despite these pressures, the majority of whites remained within the English-speaking churches. While not many were happy with the developments, at least some along with the leadership recognized the need for reconciliation between the races within the churches and the broader society. Indeed, such reconciliation became the key and much contested issue during this period. Whereas previously the focus had been on reconciliation with Afrikaners, now the focus had shifted in the opposite direction in response to the challenge of the Black Consciousness Movement. In this way, white English-speaking church leaders sought to counter the effect of black solidarity and strategic withdrawal. Thus, reconciliation became the symbol of theological and ideological divergence. This became strikingly evident in the Kairos Document, which accused the English-speaking churches of supporting a "church theology" of "cheap reconciliation," that is, reconciliation without any fundamental change in the power structures of South Africa.

If the first stage in the process where the English-speaking churches lost ethnic control was marked by tokenism, and the second was that of black consciousness, the third phase is that of Africanization. This process has deep roots, but it is only in recent times that the Africanization of the English-speaking churches in South Africa has become a major and irrevocable movement.

We can distinguish among three main positions on the subject of Africanization and its implications for the English-speaking churches. First, there is the exclusive religio-cultural understanding. Those who take this position argue that Africanization means recovering indigenous black African culture as the dominant and controlling culture. Hence there is a concerted effort to ensure the equality of indigenous languages alongside English, and traditional African religion alongside Christianity, Islam, and other imported traditions. Indigenous African languages are, of course, dominant in the vast majority of

African congregations and parishes, even though English remains the language of denominational discourse. The title, English-speaking churches, reflects the latter reality but is, as we have previously observed, a misnomer when it comes to the former. The relationship between Christianity and African traditional religion is more problematic. What, for example, is the connection between African culture and traditional religion, and in what way or ways should or does Christianity relate to it? The debate is a complex one but of considerable importance for the Africanization of Christianity and, therefore, for the Africanization of the legacy of British Christianity. These issues are now at the center of African theology, an enterprise that has not been as fully engaged in South Africa as elsewhere in sub-Saharan Africa hitherto, but one that is now very much in the fore. [7]

Second, Africanization is understood as a striving toward black majority control in all spheres. What precisely is meant by *black* is contested. Those of Indian or coloured background complain that the emphasis is on black Africans more narrowly defined. But that aside, this understanding means, for example, that the Africanization of the universities requires the striving toward a black majority among students, faculty, and administrators. Africanization is linked to affirmative action programs and the various economic development initiatives of the government and business. In many respects, Africanization in this sense has already occurred to a significant degree within the English-speaking churches. This was, after all, one of the goals of the black consciousness and black theology movements. While power still resides in white hands to a certain degree, there can be little doubt that black leadership is now firmly in place, and that issues that primarily concern the black constituency increasingly dominate the agenda of these churches.

The third understanding of Africanization may be defined as an inclusive nonracial one. This embraces all people who identify fully with Africa irrespective of race or even origin. In South Africa, this is expressed by the word *multiculturalism*.[8] During the apartheid era, when the diversity of culture was used as a justification for racial oppression, the affirmation of cultural identity and diversity was anathema to those who rejected the ideology. But it is now recognized as an essential ingredient in the development of the new South Africa. It is now possible to affirm one's own historical background, whether European or Indian or Malayan, while at the same time locating that within a broader African identity. Within this third paradigm, African culture and black control remains central, but not to the exclusion of other cultures and races. This approach to Africanization is most germane to the multiracial ethos of the English-speaking churches. The challenge facing them is how to move beyond multiracialism through nonracialism to a multiculturalism that is truly African, yet open to the legacy of other cultures including the legacy of British Christianity as expressed in the English-speaking churches. One possible clue lies in the recognition that the loss of ethnic domination can be turned into a gain, but first we need to reflect on the extent to which the English-speaking churches have lost their moral innocence.

The Loss of Moral Innocence

All the English-speaking member churches were unanimous in formally rejecting apartheid and opposing much of its legislation. But much of this was more a matter of pronouncement than of action. Synodical resolutions seldom led to an active attempt to overthrow apartheid. Having said this, we must acknowledge, of course, that churches as churches have seldom been engaged in direct political action. The way in which churches become so engaged is through their members, and invariably it is only through a relative minority of members. This can happen in various ways; for example, through participation in political organizations or through non-governmental organizations (NGOs) and the like. It is very difficult to quantify, then, the extent to which the pronouncements of the English-speaking churches actually encouraged political action against apartheid on the part of either their white or black constituency. But at least it can be said that the resolutions passed would have given them some kind of support, even if it was more qualified than they needed. Many of those who were engaged in social action, including those who belonged to such women's organizations as the Black Sash, or young white males who were conscientious objectors, were deeply committed members of English-speaking churches. Much of this was, of course, in response to the challenge presented by blacks and the political situation as such rather than in obedience to church pronouncements.

While the English-speaking churches were critical of apartheid right from the outset, their critique was more outspoken only after the Soweto uprising in 1976. This was determined to a large extent by the Black Consciousness Movement, which had inspired the Soweto uprising, providing a new and more militant direction to the churches' participation in the struggle. Ministers and priests previously educated in the moderate traditions of British theology were now trained to do theology in direct relation to the social and political context. In fact, the 1960s saw the emergence of several South African theologies. The theologies that had traditionally informed the life and witness of the English-speaking churches were no longer contextually relevant. By the late 1970s, South Africa was a melting pot of global as well as indigenous theologies and spiritualities—not only those associated with liberation and justice, but also those associated with Pentecostalism, the charismatic movement, and the "Spirit-filled" African initiated churches. In other words, both the ecclesial and theological hegemony of the English-speaking churches was gone. In what respects, then, did they still have some preeminence? Surely their critical stance against apartheid was something to which they could point, even though they were at least partly aware of its inadequacy. Of all the churches, the English-speaking churches had led the way both ecumenically and in social witness.

But a clear signal that this was not exactly the way they were perceived by those engaged more directly in the struggle against apartheid was expressed in the Kairos Document. Although the Kairos Document found some churches, such as the DRC, guilty of "state theology," a theology that supported apartheid, it also found other churches, such as the English-speaking, guilty of what they called "church theology." By this they meant that these churches despite their criticism of apartheid sought to overcome it through a process of racial reconciliation rather than by destroying its structures and building a new just society. "Prophetic theology" was, in distinction from the previous two categories, a critical theology of resistance in solidarity with all who were victims of apartheid and those who were engaged in the struggle for a just democratic society.

The depiction of the theology of the English-speaking churches as church theology may have been misleading or inappropriate, as Archbishop Tutu insisted, yet it undoubtedly touched a raw nerve within those churches. There were several reasons for this. The first was the fact that, unlike the DRC, the English-speaking churches took some pride in the fact that they were multiracial and that, despite racism and segregation in their ranks, at least they were heading in the right direction. They were the churches that promoted racial reconciliation. The second was that while the English-speaking churches were increasingly aware of their failure to put their antiapartheid resolutions into practice, they took some pride in the fact that they had adopted such resolutions. As the government itself proclaimed, they were the antiapartheid churches, the churches that were soft on communism and terrorism, the churches that were promoting revolution and anarchy whether intentionally or not. And it is true that their resolutions were not just about racial reconciliation, for if you really examine them, they said much also about social and economic justice. Yet, as we have noted, there was an undeniable gap between resolve and action, and the Kairos Document refused to let them off the hook. They might not have given theological legitimation to apartheid, but were not their many resolutions but a way of self-justification while they remained beneficiaries of the system? In other words, the Kairos Document was a challenge to the English-speaking churches' claim to innocence.

The Kairos Document, like all such confessing and prophetic statements, did not indulge in the luxury of careful qualification. Its intent was to be a sharp two-edged sword thrusting on the one side against the theological supporters of apartheid and, on the other side, against those who sought cheap solutions and who claimed the moral high ground. The fact is, to a large degree their critical stance was because of the pressure coming from the black leadership and membership within their ranks. By and large, the white constituency within the English-speaking churches—what is really meant by this description—were not only on the sidelines of the struggle when it came to action, but were compromised by their attempt to appease white sentiment even while criticizing apartheid.

At a consultation on the need for a confession of guilt sponsored by the South African Council of Churches held in Soweto in 1988, there was considerable debate on how appropriate it was that the English-speaking churches should confess their guilt for the sins of apartheid. The point was that the vast majority of the membership of the churches were themselves the victims of apartheid. Yet, at the same time, it was recognized that the churches were guilty in many ways. However, it was also recognized that their guilt was largely, though not solely, confined to their white membership.[9] Unless that distinction was made then it was very difficult to speak in terms of a confession of guilt without its being misleading and misunderstood. There is a qualitative difference between the innocent victims of apartheid and the apparent innocent bystanders and beneficiaries of apartheid. Of course, this is what began to emerge in the TRC hearings in November 1997.

Yet, there is something else that needs to be reckoned with, something that was also touched on in the submissions of the English-speaking churches, but that has not yet really come to the fore in analyses such as this. I refer to the need for the English-speaking churches to take a step back behind apartheid and recognize their guilt with regard to colonialism. It is only when they do this that these churches will finally lose their innocence and claim to a high moral ground. For what is of utmost importance in coming to terms with the past is the need for the English-speaking churches to accept the role that they played not just during apartheid, but also during the colonial period, including the South African war and the formation of the Union of South Africa. As is so clearly evident from our perspective today, virtually everything we now associate with apartheid had its origins in colonial society. The English-speaking churches were the churches of colonialism. They were, by and large, the advocates of a colonial theology. They supported both the imperial war effort and the economic forces that led to it. They also supported Milner's efforts to suppress Afrikaner identity and language. So they were not just the beneficiaries, albeit critical beneficiaries, of apartheid; they were also the supporters and sanctifiers of colonialism and, therefore, of the way in which preapartheid society was racially and economically structured. They cannot even claim to be innocent bystanders and reluctant beneficiaries. They have lost their innocence.

Turning Loss into Gain

South Africa today is a very different place to that which greeted the first British colonists and settlers at the beginning of the nineteenth century. Then everything was alien and foreboding. The planting of British Christianity within such soil was, for all its faults, remarkable in its extent and influence. South Africa today is also a very different place to what it was at the turn of the twentieth century when white English-speaking hegemony reached its zenith and the English-speaking churches were part of the dominant power. South Africa today is entering a new era of both uncertainty and promise. As a multicultural and multifaith democracy, each cultural and religious tradition has to rediscover its niche and its role and work out afresh its identity. The submissions presented by the English-speaking churches to the Truth and Reconciliation Commission were, in many respects, an attempt by them to come to terms with their ambiguous role in the history of colonialism and apartheid in South Africa. It was symbolic of their chastening and a sign of their commitment to becoming part of the process of reconciliation and nation-building. Only time will tell whether or not that commitment measures up to its promise.

The chastening of the English-speaking churches is, as I earlier suggested, a necessary prelude to their participation in the healing, reconciliation, and reconstruction process in South Africa. But that implies that they recognize that their losses can be turned around and become gains. Like whites generally in South Africa, there is no possible way in which the white constituency within the English-speaking churches can regain their dominant political status and role, nor should they seek to do so. If they are to have any political influence, then it must be as part of churches that are representative of the black majority in South Africa. But this does not mean that the English-speaking churches, now understood as black-led and black-majority churches, should seek to become the church of the new political power. If we have learned anything from the loss of political status, it is that we should never have sought it in the first place. Whether the connection is among the church and colonialism, apartheid, or the postapartheid state, its role has to be that of critical servant. This does not mean a withdrawal from the political arena onto the periphery of public life, but rather a different way of being present at the center. The fact that the English-speaking churches may become Africanized does not mean that they will automatically become more genuinely prophetic, nor does it mean that they will necessarily avoid the mistakes that they have previously made.

The loss of ethnic domination is also a gain that should be recognized. The fact is that white South Africans, and especially white English-speaking South Africans, are a relatively small minority and there is no way that they can or should control the life of the church anymore than they can control the life of the nation. They need to be set free from such pretension, for it can only lead to frustration and withdrawal. But once it is recognized that this loss is actually a form of liberation that opens up fresh possibilities, then it can become a gain. What I mean is obviously analogous to society as a whole. The real future of white South Africans lies not in their white identity, but in their participation as human beings in the shaping of the multicultural character of the new nation. This does not imply that white English speakers have nothing to contribute and therefore may as well leave the country. On the contrary, what I am saying is that we have a major contribution to make, not from an assumed position of social and cultural superiority, but as equal partners. One important way of doing this is through our participation in the life of the black majority, black-led English-speaking churches. Maybe within this context, as a minority that can never regain past power and domination, they can at least help to prevent ethnicity from becoming the controlling factor in the life and witness of the church.

In many ways it is really the recognition of the loss of innocence that is the key to all the rest. For if the white constituency of the English-speaking churches still assumes that their hands are reasonably clean, then of course there can be no way of turning loss into gain. The adage that there is no gain without pain is not only apt in this instance, but it is also biblical. Without a spirit of penitence for the past, and therefore a willingness to forgo status and domination, there is no possibility for renewal and a meaningful participation in the process of transformation and reconciliation.

Notes

1. John W. De Gruchy, *The Church Struggle in South Africa*, 2d ed. (Cape Town: David Philip, 1986), 18-41.

2. Specifically, the Church of the Province of Southern Africa (CPSA), the United Congregational Church of Southern Africa (UCCSA), the Methodist Church of Southern Africa (MCSA), and the Presbyterian Church of Southern Africa (PCSA).

3. James R. Cochrane, John W. De Gruchy, and Steve Martin, eds., *Faith Communities Face the Truth* (Cape Town: David Philip, 1999).

4. See Charles Villa-Vicencio, *Christianity and the Colonisation of South Africa*, forthcoming, and John W. De Gruchy, *Christianity and the Modernisation of South Africa* (Cape Town: David Philip, 1999).

5. John W. De Gruchy, "Grappling with a Colonial Heritage: The English-Speaking Churches under Imperialism and Apartheid," in *Christianity in South Africa: A Political, Social, and Cultural History*, ed. Richard Elphick, and T. R. H. Davenport (Cape Town: David Philip, 1997).

6. J. R. Cochrane, *Servants of Power: The Role of the English-Speaking Churches in South Africa* (Johannesburg: Ravan, 1986).

7. Tinyiko S. Maluleke, "Half a Century of African Christian Theologies: Elements of the Emerging Agenda in the Twenty-First Century," *Journal of Theology for Southern Africa* 99 (November 1997): 4-23.

8. For a helpful discussion of multiculturalism and its significance within the South African context, see the chapter by Johan Degenaar in this volume, "Multiculturalism: How Can the Human World Live Its Difference?"

9. John W. De Gruchy, "Confessing Guilt in South Africa Today in Dialogue with Dietrich Bonhoeffer," *Journal of Theology for Southern Africa* 67 (June 1989): 37-45.

Chapter Four

Ecclesiastical Racism and the Politics of Confession in the United States and South Africa

R. Drew Smith

RACE, A POLITICAL invention of western civilization, has been manipulated to particularly destructive ends in the United States and South Africa. Primarily its purpose has been to confer a sense of "otherness" upon people of color, and very little within the social life of these characteristically western nations has escaped its conceptual distortions. Churches seem to have been particularly wedded to notions of race in the two contexts—leading the way as they did in the ideological buttressing of slavery in the United States and apartheid in South Africa.

One of the legacies of the racial ideologizing of churches in both contexts has been numerous structural divisions within churches along color or ideological lines. In the United States, the Presbyterians, Methodists, and Baptists split their denominations into roughly northern, antislavery and southern, proslavery contingents during the 1800s. The Episcopalians and Lutherans also divided into regional churches with the Episcopalians reuniting in 1865 and the Lutherans reuniting in 1918. Northern and southern Methodists were not reunited until 1968, northern and southern Presbyterians were not reunited until 1983, and northern and southern Baptists were not reunited at all. In South Africa, the Dutch Reformed Church, the Apostolic Faith Mission, the Full Gospel Church, the Lutheran Church, and the Seventh Day Adventist Church have been separated into racial subsections for most or all of their existence. Initial steps toward addressing the racial divide within South African ecclesiastical and social life were attempted during the 1950s and 1960s but made little headway in the face of government enforced segregationist policies. Important progress has been made during the 1990s, however, with the 1994 merger of black and white sections of the Apostolic Faith Mission and a series of confessions by white Dutch Reformed churches.

This chapter highlights important aspects of the race-bound histories of these churches, noting ecclesiastical and social factors that contributed to racial separations and conciliatory steps by churches within both countries. The discussion situates church support of racial separation and reconciliation within a larger racial politics revolving, for segregationists, around notions of black otherness, and for persons concerned with racial reconciliation (especially between 1950 and the mid-1970s) around black empowerment. Finally, the chapter examines recent reconciliation initiatives within conservative wings of white Protestantism and the tendency to uncouple reconciliation from concrete social policy initiatives. The discussion concludes that a systematic commitment by white churches to black social and material interests is a fundamental prerequisite to genuine racial reconciliation.

Churches and the Formalization of Racial Separation

American Christianity was approached from its earliest stages out of an ethnic and racial particularism. This was evidenced even within initial settlement patterns within the country. For example, the New England colonies functioned as Protestant preserves that excluded Catholics, Presbyterians, and Quakers by law into the 1700s.[1] The religious demarcations corresponded substantially with ethnic ones, with New England comprised largely of English Congregationalists and Baptists, while the Scots-Irish Presbyterians, Irish Catholics, and German Quakers and related sectarian groups settled in colonies farther south. It was also primarily Anglicans from England who made up the original planter class that settled in the southeast, although German planters (who were mostly Lutherans) were a discernible presence by the early 1800s. With the westward expansion out of the southern coastal states during the early 1800s, large numbers of whites who were disposed toward Baptist, Methodist, and Presbyterian faith expressions flocked into the South. Given these ethnic demarcations within early American Protestantism, it comes as no surprise that race would prove an even deeper divide within churches. After all, while various ethnic whites may have been cast as economic or cultural inferiors, blacks and Native Americans were consistently viewed as ontological others.

George Fredrickson points out that Europeans, including those who eventually descended upon the indigenous populations of North America and Southern Africa, tended to view humanity through dichotomies such as "Christian and heathen" and "civil and savage."[2] In the European encounter with blacks in the two contexts, Fredrickson suggests that these dichotomies served mainly as justifications for an economic and political subjugation of blacks that was considered necessary for white social and material advancement. Others have argued, however, for a more visceral quality to the European disposition toward blacks, including Robert Hood, who makes the case for a deep-seated antiblackness within western culture dating back to the earliest foundations of western Christianity. He states that:

> deeply rooted primal myths—and therefore emotional feelings—and beliefs about the negative character of blackness precede sociological and economic factors. These beliefs, relying on ancient myths and ethnocentric claims, are a legacy that has been nourished by Christian ideas about blackness and its

attributes. In Western philosophical and religious thought, blacks and blackness have been viewed as a distinctly secondary and inferior category that always will be begrimed and on the underside of . . . European civilization.[3]

C. Eric Lincoln employed a similar interpretation to explain the exclusion of the black population from white religious life in colonial America. In assessing the reasons blacks were not welcomed into the Puritan churches of New England in any numbers, he remarks that "it was not the Puritan's Calvinism which excluded Blacks from the circle of the elect, but his unwillingness to accept the Black man's capacity for meaningful spiritual instruction and refined religious behavior." That is to say, the reasons were not related to doctrine in a generic sense but, rather, to a very particularistic understanding of the ontology of blacks as a group that would presumably exclude them from salvation. Despite the predispositions whites, and especially white Christians, held about the nature of blackness, African Americans still became widely involved in northern Baptist churches by the time of the Great Awakening in the 1740s.[4] By the early 1800s, Baptists in the North were engaged in mission efforts among blacks in the South, although southern whites, as well as white Anglicans and Catholics in the mid-Atlantic states, "responded differently to the questions of the propriety (and practicality) of bringing the gospel to the slaves."[5] Here again, the implications, were both political—it could upset the social structure defining master and slave—and ontological—blacks could not be viewed as recipients of divine grace.

More formalized concepts of separate and distinct spheres for whites and blacks emerged beginning in the first decades of the nineteenth century owing to a mostly southern, Protestant discourse that advocated a divinely intentioned hierarchy of social ranks and spheres. For example, a North Carolina Methodist named Washington .Chaffin contended that nature had "drawn lines of demarcation between [blacks] and [whites] that no physical, mental or religious cultivation can obliterate."[6] The ecclesiastical sphere obviously provided no reprieve from the oppressive racial conditions blacks encountered elsewhere within American society; in fact, churches were often active facilitators of that oppression.

By the beginning of the nineteenth century, the inability of white Protestants to act in the interests of the black population was sufficiently clear that African Americans proceeded to form independent black church communions. The first of the historically black denominations, the African Methodist Episcopal Church, was inaugurated in 1816. Before the close of the century, the African Methodist Episcopal Zion Church, the Colored Methodist Episcopal Church, and the National Baptist Convention were also formed. Having concluded in this way that black social and religious progress required separation from whites, the vast majority of black Christians would become aligned with these black communions by the end of the nineteenth century.

Nonetheless, there was also a racially progressive element within white Protestantism during the late eighteenth and early nineteenth centuries. The antislavery movement, which achieved significant momentum beginning in the early 1800s, brought race issues, and specifically the oppressive conditions endured by black slaves, into full public view. A number of northern church persons and a few southern church persons were included in the ranks of antislavery activists; nonetheless, abolitionists were still a decided minority within churches. It was also because of church engagement of abolitionism that status quo elements within the church began sounding a call for extricating the church from the conflict—purportedly as a means of "preserving the ecclesiastical peace."

Baptists, Methodists, and, to a slightly lesser degree, Presbyterians, established the precedents for regional and structural separation over the race issue. Presbyterians led the way, separating into essentially southern and northern sections in 1837 over what was officially claimed to be polity matters. Methodists in 1844 and Baptists in 1845 split along regional lines explicitly over the slavery issue. When southern states later embarked on political secession from the Union in 1861—forming what was, in effect, a separate nation—a more comprehensive regional separation within denominations took place. The division within the Presbyterian Church became even more distinctively regional, with southern Presbyterians officially cutting all ties to their national church body in 1861 and forming the Presbyterian Church in the Confederate States. In 1862, the southern dioceses of the Episcopal Church broke away from their parent body and formed the Protestant Episcopal Church in the Confederate States. Southern synods of the Lutheran Church began withdrawing from the General Synod of the Lutheran Church in 1861, leading to the organization of most of the southern synods into the Evangelical Lutheran Church in the Confederate States of America in 1863.

With the conclusion of the Civil War and the reintegration of the Confederate states into the Union, Episcopalians rejoined their national church, but separations in the other denominations remained in force. The Evangelical Lutheran Church in the Confederate States of America changed its name to the Evangelical Lutheran General Synod in North America until, along with other Lutheran groups that broke away from the parent body, a United Lutheran Church in America was formed in 1918. The Presbyterian Church in the Confederate States renamed itself the Presbyterian Church in the United States, and did not reunite with the parent church until 1987. Methodists remained divided into the Methodist Episcopal Church and Methodist Episcopal Church South until the United Methodist Church was formed in 1968. Baptists have yet to overcome their separation—the northern portion of the original denomination still operates as the American Baptist Churches and the southern portion operates as the Southern Baptist Churches.

With the defeat of the Confederate states, southern blacks enjoyed a brief moment of social progress as a result of federally mandated reforms that were enforced through military occupation of the South. However, in just over a decade, federal enforcement of southern reforms ended as suddenly as it began, and the late nineteenth century was spent reversing black social progress and suppressing discourse on race throughout the South. White churches were instrumental in consolidating the racial divisions and inequalities that would characterize American society after the Civil War and throughout the first half of the twentieth century.

Coming out of the war, Methodists maintained both a legacy of structural separation between northern and southern Methodists and an even deeper division between whites and blacks within the regional bodies. Blacks who were aligned with the predominantly white Methodist communions (the Methodist Episcopal Church, Methodist Episcopal Church South, and Methodist Protestant Church) instead of with the historically black Methodist groups (the African Methodist Episcopal Church, African Methodist Episcopal Zion Church, and Colored Methodist Episcopal Church) were first segregated into all black congregations and annual conferences within white Methodism. In 1939, white Methodists voted to unite among themselves but to force blacks, despite overwhelming black resistance, into an all-black Central Jurisdiction that, unlike all the other conferences, did not conform to geographic lines.[7]

Presbyterians, like their Methodist counterparts, also formalized racial divisions within their churches beginning in the Reconstruction period. The various branches of Presbyterianism, the Presbyterian Church (US), the Presbyterian Church (USA), and a smaller branch, the Cumberland Presbyterian Church, all supported an initiative to form black church "courts" throughout the South. These courts, predicated on the idea of establishing provisional independence for black Presbyterians in the region, were firmly in place by 1871 and endured until black members were reintegrated into white synods during the 1960s.[8]

Formalizing racial separation between black and white Baptists in the South came fairly easily after the Civil War, given that significant numbers of black Baptists were already initiating congregations independent of whites. By the 1880s, there were more than eight hundred thousand independent black Baptists; there were state organizations of black Baptists in Alabama, Virginia, and North Carolina, and in 1886 the National Baptist Convention was formed.[9] By 1890, there was not a single black member within the one million member Southern Baptist Convention and no African American congregation became a member church of the Southern Baptist Convention again until 1951.[10] Presently, the number of blacks aligned with independent black Baptist communions has grown to about twelve million, divided among four national communions, while the Southern Baptist Convention has only recently registered significant numerical gains within the black community.[11]

The situation in South Africa was a close parallel to the American situation in many respects. Much like the United States, South Africa's national project was founded upon economic and religious expansion by Europeans into lands inhabited by non-European populations, with the religious component actively reinforcing a predisposition by whites about their own superiority. Although there was a temporary Catholic presence in the Cape in the 1500s, it was the emergence of the Dutch Reformed Church in the mid-1600s and the French Huguenots and Lutherans in the late-1600s that initiated the dominant role of European Christianity in the Cape region and throughout what would become known as South Africa.

The approaches taken toward the African population differed among these various churches. For example, the Lutherans ministered among the African population, including administering baptism and communion services to slaves. The Moravians, who arrived in the early 1700s, engaged in mission work among the Khoi and San peoples. Both evangelistic efforts were opposed by the Dutch Reformed churches, or Nederduitse Gereformeerde Kerk (NGK) as they called themselves, who mainly ministered to Dutch colonists and viewed aspects of native evangelism, according to John De Gruchy, as "a threat to the social life of the settler community." De Gruchy also indicates that the Moravian "gospel of universal grace proclaimed to the indigenous peoples collided with the Calvinist orthodoxy of the Dutch church."[12] Calvinist orthodoxy here alludes, however, both to the "divine election" of certain peoples and a "divine disfavor" toward others. From the standpoint of Dutch Reformed Christians in South Africa, the latter seems to have applied, consciously or unconsciously, to the entirety of blacks as a racial group.

The arrival of significant numbers of English-speaking whites toward the beginning of the nineteenth century was coupled with the emergence of a large presence of English-speaking churches including Baptists, Congregationalists, Presbyterians, Methodists, and Anglicans. The influence and standing of the English-speaking churches increased not only as a result of the growing numbers of English-speaking Europeans in the Cape, but also because of the 1806 consolidation of British administrative control over the Cape. Tensions existed between the English-speaking and Dutch churches over issues of power, but also over the now revived issue of evangelizing the African population. As De Gruchy notes, one hundred years after their initial objection to evangelism among Africans, the Dutch churches were still inclined to believe that "Christian Natives [were] not such good servants as the wild heathen."[13]

The NGK possessed black and coloured members, but limits on ecclesiastical association between white and nonwhite members was made clear by an 1857 decision to segregate the worship life of Dutch churches along racial lines. Further structural separations between the races were formalized with the NGK's creation of a separate mission church for coloureds in 1880, the creation of an African "daughter" church (first in 1910), and the creation of an Indian daughter church in 1968.[14] Other white breakaway groups from the NGK have also maintained racial segregation within their churches.

Lutherans and Seventh Day Adventists were also among the English-speaking churches that implemented formal structural divisions along racial lines. German Lutherans arrived in the Cape in the 1700s, establishing churches among the white population. As blacks began to affiliate with Lutheranism through the mission efforts of American Lutherans in the 1900s, they were forced to form separate black synods. Seventh Day Adventists, who arrived in South Africa in 1887, separated by 1929 into the Cape Conference for whites and the Good Hope conference for coloureds, then later added the Southern conference for blacks. And although most of the other English-speaking churches would be characterized by multiracialism, there were still significant racial separations evident within these churches during the nineteenth century and into the twentieth.[15]

Even after the Boer War ended independent rule by Afrikaners in the Transvaal and Orange Free State, and after the formation of the Union of South Africa in 1910, white domination of nonwhite populations continued without interruption—and English-speaking churches proved scarcely more helpful in empowering the nonwhite populations than the NGK. The fact that the English-speaking churches were largely supportive of the 1910 constitution and of other discriminatory governmental race policies was particularly disappointing to blacks who retained hopes about the social benefits possible through affiliation with these churches.[16] Nevertheless, as Hennie Pretorius and Lizo Jafta point out, African political leaders could not distance themselves from white politics, nor from mainline churches, "if they wished to be effective."[17] In fact, most of those responsible for founding the African National Congress (ANC) in the early 1900s were black clergy aligned with mission churches.

The majority of the black masses, however, had already noticeably moved in the direction of forming their own churches by the late 1800s. By the beginning of the twentieth century there were about twenty "Ethiopian" churches in South Africa, some of which had aligned with the African Methodist Episcopal church by 1896. Ethiopianism, which was a term that came to apply to many African initiated churches was, according to Pretorius and Jafta, "a direct expression of resistance against the missionaries, white settlers, and the colonial government." Although most of these churches did not maintain their early political quality, they grew enormously, accounting for approximately nine million, or about 47 percent, of all black Christians by the early 1990s.[18]

The turn of the century ushered in an ecclesiastical development that would significantly impact the racial and religio-cultural configuration of churches in the United States and South Africa—the birth of the modern Pentecostal and charismatic movement. The modern Pentecostal movement, a successor of sorts to the American Holiness Movement, is traced by many to a Los Angeles church called Azusa Street, pastored by an African American named William Seymour. It was here that an outpouring of the Holy Spirit, characterized especially by speaking in tongues, occurred and spread throughout the United States and then around the world.[19] And although during its Azusa Street beginnings in the United States, the Pentecostal movement set new standards for interracial church interactions, it soon succumbed to the spirit of racial separation prevailing within the larger American society.

The division of black from white Pentecostal churches began in 1908 and, according to one scholar, was "formalized in 1948 . . . with the creation of the all-white Pentecostal Fellowship of North America."[20] As white Pentecostals broke fellowship with blacks, black Pentecostals continued to gather and multiply within their own Pentecostal communions. Currently, more than 3.5 million blacks are aligned with the Church of God in Christ (which predated the Azusa Street revival and is now the largest of the black Pentecostal groups), another three hundred thousand blacks are aligned with smaller black Pentecostal bodies, but only forty thousand blacks are aligned with the white Pentecostal bodies.[21]

The Pentecostal and charismatic movement in South Africa, which also began in the early twentieth century, stemmed from a number of sources including Ethiopianist and Zionist churches; the Azusa Street phenomenon in Los Angeles and something of a counterpart movement in Wakkerstroom, Transvaal; and also from subsequent North American and European missionary activity. Many of these groups, including the Apostolic Faith Mission and the Full Gospel Church, marginalized blacks within their ecclesiastical life from the start. From its founding in 1908, the Apostolic Faith Mission maintained a whites-only membership policy in its official ecclesiastical body where all of the executive powers resided—restricting African, coloured, and Indian converts to separate mission sections.[22] The Full Gospel Church was similarly structured into a white "official" section and separate black and Indian sections. Not surprisingly, the racial segregation of these major Pentecostal bodies further escalated what was already a significant black momentum toward Pentecostal and charismatic assemblies under their own control.

Martin Luther King Jr. once stated that eleven o'clock on Sunday morning was the most segregated hour in America. The same could be said of South Africa, with the tragic implication of the statement being that racial divisions in both contexts have been more manifest in churches than in any other sector of the society. This has evolved in the two countries out of a deep-seated ideological disposition toward racial separation among churches that went largely unchecked through the opening decades of the twentieth century. Perhaps no institution other than churches within the two societies has had such large numbers of people engaged in such comprehensive group definition with so little accountability to anything other than their own internal imperatives. And while large numbers of white Protestants in both contexts have used this social freedom and influence to perpetuate racial division and animosity, there have also been church persons of all races whose ideas of community and commonwealth have not been so contorted. This was indeed the case with ecumenical and desegregationist movements within twentieth-century South Africa and the United States that, in numerous ways, embodied a Christian spirit inclined in a considerably more progressive social direction.

Movement toward Progressive Racial Politics within Church Communions and Ecumenical Circles

If the opening decades of the nineteenth century laid the foundations for ecclesiastical atomization within the United States and South Africa, then the opening decades of the twentieth century and the growing ministerial and social complexities that accompanied this period established the groundwork for more coordination between ecclesiastical bodies. This coordination and cooperation within churches paralleled similar dynamics within ihe larger civil society, with emerging black organizations such as the National Association for the Advancement of Colored People (NAACP) in the United States, and the African National Congress (ANC) in South Africa, and inspired some of the terms of the ecclesiastical and civic discussion. For both of these organizations the discussion necessarily revolved around black empowerment.

The prevailing ideological framework for a black empowerment politics in the United States and South Africa has been that of "democratic liberalism." For those committed to black empowerment, the tendency to define it in liberal terms has been occasioned by both a resonance with its ideological emphases and by the strategic necessity of locating black politics within the national mainstream in either context.[23] Liberal tenets within the South African mainstream have included: "a belief in the importance and dignity of the individual . . .; [an] emphasis on equality of opportunity . . . and the rule of law; and the conviction that society can achieve political stability, economic prosperity and social justice by human effort and at an evolutionary pace."[24] Similarly, liberalism has been defined within the American context as a "belief that individuals and institutions, including governments, should so act—or refrain from acting—as to liberate as many individuals from as many shackles as possible, without overturning basic social machinery."[25] Liberalism, then, with its stress on rights and liberties, has provided the central ideas on which western democracy has been built, yet one of the ironies of the American and South African contexts has been the extent to which commitments to liberalism have proven capable of sustaining both segregationist and desegregationist politics. Nevertheless, throughout the period of formalized segregation in the United States and South Africa, black empowerment politics has drawn generously on liberal doctrines in what has been primarily a pursuit of desegregation by black and white and church-based and nonchurch-based activists.

Within the United States, the years just prior to and after World War I were years of significant social ferment and realignment that began to break race activism free from some of the stifling social forces deployed against it after Reconstruction. Dramatic numbers of blacks physically broke free from the stultifying context of the South via massive migrations to the North. This contributed greatly to a rapid escalation in the numbers and influence of the emergent NAACP, formed in the 1910s, as well as groups such as the Urban League, formed shortly afterward. These interracial, but predominantly black, organizations served as major public policy platforms on race and became the primary vehicles through which black churches could voice their racial concerns.

During this time, the ecumenical movement emerged as well and provided a major impetus for changes in race relations within church and society—first by providing a highly visible, broad-based platform from which race issues could be pursued. The major Protestant ecumenical group in the United States was the Federal Council of Churches, formed in 1908, as forerunner to what later came to be known as the National Council of Churches. Even in its formation process, it augured shifts in mainline Protestantism's approach to race relations by inviting the historically black Methodist churches and historically black National Baptist Convention to play an active part in the proceedings. By 1920, the council had targeted improvements in race relations as one of its specific objectives. As C. Gregg Singer points out, the treatment of black troops in World War I and the work of a government study commission on the issue just after the war elevated race relations to a new level in the thinking of the American public. In response to these developments, the Federal Council issued a statement in support of integration, which was the first of its kind by any ecclesiastical body.[26]

The following year the Federal Council created a Commission on the Church and Race Relations that sponsored conferences on racial matters, served as a clearinghouse for agencies concerned with race relations, and issued numerous public statements, including calls for church cooperation across racial lines. The council also issued theological rejoinders to white supremacist inclinations within white churches, calling specifically for white churches to devote themselves to policies and actions aimed at the social welfare of the black population. The council stated, for example: "Recognizing one God as the Father of all, and conceiving mankind as his family, we are convinced that all races are bound together in an organic unity (and) only on the basis of brotherhood can satisfactory relations be secured."[27] Other race relations initiatives carried out by the council during the 1920s included the creation of an annual Race Relations Sunday that survived more than fifty years. However, as one observer notes, the council's race relations initiatives during the 1920s "met with only limited success and much opposition."[28] Nevertheless, what these early ecumenical efforts did accomplish was to provoke a public discussion of race in a manner that began to shift black status from an otherness designation to something approaching rightful membership in the ecclesiastical and social community.

The early stages of ecumenical activity in South Africa revolved less around social reform than was true of nascent ecumenism within the United States. Daryl Balia points out that at the beginning of the twentieth century, South African churches "largely ignored" social justice issues, concentrating instead on "promoting 'cooperation and brotherly feeling' among the different missionary societies." It was this missionary instinct, and a specific concern with evangelizing the "native races," says Balia, that gave birth to ecumenism in

South Africa.[29] A General Missionary Conference was formed in 1904 by the English and Afrikaans churches with an agenda that included fostering "self-supporting" and "self-propagating" black churches. And although some attention was also given to influencing legislation on behalf of blacks, Balia comments that "while the interests of Blacks were acknowledged, they did not provide the focus for the organizations of the conference, nor did they ever feature prominently in its activities."[30]

The Christian Council of South Africa was soon formed and, unlike the General Missionary Conference, it appeared sufficiently reformist to inspire ecclesiastical hopes among black South Africans. At the very least, its attention to racial reform generated enough unease among Dutch Reformed churches that they withdrew from the Christian Council and formed an alternative group called the Federal Mission Council. The two councils proceeded to move in opposite directions, with the Christian Council convening in the 1940s to discuss preliminary steps toward racial reform in South Africa and the Federal Mission Council rallying its forces around policies of "separate development." But as the Christian Council was characterized overall by a racial gradualism, and the Federal Mission Council advocated an "apartheid" policy, black South African ecumenical hopes were left frustrated throughout the first half of the twentieth century.[31]

Momentous political reconfigurations would be responsible for defining in large part the midcentury contexts of ecclesiastical activity within the United States and South Africa. In South Africa, government-enforced segregation achieved new levels of formalization with the 1948 advent of apartheid. In the United States, government-enforced segregation signaled its retreat with the 1954 Supreme Court ruling, *Brown vs. the Board of Education*, which declared longstanding "separate but equal" educational policies unconstitutional given the inherently unequal black and white educational opportunities resulting from these policies. These developments had the effect, within both the United States and South Africa, of generating significant ecumenical ferment around race issues in ways that moved churches toward a more explicitly black empowerment-oriented politics.

The National Council of Churches (NCC) of the United States, which formed in 1950 as a successor to the Federal Council of Churches, led the way among mainline Protestants in endorsing the 1954 Supreme Court action. It issued the following unequivocal condemnation of segregation: "Racial prejudice in any and all forms is contrary to the will and design of God. It is not merely bad, unfortunate, unrighteous—it is a sin."[32] The National Council's response to the Supreme Court ruling followed up on an earlier council resolution in 1952 on churches and segregation. The 1952 resolution outlined church complicity in discriminatory racial practices and laid out specific proposals for how churches could work toward a "non-segregated church and a non-segregated community."[33] The NCC issued many other resolutions on racial issues during the 1950s—two dozen altogether between 1950 and 1958.[34]

Other church councils, including local councils and the World Council of Churches, also came out in immediate support of the Supreme Court ruling. The World Council proclaimed that "segregation in all its forms is contrary to the Gospel, and is incompatible with the Christian doctrine of man and with the nature of the Church of Christ." The Washington, D.C. Federation of Churches circulated a treatise among its member churches that included the following statements: "Our churches will be fulfilling their duty to evangelize all people only when they sincerely and personally offer church membership to all persons living within the communities served by them. We call upon all Christians to work for, not to wait for, a church and a society which rise above racial restrictions."[35]

The Court's ruling also mobilized African American churches that took the fight against segregation to entirely new levels through direct action protests, including a 1955 boycott of public buses in Montgomery, Alabama, which thrust black civil rights and church involvements in civil rights activism into the national spotlight. The protest efforts of an impressive number of black as well as white church persons over the next decade provided the impetus for legislation, such as the 1964 Civil Rights Act and the 1965 Voting Rights Act that effectively removed the legal props for racial discrimination in the United States.

The desegregationist momentum among progressive black and white Protestants, whether aligned with emerging ecumenical organizations or not, increasingly swept aside layers of resistance among some churches previously ambivalent toward the cause of racial progress. A number of Southern Baptist leaders responded favorably to the Court's ruling, including the convention's Christian Life Commission that declared that the ruling was "in harmony with the constitutional guarantee of equal freedom to all citizens, and with the Christian principles of equal justice and love for all men." The commission also urged the Southern Baptist membership and all other Christians to fully comply with the ruling. State associations, such as the Virginia and North Carolina Associations, encouraged their constituents to accept the ruling as both a religious and political imperative. Moreover, a resolution was adopted by the Convention at its 1954 assembly consistent with the theological and political support of the ruling expressed in these other Southern Baptist leadership sectors. It is important to note, however, that a number of state associations and individual clergy vigorously opposed the Court's ruling and the convention's support for the ruling.[36]

Although somewhat belated, in 1958, the bishops of the United Methodist Church issued a statement endorsing integration and the 1954 Supreme Court ruling. They stated:

> We earnestly urge all our people to accept the ruling of the court in good faith. We heartily commend those lay people, pastors and bishops who have demonstrated Christian courage in critical areas. In these days of extreme tensions we commend our people who, while not always sharing the same

attitude on integration, are determined to demonstrate in their own lives the qualities of understanding, tolerance and brotherhood.[37]

The Supreme Court decision and southern civil rights activism also encouraged some movement toward desegregation within the churches themselves. In early 1955, the Lutheran Church's executive secretary of the Division of American Missions declared that the Lutheran Church would be opening its doors to blacks "in a dramatic break with the past when separate congregations were the rule."[38] The Lutheran leader tied his declaration to racial progress made by Lutheran churches over the previous five years where "dozens" of Lutheran churches accepted black members and many more actively considered "seeking (blacks) for membership."[39] The Presbyterian Church (USA) began desegregating its synod structure in 1957 and completed the process in 1964, while the Presbyterian Church (US) took preliminary steps toward integrating their black member churches into the white synods as early as 1946—completely dissolving the black southern synod and integrating black churches into the regular synod structure by 1968.[40]

Among Methodist churches, the Methodist Women's Society of the Southeastern Jurisdiction adopted the Charter of Racial Policies in 1955 that called for "the integration of all groups into the life and work of the church" and stated further that "where law prohibits or customs prevent [integration], workers and local boards are charged with creating a public opinion which may result in changing such laws and customs."[41] At their 1956 general conference meeting, Methodist delegates unanimously passed an amendment that "opened the door" to full integration by "easing the procedure" by which black churches could transfer into the regular jurisdictions. Unfortunately, delegates voted to set up a commission to study the issue and the all-white study commission recommended that no basic changes be made in the denomination's jurisdictional system, preferring instead to let the system "die out gradually when white church groups are ready to accept Negroes." The system did indeed "die out gradually" given that the integration of black conferences into the regular geographic conferences did not begin until 1964 and was not completed until 1973—five years after the United Methodist Church was officially formed.[42]

These structural and social reforms were important, but there were limits, even within progressive circles, to how far churches were willing to go in pursuit of racial reconciliation and black empowerment. The Black Power and black theology movements within the United States during the latter 1960s and, to some extent, parallel black theology and the Black Consciousness Movement in South Africa, evoked responses that made these limits abundantly clear. Common to these initiatives was a severe assessment of the pervasiveness of white racism and aggressive calls for black intellectual and institutional self-determination in ways that threatened, particularly in the American context, to break with pluralist commitments to interracialism and with liberal commitments to a democratic-procedural approach to social change. The indictments of white Christianity and the breaks with liberal-pluralism caused a number of white Christians in the United States to begin drawing back from the interracial cooperation that had characterized the desegregation movement. By the close of the 1970s, interracial church activism stalled with respect to racial reform in America, because, as many of these activists sensed racial reform had reached its legislative limits within the United States constitutional framework and that moving beyond the liberal-pluralist model, as some black leaders were advocating, was not an alternative most were willing to entertain. Nevertheless, what is clear about America's mid-twentieth century desegregationist movement was that it brought about important connections between commitments to racial reconciliation, on the one hand, and concrete social policy and social institutional reforms, on the other.

At about the same time that the civil rights movement was being launched in the United States, progressive forces in South Africa were mobilizing against apartheid under the banner of the Defiance Campaign. Organized by the ANC in 1952, this coordinated protest mobilized tens of thousands of black freedom fighters, although it gained far less support among the white church community than American civil rights protests did during the 1950s. As Charles Villa-Vicencio points out, despite the existence of a few white clergy allies of the campaign, white churches largely rejected the campaign, branding it as "excessive and responsible for unnecessary suffering."[43]

The white English-speaking churches in South Africa limited their resistance activities from the early years of apartheid until its demise in the early 1990s mainly to declarations and consultations. The Freedom Charter was one of the initial declarations during the 1950s, focusing attention on racism within church and society. It was a broad manifesto of "nonracialism," written by a black, South African clergyman, and widely endorsed by the liberal, English-speaking churches. Many of these same churches would also shortly embrace the Cottesloe Statement and calls for confession issued by the Christian Institute. The Cottesloe conference was a 1960 gathering of World Council of Churches member churches in South Africa, including the NGK, convened in response to the Sharpeville massacre and a demand by the Anglican archbishop of Cape Town, Joost de Blank, that the Dutch Reformed Church be expelled from the WCC. The Cottesloe delegates advanced a number of important declarations about race, including that apartheid policies were reconcilable with Scripture, that political rights for coloureds should be pursued, and that persons should not be barred from church membership based on race or color.[44]

The Christian Institute (CI), founded in the early 1960s by Dutch Reformed clergyman Beyers Naude as a follow-up to Cottesloe, immediately produced two important statements that challenged the theological basis of apartheid—the 1965 Call for Confession and a 1968 publication coauthored by the South African Council of Churches (SACC) entitled *The Message to the People of South Africa*. The SACC and CI collaborated throughout the 1960s around additional antiapartheid dialogue and action. These various initiatives emanating from English-speaking churches from the 1940s through the 1960s served as the beginning steps of a South African "confessional movement." The initiatives gained greater formalization through Bishop Manus Buthelezi's successful efforts to have the South African racial crisis declared a *status confessionis* by the Lutheran World Alliance in 1977 and through Dr. Allan Boesak's analogous success with the World Alliance of Reformed Churches in 1982.

While not all antiapartheid discourse within English-speaking churches translated into concrete ecclesiastical reforms during the apartheid era, some initiatives do stand out in this regard. For example, English-speaking churches offered up sufficient resistance to the Native Laws Bill of 1957 (which contained a "church clause" that made it "virtually impossible for black people to worship in churches located in white areas") that it was slightly modified. The Methodist Church, in particular, had already formally announced that it would not comply with the bill and that racial unity would stand as official policy within their communion.[45] A more significant step toward ecclesiastical reconciliation was taken in 1967 by the London Missionary Society, the Bantu Congregational Board, and the Congregational Union of South Africa. The churches agreed to unite as the United Congregational Church of Southern Africa (UCCSA) and immediately invited the Anglicans, Presbyterians, and Methodists to join the union. The following year the UCCSA endorsed the *Message to the People of South Africa*, stating that "racial separation must ultimately require that the Church cease to be the Church if applied to its members."[46] The South African Association of the Disciples of Christ would later join the UCCSA in 1972.[47]

Racial activism among South African and American churches fed off each other at times from the 1950s through the mid-1970s—due in part to a global awareness of race problems by leaders such as Martin Luther King Jr. in the United States, and Desmond Tutu and Allan Boesak in South Africa. But as racial activism died down in the United States toward the mid-1970s, many activist churches in the United States shifted their focus to the South African racial context owing largely to the fact that the reformist potential of liberal pluralism did not appear close to being exhausted within South African politics or within the thinking of its key black church activists. Consequently, as interracial church coalitions that were built around racial reform dissipated in the United States, they held strong throughout the 1980s and into the 1990s in South Africa, motivated by the urgencies and strategic opportunities of the antiapartheid struggle and bolstered by new support from churches in the United States and elsewhere.

Contemporary Disconnections between Confession and Black Empowerment

Some of the politically conservative branches of white Protestantism that distanced themselves from progressive racial reform during most of the twentieth century have emerged during the 1990s with racial reform initiatives of their own in the United States and South Africa. This would include a range of white evangelical, Pentecostal, and charismatic churches in the United States, and white Dutch Reformed, Seventh Day Adventist, Lutheran, and Pentecostal/charismatic churches in South Africa. The factors motivating this recent round of confessions differ from the one national context to the other, although the fact that in both instances the confessions came only after the eradication of governmentally sanctioned segregation has led some to view these actions as driven more by an attempt at some strategic advantage than by genuine remorse.[48] What is of more concern here than potential motives, however, is the degree to which admissions of racism in these instances have noticeably divorced themselves from the kind of black empowerment-oriented social policies that were characteristic of preceding generations of ecclesiastical confessions.

An example from the American context is suggestive of the pattern. The largely white National Association of Evangelicals (NAE) issued a statement on race in 1956 that declared: (1) that discriminatory racial practices "in many, if not all, sections of [the United States]" violated the teachings of Christ; (2) that the teachings of Christ emphasize the "inherent worth and intrinsic value of every man regardless of race, class, creed or color"; and (3) that "every legitimate means to eliminate unfair practices" should be pursued by the NAE. This legitimate means clause was qualified, however, by the phrase: "we deplore extremist tactics by any individual or organized group." Given that the NAE issued this statement as the campaign of direct-action, civil rights protest was getting under way, and then reissued it in 1963, a year that produced pivotal civil rights protests actions in Birmingham as well as the march on Washington, the reference to "extremist tactics" by "organized groups" was undoubtedly a veiled criticism of the protest campaign. In fact, rank-and-file white evangelicals were frequently among those involved in criticisms of the protest campaign for what they considered to be "extremism."

It has been precisely this formula of verbally condemning racism, encouraging reform in theory but then opposing concrete reformist actions and policies, that has allowed many conservative churches to appear to support positive change while remaining tied to policies and structures that undermine black social progress. In some sense, this posture stems from the notion that a political neutrality is achievable through disengagement from political controversies. Given the controversial nature of race policy within American life, as conservative churches were finally pushed toward lending a degree of support to racial reforms during the 1950s and 1960s, it tended to be in a rather distant, contradictory way.

By the mid-1970s, however, conservative churches began ridding themselves of any reluctance they may have had about appearing too "political," or too out of step with progressive political currents within the American mainstream. America's rightward backlash against the reforms of the 1960s and the related dynamic of the ecclesiastical and political decline of white liberal churches created a significant opportunity for conservative churches to move onto center stage within American politics. Groups such as the Moral Majority, an activist group comprised mainly of white evangelicals, convinced their constituencies that the time had come to assert their influence in electoral affairs. Throughout the 1980s, this new evangelical activism was wedded largely to the conservative Republican "revolution," which placed a great deal of emphasis on reversing policies such as affirmative action and electoral procedural shifts beneficial to blacks.

During the 1990s, white evangelicals retreated again from the national political stage, due partly to the fact that Democrats regained the White House and partly to the strong pull toward privatistic piety among conservative churches. A politics that seemed more compatible with their central ecclesiastical concerns at this point, particularly given the increasing stress within American Protestantism on church-growth philosophies and the mega-church model, was a politics of racial reconciliation. In 1990, the NAE along with the National Black Evangelical Association (NBEA), which split from NAE in 1964, jointly issued one of the first of this new generation of formal statements on race. The statement, though not a binding, officially endorsed resolution, addressed issues such as the need for whites to: (1) confess the racism of American society throughout its history and in all of its institutional and ideological manifestations; (2) admit that racism is a sin that whites must collectively repent of; (3) "remove the institutional barriers which hinder progress for blacks and other people of color"; and (4) "work to make restitution and repair as soon as possible."[49] The document, which largely reflected the thinking of the black churchmen around the table, has produced very little concrete follow-through other than a series of task force meetings between the leadership of the two organizations and the initiation of a racial awareness Sunday that has been observed each year by the member churches.

Southern Baptists, who have a number of churches active in NAE circles, adopted their own resolution on racism at the Convention's sesquicentennial meeting in 1995. This far-reaching resolution admitted to the Convention's complicity, since its beginnings, in the practice and defense of slavery; the Convention's opposition to black civil rights initiatives; the "intentional and unintentional" exclusion of blacks from worship, membership, and leadership in Southern Baptist churches; and to "distortions" of Scripture by some Southern Baptists in support of racial prejudice and discrimination. It went on to condemn racism in all forms as a deplorable sin; "repudiate" slavery as a "historic act of evil" that "plagues our cultures today"; apologize to African Americans for perpetuating racism; and commit to eradicating racism "from Southern Baptist Life and Ministry." Nevertheless, Andres Tapia observes that there are "rumblings" among black Southern Baptists, as well as among members of the NBEA, that structural changes have "stalled" within Southern Baptist and Evangelical Association circles and that white church leaders are going back to "business as usual."[50]

Racial reconciliation between Pentecostal churches began in earnest in 1992 when the all-white Pentecostal Fellowship of North America's Board of Administration voted to "pursue the possibility of reconciliation with our African-American brothers."[51] Subsequently four meetings were held over the next two years between key black and white Pentecostal leaders leading up to a major conference between black and white Pentecostal churches in Memphis held in October of 1994. The conference, entitled "Pentecostal Partners: A Reconciliation Strategy for Twenty-First Century Ministry," attracted three thousand delegates who unanimously approved a "Racial Reconciliation Manifesto" and voted to replace the all-white Pentecostal Fellowship of North America with a new interracial fellowship called the Pentecostal and Charismatic Churches of North America (PCCNA). The organization then established a board of directors comprised of equal numbers of blacks and whites, selected an African American to be president of the board, and went on in 1998 to initiate an official organizational journal whose focus and title is *Reconciliation.*

The manifesto itself was also quite impressive in its confession of the racial sins of white Pentecostal Christians. It condemned racism as a sin that has "hindered . . . spiritual development and mutual sharing among Pentecostal-Charismatic believers for decades"; it confessed the harm white church "participation in the sin of racism" has brought to "generations born and unborn"; it pledged opposition to racism "within and without the Body of Christ" including "all forms of personal and institutional racism"; it pledged to appeal throughout the various constituencies of their fellowship for "logistical support and intervention as necessary in opposing racism"; and it pledged its allegiance to the model of evangelism, justice, holiness, renewal, and reconciliation embodied in their common mother church, the Azusa Street Mission. Nevertheless, as David Daniels notes, black Pentecostals have registered a number of concerns including that psychological rather than institutional definitions of racism have dominated the PCCNA conversation, financial resources have remained disproportionately under the control of white PCCNA churches, and reconciliation initiatives have not developed toward specific actions.[52]

One of the more visible reconciliation initiatives among conservative Protestants has been the Promise Keepers movement, a large men's movement founded in 1991 by former University of Colorado football coach Bill McCartney primarily to promote male spirituality and biblical concepts of male leadership in the home and the society. More recently, Promise Keepers has made racial reconciliation a centerpiece of the movement and has provided the issue with high profile attention at the mass men's gatherings they hold at sports stadiums across the United States.

Stadium attendance, for example, numbered at 1.1 million men in 1996 and seven hundred thousand in 1997. Hundreds of thousands attended a single October 1997 rally at Washington, D.C.'s National Mall, patterned after similar gatherings by civil rights movement activists and, more immediately, by black men who attended the Million Man March in 1996. The crowd at the Washington event was estimated to be 80 percent white, 14 percent black, and 2 percent Asian. The organization also intends to hold massive assemblies at every state capital building on January 1, 2000, to demonstrate, according to McCartney, that "the giant of racism is dead in the church of Jesus Christ."[53] The attention Promise Keepers has received among white conservative Protestants has been noteworthy, but the movement has not gained much support within historically black denominations. A bishop in the predominantly black Church of God in Christ is the chairman of the board but, other than that, Promise Keepers can point to little else approaching official recognition or endorsement by the historically black denominations.[54]

In South Africa, it has been the Dutch Reformed, Seventh Day Adventist, Lutheran, Pentecostal, and charismatic churches that have remained largely segregated along race lines throughout most of the twentieth century. The Dutch Reformed churches made some efforts during the 1950s to face up to racial divisions, including five conferences on race convened by the Federal Missionary Council of the Dutch Reformed Churches between 1950 and 1953. Dutch Reformed churches also participated in the Cottesloe conference of 1960, endorsing many of its racial reforms, but eventually recanting and resigning its World Council of Churches' membership after the conference was roundly condemned by South Africa's prime minister, Hendrick Verwoerd. The first significant movement by the white Dutch Reformed Church toward racial reconciliation did not take place until after the NGK was suspended from the World Alliance of Reformed Churches in 1982 for its racial policies. In 1990, the NGK and the coloured "daughter" church agreed to unite and form the United Reformed Church (the VGK)—though choosing not to unite at the time with the black daughter church. And while a statement was adopted at the time by the VGK that declared apartheid to be a sin, the VGK's failure to really confront the racial issue, given its exclusion of black churches, apparently led to an alternative alliance in 1994 between black and coloured churches that took on the name of the Uniting Reformed Church of Southern Africa.

A church conference, held in the South African town of Rustenburg in 1990, served as a setting for significant new breakthroughs on racial reconciliation among a number of the racially divided churches. Rustenburg, which was hailed as a "conference of confessions," reportedly brought together "approximately 230 church leaders from more than 80 denominations and para-church organizations," representing "more than 90% of Christians in South Africa."[55] The tone of the event was established the first morning by a confession of the NGK's "guilt of negligence" relative to apartheid. Although the confession was warmly received by many, the black and coloured Dutch Reformed churches approached it with skepticism, sensing that the confession, "like others they had heard before, was too general and all-inclusive." Apparently neither the South African Council of Churches (SACC) nor the World Alliance of Reformed Churches (WARC) was totally persuaded by the confession either. For instance, at the SACC's annual conference a few months after Rustenburg, the SACC turned down a request by the NGK for observer status pending further progress by the DRC in concretely opposing apartheid and desegregating its churches.[56] As late as 1997, the WARC refused to readmit the NGK until it condemned apartheid "in its fundamental nature," something the Rustenburg apology was not believed to have done.[57] It was not until October 1998 that the NGK resolved that "apartheid [w]as wrong and sinful, not simply in its effects and operations, but in its fundamental nature." Even here, the NGK maintained its resistance to the idea of uniting with its black daughter churches.[58]

The NGK was not the only church in South Africa that continued to drag its feet on racial reform through the 1990s. Efforts to unite black and white Lutheran churches during the 1970s failed due to resistance by whites and resulted in further ossification of racial divisions between white Lutherans and the four independent black synods. Eventually black synods abandoned hopes of racial reconciliation and organized apart from white Lutherans into the Evangelical Lutheran Church of South Africa.[59] Meanwhile, white South African Lutherans were viewed as increasingly out of step with their larger Lutheran communion, the Lutheran World Federation (LWF). At its 1977 assembly in Dar es Salaam, the LWF delegates accepted a confessional statement that called on their churches in southern Africa to demonstrate their Christian unity by unequivocally rejecting apartheid. The failure by white churches to do this led delegates at the 1984 LWF assembly to pronounce white Lutheran churches in southern Africa officially withdrawn from LWF membership, given their unwillingness to unify Lutheran churches within the context.[60]

Pentecostal and charismatic churches also maintained various degrees of support for apartheid throughout the 1970s and 1980s. As J. Nico Horn points out, as late as 1989 a conservative Pentecostal/charismatic fellowship known as Christian Action for South Africa (CASA) "encouraged the government to continue the ban on the African National Congress and the Pan African Congress, to retain Mr. Nelson Mandela until he had renounced violence, and to keep the death penalty intact."[61] The Full Gospel Church is another Pentecostal communion that has consistently resisted pressure from black churches to eradicate formal racial divisions within its ecclesiastical life. A 1990 date had been set for uniting the church but was delayed indefinitely by whites who opposed the action and, in response to this, most black churches (along with a few sympathetic white churches) formed a separate body called the United Assemblies Association of the Full Gospel Church. Most of the other white churches along with a small number of black churches formed what was called the Irene Association.[62]

Nonetheless, the late 1980s and early 1990s represented a period of progress on race issues among a number of Pentecostal and charismatic churches. First of all, a progressive Pentecostal group calling itself Relevant Pentecostal Witness was organized in May of 1989 and immediately countered

CASA's proapartheid policies by calling for the government to "lift the ban on political parties, to release Nelson Mandela and to repeal the death penalty." The broad involvement by Pentecostal and charismatic churches in the Rustenburg Conference was also regarded by many as an important step forward. Undoubtedly, the most concrete racial reconciliation initiative within Pentecostal churches to date was the Apostolic Faith Missions decision in 1994 to unite the historically separated black and white sections of its denomination.

Seventh Day Adventist (SDA) churches have moved forward in their race policies as well during the 1990s. The Cape (or coloured) conference of the SDA, who had been petitioning without success for the merger of the separate white, coloured, and African conferences at each of the annual conferences since 1970, finally succeeded in 1994 in getting SDA churches to establish a merger committee. This led over the next two years to the merger of their racially distinct conferences throughout South Africa, with the exception of the Cape where, ironically, white members voted the merger down. Those resisting the merger argued that it had to do with finances and not race given that virtually all the churches in the Cape conference already had some coloured or African members.[63]

There are close parallels between the experiences of conservative churches in South Africa and the United States over the last few years, just as there were close parallels between liberal churches in the two contexts during the 1950s and 1960s. In both instances South African churches did not move quite as far as their American counterparts on race issues, but then South Africa has generally lagged well behind most other places in the world on race issues. Nevertheless, there is one respect in which conservative churches in South Africa may actually enjoy a better positioning with respect to racial reconciliation than conservative churches in the United States. Given that the broader South African society has only moved beyond formal segregation within the past five years, conservative churches in South Africa may be perceived as not quite so far behind their national social curve as the conservative churches in the United States (who many black churches regard as at least thirty years too late in their reconciliation initiatives). An important lesson for South African churches is that the more time they allow to pass between the formal overturning of segregation within the society at large and their own ecclesiastical desegregation the less hope there may be for racial reconciliation.

In the end, the historical dimensions may prove less central to the prospects for reconciliation among conservative, as well as among liberal churches, than the ability of churches to embrace social and ecclesiastical agendas that concretely move blacks into full social partnership. There is a well-known adage within political life, equally applicable to ecclesiastical life, that states that "there is no such thing as permanent friends (or enemies)—only permanent interests." When white churches show themselves to be systematically supportive of not only the spiritual but the social and material interests of blacks, then reconciliation between the two racial groups may not seem such a difficult reach.

Notes

1. J. Owens Smith, *The Politics of Racial Inequality: A Systematic Comparative Macro-Analysis from the Colonial Period to 1970* (New York: Greenwood Press, 1987), 29.
2. George M. Fredrickson, *White Supremacy: A Comparative Study in American and South African History* (New York: Oxford University Press, 1981), 7-8.
3. Robert E. Hood, *Begrimed and Black: Christian Traditions on Blacks and Blackness* (Minneapolis: Fortress, 1994), 20-21.
4. C. Eric Lincoln, "The Development of Black Religion in America," in *African-American Religious Studies: An Interdisciplinary Anthology*, ed. Wilmore Gayraud (Durham, N.C.: Duke University Press, 1989), 15, 18.
5. Lincoln, "Development of Black Religion," 12.
6. Washington S. Chaffin, *Sermons*, January 1845-June 1862, in W. S. Chaffin Papers, Duke University Manuscript Department, Durham, N.C., 77-78.
7. James S. Thomas, *Methodism's Racial Dilemma: The Story of the Central Jurisdiction* (Nashville: Abingdon, 1992), 43.
8. Joel Alvis, "Ecclesiastical and Social Racial Policy," in *The Diversity of Discipleship: The Presbyterians and Twentieth Century Witness*, ed. Milton Coalter and John Mulder (Louisville: Westminster/John Knox, 1991), 201-202.
9. John Eighmy, *Churches in Cultural Captivity: A History of the Social Attitudes of Southern Baptists* (Knoxville: University of Tennessee Press, 1987), 32.
10. Joe Maxwell, "Black Southern Baptists," *Christianity Today*, 15 May 1995, 27-28.
11. C. Eric Lincoln and Lawrence H. Mamiya, *The Black Church in the African American Experience* (Durham, N.C.: Duke University Press, 1990), 407.
12. John De Gruchy, *The Church Struggle in South Africa* (Grand Rapids, Mich.: Eerdmans, 1979, 1986), 2.
13. De Gruchy, *The Church Struggle in South Africa*, 2.
14. The first "daughter church" was created in the Orange Free State in 1910; later in the Transvaal in 1932, the Cape in 1951, Natal in 1952, and a combined synod in 1963.
15. De Gruchy, *The Church Struggle in South Africa*, 16.
16. John De Gruchy, "Grappling with a Colonial Heritage: The English-Speaking Churches under Imperialism and Apartheid," in *Christianity in South Africa: A Political, Social, and Cultural History*, ed. Richard Elphick and Rodney Davenport (Berkeley: University of California Press, 1997), 156-57.
17. Hennie Pretorius and Lizo Jafta, "'A Branch Springs Out': African Initiated Churches," in *Christianity in South Africa*, 215.
18. Pretorius and Jafta, "African Initiated Churches," 211, 213.
19. For example, see Harvey Cox, *Fire from Heaven: The Rise of Pentecostal Spirituality and the Reshaping of Religion in the Twenty-First Century* (Reading, Mass.: Addison-Wesley, 1995).
20. Vinson Synan, "Memphis 1994: Miracle and Mandate," *Reconciliation* (Summer 1998): 14.

21. Lincoln and Mamiya, *The Black Church in the African American Experience*, 77-80.

22. Allan Anderson and Gerald Pillay, "The Segregated Spirit: The Pentecostals," in *Christianity in South Africa*, 229, 235.

23. It is important to note, however, that black nationalist understandings of black empowerment have had strong backing among a minority of blacks within both contexts.

24. Mandy Goedhals, "From Paternalism to Partnership: The Church of the Province of Southern Africa and Mission, 1848-1988," in *Bounty in Bondage: The Anglican Church in Southern Africa*, ed. Frank England and Torquil Paterson (Johannesburg: Raven Press, 1989), 112.

25. William Gerber, *American Liberalism: Laudable End, Controversial Means* (Lanham, Md.: University Press of America, 1987), 11.

26. C. Gregg Singer, *The Unholy Alliance* (New Rochelle, N.Y.: Arlington House Publishers, 1975), 74.

27. Federal Council of Churches, *Annual Report* (1921). 79-80.

28. Singer, *The Unholy Alliance*, 75.

29. Daryl Balia, *Christian Resistance to Apartheid: Ecumenism in South Africa 1960-1987* (Ammersbek b. Hamburg: Verlag an der Lottbeck, 1989), 25.

30. Balia, *Christian Resistance to Apartheid*, 26.

31. Balia, *Christian Resistance to Apartheid*, 26.

32. *Indianapolis Recorder*, 12 February 1955, 1.

33. Cited in James Findlay, *Church People in the Struggle: The National Council of Churches and the Black Freedom Movement, 1950-1970* (New York: Oxford University Press, 1993), 14.

34. Findlay, *Church People in the Struggle*, 14.

35. *Indianapolis Recorder*, 5 March 1955, 10.

36. George Kelsey, *Social Ethics among Southern Baptists, 1917-1969* (Metuchen, N.J.: Scarecrow Press, 1973), 231-35.

37. *Indianapolis Recorder*, 22 November 1958, 1.

38. *Indianapolis Recorder*, 12 February 1955, 1.

39. *Indianapolis Recorder*, 12 February 1955, 10.

40. Alvis, "Ecclesiastical and Social Racial Policy," 202.

41. *Indianapolis Recorder*, 12 February 1955, 1, 8.

42. Thomas, *Methodism's Racial Dilemma: The Story of the Central Jurisdiction*, 131.

43. Charles Villa-Vicencio, *Trapped in Apartheid: A Socio-Theological History of the English-Speaking Churches* (Maryknoll, N.Y.: Orbis, 1988), 77.

44. Gustav Gous, "From the Church Struggle to a Struggling Church: A Tale of Three Conferences: Cottesloe, Rustenburg, and Cape Town," *Missionalia* 21, no. 3 (November 1993): 255.

45. Villa-Vicencio, *Trapped in Apartheid*, 19.

46. Quoted in Desmond van der Water, "Born Out of Unity and for Unity: The Witness of the United Congregational Church of Southern Africa in South Africa," *International Review of Mission* 83, no. 328 (January 1994): 159.

47. Other historic English-speaking churches, such as the Anglicans, maintained a largely paternalistic and gradual approach to racial reform through the mid-1970s, despite prodding by black Anglicans and progressive white Anglican clergy. The latter included Michael Scott, who organized a Campaign for Rights and Justice in 1944 that challenged

racist practices in both church and society, and Trevor Huddleston who, among other things, published an article condemning the political gradualism of churches on race issues.

48. Nancy Wadsworth suggests, for example, that one possible motive conservative churches may have for their heightened emphasis on racial issues is to play racial claims against sexuality-based claims "as a primary strategy for opposing gay and lesbian civil rights." "Reconciliation Politics: Conservative Evangelicals and the New Race Discourse," *Politics and Society* 25, no. 3 (September 1997): 342.

49. National Association of Evangelicals and National Black Evangelical Association, "Statement on Prejudice and Racism" (26-27 January 1990).

50. Andres Tapia, "After the Hugs, What? The Next Step for Racial Reconciliation Will be Harder," *Christianity Today*, 3 February 1997, 54-55.

51. Synan, "Memphis 1994," 15.

52. Interview with church historian Dr. David Daniels, McCormick Theological Seminary, November 1998.

53 Joe Maxwell, "Will the Walls Fall Down?" *Christianity Today*, 17 November 1997, 62.

54. Maxwell, "Will the Walls Fall Down?" 62.

55. Gous, "From the Church Struggle to a Struggling Church," 258.

56. Gous, "From the Church Struggle to a Struggling Church," 260, 263.

57. Rehana Rossouw, "Adventists Vote for Segregation," *Weekly Mail and Guardian*, 25 October 1996.

58. *Electronic Mail and Guardian*, "NGK Denounced Apartheid at Last," 14 October 1998.

59. De Gruchy, *The Church Struggle in South Africa*, 100.

60. Peter Lodberg, "Apartheid As a Church-Dividing Ethical Issue," *The Ecumenical Review* 48 (April 1996): 73.

61. J. Nico Horn, "After Apartheid: Reflections on Church Mission in the Changing Social and Political Context of South Africa," *Transformation* 11, no. 1 (January-March 1994): 25.

62. Anderson and Pillay, "The Segregated Spirit: The Pentecostals," 235.

63. Rossouw, "Adventists Vote for Segregation," The Mail & Guardian Archive, http://web.sn.apc.org/wmail/issues.

Chapter Five

Building a Pluralist Democracy: An Examination of Religious Associations in South Africa and Zimbabwe

Tracy Kuperus

BEGINNING IN 1990, South Africa entered a transition away from authoritarian rule that culminated in the first multiracial, democratic election in April 1994. South Africa is currently in the midst of consolidating its democratic gains.[1] Observers who comment on South Africa's democratic experience concentrate mainly on the domestic factors that have contributed to or are contributing to South Africa's democratic successes. Case studies from neighboring countries, however, provide important insights, and in this sense, Zimbabwe offers poignant lessons for South Africa. Although Zimbabwe sustained a transition in 1980, its experimentation with regime change led to a restrained democracy, or more accurately, a de facto one-party state.[2] How will South Africa's consolidation phase differ from Zimbabwe's, and what can it learn from Zimbabwe's experiences?

One way to explore the dynamics of regime change is through the lens of civil society. Civil society has become an important factor in understanding regime change because many claim that civil society strengthens already existing democracies and demands democratic change from authoritarian regimes. This chapter explores a number of questions in an attempt to develop a framework for analyzing the role played by South African and Zimbabwean civil society institutions in general and by religious associations in particular in the process of democratic change. The first three questions relate to the process of political change and the role of civil society in both countries: What is the nature of civil society? What is its purpose? How effective are religious associations, as examples of civil society, in building or strengthening democracy? The last question has to do with the impact of political change and democratic consolidation on state civil society relations.[3] The answers to these questions are useful for explaining the unique outcomes in Zimbabwe and South Africa: Zimbabwean civil society, but religious associations in particular, have a more difficult time promoting and institutionalizing democratic change than does South African civil society because of the restrictions placed on Zimbabwean societial activities by the current regime.

As important as an autonomous, inclusive civil society is to the health of democracy in South Africa and Zimbabwe, I will argue that the organs of civil society cannot and will never serve as a panacea for democratic consolidation. Moreover, governments must not only learn to coexist with pluralism, but also to respect it. The latter demands a careful critique of the notion of governance and the proper role of the state vis-à-vis other societal arenas. Until this occurs and policies are implemented that uphold a pluralist democracy, South African and Zimbabwean attempts at building democracy will suffer.

State-Civil Society Approaches in the Context of Democratization

Civil society has become an important factor in understanding regime change related to "democracy's third wave," joining other variables like the existence of a middle class and high levels of economic development.[4] While "civil society is suddenly all the rage in social science and comparative politics circles," the philosophical and historical context of this concept is rich, rooted mainly in European developments.[5] A variety of authors have provided a thorough review of the meaning of civil society in European philosophy, and many scholars today adopt definitions of civil society based in these philosophical contexts.[6] Liberal or mainstream scholars provide the dominant insights concerning the proper definition, function, origin, or historical status as well as the western specificity of civil society.[7]

This approach generally argues that civil society is a necessary but not sufficient condition to the establishment of democracy. Democracy is defined as "a system of institutionalized competition for power (with broadly inclusive political participation and effective guarantees for civil and political rights)."[8] Civil society is noted as a sphere of activity or conglomeration of associations that can resist an authoritarian regime, thus creating a conducive environment for political liberalization and abetting a democratic transition, or civil society is viewed as a particular mix of associational life that helps strengthen or consolidate democracy by fostering civility or holding an overcentralized state accountable. To be effective, civil society must be liberated from an overcentralized state—it must be relatively autonomous and independent from the state. Contrarily, civil society cannot be "a substitute for state power, . . . an alternative to effective state democracy, or . . . a new form of non-state direct democracy."[9]

Scholars like Larry Diamond, Guillermo O'Donnell, and Donald Rothchild grapple with the relational dynamics among state, civil society, and democracy.[10] Concerning liberal democratic transitions and consolidation, Larry Diamond defines civil society as "the realm of organized social life that is voluntary, self-generating, [largely] self-supporting, autonomous from the state, and bound by a legal order or set of shared rules."[11] Democratic transitions are based mainly on the strategic choices made by elite actors and the negotiating that follows, but civil society is credited with providing some of the stimulus for democratization. Liberals see the primary function of civil society as restraining the power of the state in the process of consolidation. It is also engaged in fostering tolerance, generating a democratic political culture, enhancing the freedom of association, and providing an outlet for marginalized groups. This perspective cautions against antistatist, romantic perspectives of civil society rooted in the Lockean tradition wherein the state is viewed as a suspicious, if not oppressive, institution that must be countered by a democratic civil society. Some scholars have stated that relations between state and civil society can go beyond conflict to include cooperation or a mix of the two;[12] however, conceptual clarity on this continuum of relationships has been lacking.[13] Moreover, while state-civil society literature has made great strides in explaining the role of civil society in democratic societies, considerable debate remains concerning the attributes of civil society in an authoritarian context. How does the nature and purpose of civil society differ in an authoritarian context relative to a democratic context? Must civil society always support universal norms like tolerance and civility? For example, does civil society include all associational life and interest groups that take part in rule-setting activities, even those as "undemocratic" as the Ku Klux Klan, the John Birch Society, and the Afrikaner Broederbond (Afrikaner Brotherhood)? Or, can civil society actually discourage the establishment of democracy?

Michael Bratton, in a case study of Zimbabwean farm unions, demonstrated that "associational life does not always pluralize the political environment and generate a set of alternative values and practices which can be a force for the democratization of African politics."[14] Bratton concentrated his study on the Zimbabwean government's effort in the 1990s to create one agricultural union out of the three existing unions that represented large-scale commercial farmers, black smallholders, and peasants on land-resettlement areas. Over time an agricultural union developed among the latter two organizations, but the union leaders who agreed to the merger did so in an effort to bolster their interests through the possibility of well-paid positions and access to material spoils. The ties of neopatrimonialism superseded broader political interests, the result being reduced participation for smallholder farmers in Zimbabwe. Bratton's startling conclusion showed that, "the institutions of civil society in Africa do not always provide protection against autocracy."[15]

Africanists have also questioned whether civil society can actually contribute to the consolidation, not the mere emergence, of democracy in Africa. Although the second wave of democratization in Africa arose in part due to the vibrancy of civil society, some analysts are pessimistic about the ability of African civil society to consolidate and sustain democracy. In the words of E. Gyimah-Boadi, "Civil society remains too weak to be democracy's mainstay."[16] Peter Lewis makes a similar argument when stating that Africa lacks the historical conditions that would foster a vibrant civil society, namely a legitimate and hegemonic state, political inclusion, and political engagement.[17] Further investigation into the political context and the kind of institutionalization that coexists with the varieties of associational life is needed to clarify how civil society can help give rise to a strong state and democracy as well as the consolidation of a democratic regime.

Scholars who analyze civil society, then, agree that civil society can play a key, but not leading, role in fostering and consolidating democracy, and they agree that civil society arises when a variety of autonomous, mediating institutions exist, distinguishable from but interacting with the state, that mobilize, aggregate, and define opinions vis-à-vis public policy. However, considerable ambiguity exists concerning conceptual clarification on state-civil society relationships. Moreover, civil society literature accurately explains the nature, role, and purpose of civil society in a society constructed along liberal democratic lines, but it has not explained extensively the role, nature, and purpose of civil society in an authoritarian context or weak democratic context.[18] An examination of state-civil society relationships in South Africa and Zimbabwe enlarges these ongoing debates by comparing and contrasting the historical development of civil society in two countries that have experienced regime change from authoritarianism to a form of democracy, and in Zimbabwe's case, a gradual move toward authoritarianism again.

This chapter assumes that the state is a contested entity and an essential element of current society that must be balanced by the organs of civil society. The state, based on a Weberian understanding and Joel Migdal's work, is "an organization, composed of numerous agencies led and coordinated by the state's leadership [executive authority] that has the ability or authority to make and implement the binding rules for all people as well as the parameters of rule making for other social organization in a given territory."[19] The term *civil society* refers to formal associations, societal spheres, and institutions engaged in activities like economic and social production, civic education, family maintenance, or religious training in an effort to preserve societal identity, reach collective goals, demand government responsiveness, or hold the state accountable. Civil society can include but is not limited to trade unions, churches, women's groups, religious organizations, cultural organizations, neighborhoods, schools, and families. In this conceptualization, civil society combines a consideration of autonomous, pluralistic interests outside the state as well as aspects of civil society that penetrate, transform, or emerge from within the state.[20]

This focus on state-civil society relations regarding regime change excludes other variables, for example, the globalization of capitalism or specific class relations, but the purpose of this chapter is to examine the role, function, and purpose of religious associations as examples of civil society in Zimbabwe and South Africa regarding regime change. Given this framework, what do specific state-civil society relations in these two countries reveal concerning democratization efforts?

South Africa's and Zimbabwe's State-Civil Society Relations

South Africa and Zimbabwe contain many similarities regarding their history and democratization process. Both countries experienced a white-settler colonial heritage associated with an oligarchical form of governance that was accompanied by institutionalized racism whereby the vast majority of people were denied their basic civil, political, and economic rights. In addition to constitutionally entrenched racism, white-settler colonialism was premised on the idea that European settlers needed to be coddled and protected. The state assumed intervention on their behalf. This was evident in the state's protection of industry, in its provision of credit and marketing for farmers, and in its protection of an artificially high standard of living for whites.[21] This is not to say that the settler state was homogeneous in its class and economic interests. Indeed, power plays resulted among various factions, for example, industrial versus agricultural economic sectors, but overall the settler state implemented policies that appeased white interests within a heavily protected "capitalist" mode of production.

White minority rule also impacted the nature of civil society in South Africa and Zimbabwe, that is, both countries contained a divided civil society. A rich variety of civic institutions existed for white South Africans and white Zimbabweans that interacted with the state, and the individuals associated with them promoted virtues like tolerance and civility (among whites). In nonwhite sectors, however, civil society associations were either limited, excluded from participation in society, or banned and forced underground. The significance of this distinction is that often the most active, aboveground civil society institutions were the greatest obstacles to the achievement of widespread democracy because of their connections with and commitments to ethnic, parochial interests and/or their co-optation by an authoritarian state.

Finally, the periods of nationalist struggle and independence in Zimbabwe and South Africa were similar in that the dominant liberation movements, African National Congress (ANC) and Zimbabwe African National Union (ZANU), sought to replace white minority rule with some form of socialism. Both ZANU and the ANC transformed themselves into legitimate negotiating partners within a democratic transition, Zimbabwe from 1979 to 1980 and South Africa from 1990 to 1994, and both movements evolved into political parties that led the governments of the first nonracial democracy.[22]

In contrast to their similar histories of white minority rule and the liberation struggle, the outcome of regime change has differed between these two countries in that Zimbabwe exhibits a severely restrained "democracy" while South Africa has, up to this point, maintained and established a liberal democracy.[23] Other differences that distinguish the countries include the timing of their respective transitions, the type of negotiated transition transfer, the impact of external, economic processes, and the dynamics of civil society relations in the postliberation phase. Regarding the latter, how does civil society affect democratic processes in Zimbabwe and South Africa?

In Zimbabwe and South Africa, a vibrant, diverse civil society exists that strengthens democratic possibilities. However, Zimbabwean civil society is more restricted for reasons that include regime type, legislative impediments, and dire socioeconomic circumstances. Zimbabwean civil society has increased in strength (i.e., the ability to carry out actions and policies effectively) in the last few years, but the limitations it faces are caused mainly by the restraints placed on Zimbabwean civil society by a government with authoritarian tendencies. This contrasts to South Africa's long history of antiapartheid resistance that nourished a vibrant civil society as well as a new government that is seemingly more open to civil society's voice.

Some scholars, for example, credit South Africa's long liberation struggle, coupled with the demands of South African industrialization and urbanization, with the formation of vibrant, popular-based associational organizations, especially by the 1980s. The state disenfranchised the majority of citizens and banned national movements, but the basis of civil society's infrastructure was nourished within the struggle. Mark Swilling's work suggests that "during the 1980s, resistance activity was led by social movements, professional groups, churches and unions operating within the country, many of whom coalesced in the United Democratic Front."[24] Even though these civil society institutions were not created in ideal situations (i.e., democratic socialism), they were voluntary organizations that existed to temper and replace state power in an effort to establish full-scale democracy.[25]

But other scholars argue that the apartheid era of South Africa hardly modelled a vibrant civil society. Khehla Shubane states that a healthy, democratic civil society did not exist in South Africa among the black population during the apartheid years. Evidence of civil society actually constituted popular movements involved with the liberation struggle that wanted to replace the state. Additionally, these movements sought to co-opt civil society once apartheid passed away.[26] Shubane argues that South Africa's oligarchical, racist government disenfranchised millions of South Africans. The majority, then, were excluded from forming civil society and instead joined the liberation movement, which arose out of force, not volition. According to Shubane, liberation movements lacked the plurality and autonomy that civil society assumes. The tension between these two positions is significant, and although an independent, strong civil society did not exist until the 1990s among black South Africans because of the restrictions placed on it by the state, I would argue that civic activity among weak civil society institutions *did exist* and was vibrant in antiapartheid South Africa throughout the struggle. These civic bodies, including churches, familial associations, and student organizations, formed the basis of South Africa's diverse civil society today.[27] This contrasts to Zimbabwe's shorter liberation struggle and a weaker civil society infrastructure immediately after independence was achieved.

Zimbabwean state-civil society relations after independence could be described as co-opted or consensus driven.[28] In an attempt at building national unity and strengthening development and political stability, the government purposely sought the support of civil society organizations (e.g., trade unions, religious associations, student bodies, and civic groups) for the purposes of legitimacy and ideological credibility. These organizations, by and large, opted for solidarity with the ruling party (ZANU) and state because of clientalist benefits, but more so because the new government's policies embraced the norms of equality and justice promoted by the liberation struggle. Only in the last ten years has Zimbabwean civil society regretted its passive acceptance of government policies during the early years of independence.

The relative weakness of Zimbabwe's civil society after independence helps explain its activities in the 1980s, but the limitations it faces presently are related to the status of Zimbabwe's democracy. Instead of democratic socialism or liberal democracy, Zimbabwe exhibits a severely restrained democracy.[29] Although the government holds regularly scheduled, competitive elections, there is an absence of true freedom for opposition parties and overbearing party and elite dominance (through Zimbabwe African National Union-Patriotic Front [ZANU-PF]). For example, in the 1995 general election, ZANU-PF captured 82 percent of the vote in a turnout of 57 percent and won 118 of 120 seats in parliamentary balloting.[30] The great majority of eligible seats in Parliament were automatically won by the ruling party as opposition parties failed to field candidates. Many observers comment on the lack of a viable opposition in Zimbabwe due to scare tactics, intimidation, and skewed electoral rules and constitutional limitations. Regarding the latter, Zimbabwe's first-past-the-post electoral system discourages opposition parties from investing the time and resources into fielding candidates who will likely lose electoral contests. There is also a constitutional provision (section 38) that allows the "president to appoint directly twenty members of parliament [eight provisional governors, twelve individual societal members]"[31] while another ten are "appointed from traditional chiefs elected by the Council of Chiefs sitting as an electoral college,"[32] effectively making them Mugabe appointees. Since the absorption of Patriotic Front-Zimbabwe African People's Union (PF-ZAPU) and its leadership in 1987, ZANU-PF has been unrivaled in political power, moving toward an ideal of a one-party state for purposes of national unity and political efficacy— all of which stifle citizen involvement and civil society.[33] As Dr. Welshman Ncube, professor of legal studies at the University of Zimbabwe states:

> From a superficial point of view, we look democratic. Like in non-election years, people assume Zimbabwe is very democratic—no detentions, no real violence, etc. But democracy should be judged when there is conflict of ideas or difference. People should agree to disagree and during elections, this doesn't happen at all. There is a labyrinth of legislation that is in direct conflict with true democracy, for example, the Presidential Powers (Temporary Measures) Act or the Political Parties (Finance) Act, which grant excessive power to the governing party and the executive.[34]

Although many political commentators define Zimbabwe as a democracy, it is far more accurate to describe it as a de facto one-party state. Zimbabwean citizens suffer through the lack of leadership turnover and the dominance of one party, the excessive powers granted to the executive branch within the constitution and through subsequent legislative acts, the lack of checks and balances in the political system, and the use of force and intimidation tactics by the police against those who oppose the regime. Zimbabwe is a neoauthoritarian state on the verge of redemocratizing rather than democratizing or consolidating its gains.[35]

Because of Zimbabwe's regime status, the efforts by civil society to hold the government accountable are often thwarted by the state. Mike Auret, national director of the Catholic Commission for Justice and Peace, remarked in 1996 on the inability of civil society to freely express itself due to structural impediments on the part of the government:

> Civil society is alive and well in Zimbabwe if you look at numbers and types of organizations. However, if you look more closely, we are mere window-dressing for the government's claim to be a democratic government. . . . The government is trying to control civil society! We're living under a *de facto* one-party state if you look at the electoral laws, media control, intimidation tactics and so forth.[36]

Recent actions in Zimbabwe give evidence to a government willing and able to suppress civil society if it threatens the party's hold on power. On December 1, 1998, Mugabe used his extensive presidential powers to amend the Labor Relations Act in ways that ban "collective industrial action meant to put pressure on the government to change laws."[37] This action places serious limits on the Zimbabwe Congress of Trade Unions' ability to demonstrate against work relations, tax increases, or related issues. More ominous was the government's tacit support of the army's arrest and torture in January 1999 of two journalists who wrote in the independent press about an apparent coup attempt.[38]

Despite the limitations Zimbabwe's civil society organizations face, events in Zimbabwe have led to a rekindling of associational activity. The state's legitimacy is increasingly called into question by Zimbabweans because of corrupt government–business deals (for example, the Harare Airport terminal reconstruction contract), the government's mishandling of compensation for excombatants and land reform policy, the ongoing economic crisis, and the costly involvement of Zimbabwean troops in the Congo war.[39] Organizations like ZimRights, the Catholic Commission for Justice and Peace (CCJP), the Zimbabwe Congress of Trade Unions (ZCTU), the Zimbabwean Women's Resource Centre and Network (ZWRCN), and the Zimbabwe Council of Churches (ZCC) have called for significant change through actions such as work stayaways, campaigns to repeal repressive legislation, and conferences aimed at constitutional restructuring.[40] John Makumbe, a political scientist at the University of Zimbabwe, commented on the growing influence of civil society in these words:

> Civil society has changed dramatically over the last two years. Civil society is a force to be reckoned with. Civil society has helped support ZCTU job stayaways which have hurt the economy. The government pays attention to us. They did a survey recently and they found out that people felt too much

power had been given to one party/person. The people want real change; including constitutional change. Civil society today is quite capable of making the government listen and respond.[41]

In contrast to Zimbabwe, South African civil society organizations do not operate in a context of authoritarianism. Since 1994, majority rule emerged out of South Africa's three-year negotiation process that led to an eventual agreement between the ANC and the NP (National Party) on the form of government—a nonracial liberal democracy protecting group rights within a capitalist economy—that South Africa would adopt. South Africa's first nonracial election from Tuesday, April 26 to Friday, April 29, 1994, ushered in the new regime. South Africa's transition mirrored a "picture-perfect" model.[42] It was gradual, many parties were involved, and pacts were built between opposing parties that led to successful compromise. Moreover, the government has made proper room for the diversity of civil society in South Africa. Steven Friedman, director of the Center for Policy Studies, says that:

> There are no legal mechanisms which restrict civil society today. The government. in that sense. has made room for civil society. However. we're a polarized society and this has obvious implications. There are parts of civil society the government will listen to and others that it won't, but this is part of any society. . . . Our country has a diverse civil society arrangement that has a complex relationship with the government.[43]

The new era of liberal democracy in South Africa will see the proliferation of civil society institutions, some of which will develop an intense loyalty to the state because of links with political leaders who used to comprise the liberation movement, others that will remain silent and take a decidedly apolitical stance, and still others that will present a vocal, independent voice to the South African state. In a revealing study of South Africa's Civic Association Movement, Kimberly Lanegran points to the dilemma that ANC-aligned civil society institutions face. Lanegran states that Civics *may willingly* trade in their autonomy for the benefits that accrue from political and economic power.[44] Actions by associational groups with links to the ANC that sacrifice independence and autonomy for selfish gains could ironically mimic the negative repercussions associated with civil society institutions that collaborated with the state (e.g., the Dutch Reformed Church) during the apartheid years to enhance group interests at the expense of democracy for the greater numbers, or they could resemble the co-opted state-civil society relations found between state and civil society organs in Zimbabwe in the early years of independence.[45]

Nevertheless, a broad overview of civil society activity in South Africa reveals a multitude of institutions and organizations that display an unanticipated independence and willingness to hold the government accountable for the benefit of the citizenry at large. The trade union movement, COSATU (Congress of South African Trade Unions), has chided the government for adopting GEAR (Growth, Employment and Redistribution), a neoliberal macroeconomic strategy intended to reverse South Africa's anemic economy.

COSATU, whose connections with the ANC during and after the liberation struggle would have analysts assume collaboration with the government, has not hesitated to criticize governmental policies. The Institute for Democracy in South Africa (IDASA), a nonprofit organization, engages in a variety of actions that monitors parliamentary and government progress, and the SACC (South African Council of Churches) has also critically engaged with the state on issues ranging from the appropriate amount of defense spending to the adoption of neoliberal market reform.

A much more thorough assessment of South Africa's and Zimbabwe's civic associations is needed to confirm the above observations, but the analysis so far suggests the following: Civil society cannot be romanticized as a panacea for bringing democracy to places like South Africa and Zimbabwe. However, civil society's "watchdog" function will likely be encouraged in South Africa more so than Zimbabwe for reasons that include the nature of South Africa's regime and the new government's commitment to the establishment of an environment that leads to an autonomous civil society, at least at the present. These later points can be further examined by an analysis of the nature of South Africa's and Zimbabwe's religious associations.

Religious Groups in Zimbabwe and South Africa

Churches and religious groups represent one of the most encouraging signs of a vibrant civil society in the developing world. Christian churches and their national associations have actively fought authoritarianism and supported democracy in African countries as diverse as Kenya, Malawi, Madagascar, and Nigeria. Malawi's Catholic bishops, for example, produced a pastoral letter in 1992 criticizing political repression and the government's mismanagement of the economy, and many countries in West Africa asked respected churchmen to preside over their national conferences.[46] E. Gyimah-Boadi notes, "These religiously based civil society groups played key roles not only in starting but also in guiding the process of political opening" due to their organizational strength, financial resources, and social credibility.[47] Religious groups in South Africa and Zimbabwe, too, have played a key role in achieving and sustaining democracy.

The strategies that religious groups in Zimbabwe and South Africa adopted vis-à-vis the state have followed a similar pattern. More specifically, the Catholic Commission for Justice and Peace (CCJP), the Zimbabwe Council of Churches (ZCC), the Southern African Catholic Bishops' Conference (SACBC), and the South African Council of Churches (SACC) opposed white minority rule and accepted strategies of state resistance until national liberation was achieved. After liberation, church groups changed their strategies to reconstruction with the new state and/or government. Zimbabwean religious groups, however, have moved back to a strategy of steady resistance to the authoritarian tendencies of the Zimbabwean state while South Africa's religious groups are critically supportive of the democratic gains in the new state.

Zimbabwe contains numerous religious groups, including several that, among other things, serve as a watchdog on government activities. One of the most significant of Zimbabwe's religiously based civil society institutions is the Catholic Commission for Justice and Peace (CCJP).[48] Founded in 1972 under the auspices of the Rhodesian Catholic Bishops' Conference (RCBC), CCJP opposed the atrocities of white rule and the sham internal agreements among Ian Smith's Rhodesia, liberation movements like the African National Council, and the United Kingdom. The Rhodesian Catholic Bishops' Conference and CCJP "began to recognize the Patriotic Front, comprising both ZANU and ZAPU, as the potential government to be" in the 1970s.[49]

The Zimbabwe Christian Council (ZCC), otherwise known as the Zimbabwe Council of Churches, emerged in 1964 as an ecumenical organization representing mainline Protestant denominations. Its goals include inspiring "churches to engage in a sustained effort to bring total salvation to all and total elimination of poverty, and moving towards self-actualization and sustainable development."[50] The ZCC took a more moderate position relative to the CCJP during the liberation struggle because of the influence of and loyalty toward Ian Smith, a Protestant, and Bishop Abel Muzorewa, a United Methodist minister and leader of the African National Council. While the RCBC and CCJP rejected the internal settlement of 1977-78, the ZCC gave conditional support for it, and it encouraged reconciliation between warring parties, hoping that peace could be achieved among all sides through trustworthy dialogue.[51]

Immediately after independence, the ZANU-led government adopted a constitution that entailed church-state separation; however, it encouraged churches to be involved in efforts of national reconstruction. The Roman Catholic Church, of which Mugabe is a member, was given new opportunities to engage with the new administration, and, for a time, the Zimbabwe Catholic Bishop's Conference (ZCBC) supported the new government's efforts at redistributing resources through things like the establishment of the Catholic Commission of Social Service and Development.[52] The ZCC also took part in reconstruction tasks after initial tensions between it and the state, related to the ZCC's reluctance to support ZANU during the liberation struggle, were resolved. Indeed, the ZCC was nearly forced into adopting the state's strategy of development when governmental leaders like President Canaan Banana charged the ZCC with "straddling the fence" and encouraged a non-Muzorewa leadership change in the organization.[53] Both the ZCC and the CCJP supported the government's agenda for the first five years of its existence; however, it was not long before the ZCBC, essentially through CCJP, and to a lesser extent the ZCC, criticized the state for human rights abuses and the concentration of political power. CCJP's prophetic voice steadily increased throughout the 1980s as it pointed to the atrocities committed by the state in the Matabeleland uprisings of the 1980s, as it challenged the government's movement toward a one-party state, and as it called for electoral and constitutional changes that would increase governmental accountability.[54]

In the 1990s, the ZCC joined the CCJP in backing away from co-optation with the state in the face of increasing authoritarianism. Religious organizations have criticized the state's undemocratic tendencies when they describe the political situation in the following way:

> The imposition of candidates by political parties leaves people little freedom of choice and causes despondency. . . . The emergence of a *de facto* single party system leaves only internal party dissent to act as a political watchdog. Opposition parties have been operating under severe disadvantage.[55]

Beyond their criticism of the political system, the CCJP and the ZCC have engaged in actions that try to hold the state accountable. For example, they have established legal units that serve as a human rights watchdog for state torture and detentions without trial, but they also monitor existing and proposed legislation.[56] One piece of legislation that the CCJP and the ZCC opposed was the Political Parties (Finance) Act (1992) that, until recently, permitted each registered party state funds if it won at least fifteen seats in parliament, a virtual impossibility considering the barriers that opposition parties face. Due to a supreme court ruling that declared the act unconstitutional, the act has been changed such that the benchmark for political parties receiving state funds is now 5 percent of votes in the general election.

In a more recent challenge to the ruling party, the CCJP, working with the Legal Resources Foundation, published a report in July 1997 ("Breaking the Silence") that implicated Zimbabwe's rulers for sanctioning the mid-1980s campaign that brutally suppressed ZAPU supporters in Matabeleland and the Midlands. Mugabe responded by deriding the report's authors for dividing the nation. He criticized "people who wear religious garb and publish reports that are decidedly meant to divide us," and said, "If we dig up the country's history in this way, we wreck the nation and we tear our people apart into factions."[57]

But these responses from national leaders have not stopped religious organizations' interest in redemocratizing the state. In fact, the CCJP and ZCC are providing the most noticeable leadership in an effort aimed at devising a new constitution for Zimbabwe. Recognizing that Zimbabwe's present constitution is a neocolonial holdover—written without the people's participation and oriented toward a transfer in power, not the consolidation of democracy—that has been amended in ways that increase the ruling party's power at the expense of the people, civil society organizations with the ZCC and CCJP at the helm established the National Constitutional Assembly (NCA), a nonpartisan open forum, in May 1997 to initiate discussions and to organize debates around a new constitution that will promote good governance, accountability, the rule of law, and political pluralism. The NCA sponsors workshops and assemblies throughout the country that discuss constitutional reform, and it supports an appropriate legal framework that will establish an elected Constitutional Assembly and a Constitutional Commission that will devise a Draft Constitution to be voted upon by the people.[58] The government has responded to these efforts by commissioning its legal department, under the leadership of Eddison Zvobgo, to "draft a parliamentary White Paper outlining a new constitution that will consult the people on their proposals,"[59] but civil society organizations remind the government that the new constitution will be viewed as legitimate only if the people are *involved* in the process. Consultation is not enough.

As religious organizations like the ZCC and the CCJP effectively articulate messages and engage in activities that demand democratic accountability from the Zimbabwean state, the state has become increasingly suspicious. In July 1998, ZANU-PF secretary for administration, Didymus Mutasa, stated that churches and church organizations were overstepping their boundaries by their involvement in political matters. In his words, "The Zimbabwe Council of Churches' primary concern should be the spiritual well being of the nation and politics should be a secondary concern. Churches must leave political issues to people with the political responsibility."[60] Mutasa went on to issue "a thinly veiled warning that the government might crack down on those clerics who had teamed up with politicians, trade unions, and other groups in campaigning for a new national constitution."[61] In the end, religiously based civil society institutions in Zimbabwe offer an independent voice in a restricted political environment, and they have clearly demonstrated courage in trying to hold the state accountable, but the ZANU-led government has resisted people-centered efforts concerning constitutional and democratic reform up to this point.

South Africa's religious associations also serve vital accountability functions. South Africa's religious groups opposing white minority rule, like Zimbabwe's CCJP and ZCC, experienced a strategic shift vis-à-vis the state, from resistance to reconstruction, but unlike Zimbabwe's groups, they have not returned to a strategy of resistance.

The most well-known religious associations in South Africa are the South African Council of Churches (SACC) and the Southern African Catholic Bishops' Conference (SACBC). Many of the English-speaking churches in South Africa belong to the SACC, an ecumenical body representing over fifteen million churchgoers, established in 1968 to foster black leadership and interchurch cooperation. Its predecessor was the Christian Council of South Africa (CCSA), an organization founded in 1936 that mainly represented the white leadership of the English churches. In 1968, the CCSA changed its name to the SACC and issued, along with the Christian Institute, the controversial *Message to the People of South Africa*. This was the beginning of the SACC's sustained campaign against apartheid. The *Message* declared that apartheid was an unjust political policy and contrary to biblical messages because it substituted the ideology of separate development for the gospel's reconciliation.[62]

Throughout the 1970s, black leaders like Desmond Tutu, Alan Boesak, and Manas Buthelezi replaced the majority of white leaders in the SACC. The organization took a firm stance against apartheid and was beginning to develop a prophetic voice through the rise of black theology that developed many of its tenets from the overall principles of liberation theology—the promotion of a contextual theology rooted in the recognition of poverty due to oppressive structures and the call for activism. Black theology lamented the oppression that blacks suffered, it distinctly denounced the tenets of the Afrikaner theological worldview, and it forwarded the idea of "religious empowerment in the interest of economic, social, and political liberation."[63]

During the 1980s, the SACC was one of the few unbanned liberation-oriented institutions in the country. Leaders like Desmond Tutu, Beyers Naude, and Frank Chikane continued to forward the SACC's critique of apartheid's political, social, and economic structures.[64] Throughout the 1980s, as political oppression increased, the SACC provided support for conscientious objectors to military service, opposed foreign investment in South Africa and supported sanctions, and resolved that churches should withdraw from cooperation with the state in all those areas and organizations where the law of the state contradicted the law of God's justice. The SACC's actions were directed toward transforming white power structures and mobilizing the resources of the oppressed communities.

For purposes of brevity, a thorough examination of the SACBC will be omitted, but it is important to note that as apartheid's brutality increased throughout the 1980s, the SACBC worked closely with the SACC, even though its actions and pronouncements were not as vocal.[65] While the laity and parishes lagged in their support for contextual theology and the liberation struggle, the leadership of the SACBC offered strong backing for prophetic theology in the form of letters and reports throughout the 1980s that, among other issues, condemned the 1983 constitution, revealed acts of police brutality, and attacked government policies of relocation.[66] Justice and Peace Commissions were set up in many of the dioceses in the late 1980s in an effort to involve the laity in social justice activities. While the SACBC's actions contributed significantly to the liberation struggle, the SACBC organized many of its activities under the SACC's auspices.

Because the SACC was sympathetic to the ANC during the apartheid years, endorsing the Freedom Charter as a document that embraced a just vision of the future and supporting the aims and goals of the liberation struggle instead of presenting a Christian "third way,"[67] one would expect the SACC's relationship to the current government to be one of strong support, or the "ANC at prayer." However, the SACC has tried not to be an instrument of the state. Its leaders today realize the complex arrangement they find themselves in, and they have tried to maintain a critical distance from the ANC-dominated state to maintain their legitimacy, even as they support the state's overall goals concerning nation-building and reconstruction. More specifically, in the early 1990s, religious leaders, especially those connected with the SACC, decided that a different contextual theology—a theology of reconstruction (rather than resistance)—was needed to ground the churches' goals and purposes in the new South Africa.

Charles Villa-Vicencio described this prophetic "theology of reconstruction" as one that denounced all forms of exploitation but simultaneously affirmed the process of nation-building in a democratic society when it involved "meaningful political, socioeconomic and cultural changes such as one-person-one-vote, economic justice, ecological renewal, gender sensitivity, and so on."[68] A theology of reconstruction involves churches that are in *critical solidarity* with a democratically elected government.[69] Churches and religious organizations cannot simply retreat to saving souls and letting politicians do the politicking, nor can they continue criticizing and resisting the state by making unrealistic utopian demands. Instead, the church "must be critical, but from within the context of solidarity and support for what is good and laudable in the government's programmes."[70] In Charles Villa-Vicencio's words:

> The call to prophetic ministry requires the church to be both a social critic and a partner in the building of the nation. At times the church will be required to pay a heavy price for rendering this ministry. At times it will receive national acclaim. It is required theologically never to allow itself to be seduced by either response.[71]

How effective have religious associations been in critiquing the government within an environment of solidarity? Religious associations like the SACC and SACBC continue to keep alive a social vision that avoids the twin evils of exploitative laissez-faire capitalism and dogmatic socialism. This vision is not afraid to give special recognition to the poor through, for example, race and gender preferences because of their marginalization. It also upholds notions of human dignity and human rights. Conferences in the 1990s, like Cottesloe II and Kairos II, reaffirm the prophetic churches' original commitments to stamping out racial and economic oppression and supporting the path to a true, uninhibited democracy.

The SACC and SACBC have also been involved in specific actions that have contributed to the state's nation-building actions. Both religious organizations have set up Parliamentary Liaison Offices in Cape Town that are staffed by individuals who monitor parliamentary legislation that can "enable church leadership to influence the formation of public policy" and help "build up the capacity of the church as a part of civil society to ensure that the standards and norms of parliamentary democracy are upheld."[72] One piece of legislation that both Parliamentary Liaison Offices supported was the Employment Equity Bill that addressed unfair discrimination in the workplace and supported affirmative action policies. The SACBC and SACC felt the bill worthwhile because it upheld the notion of work as a "sacred human activity" and it helped achieve "social and economic justice and the promotion of reconciliation and unity."[73]

Other examples of religious organizations' involvement in South Africa's nation-building endeavors was their support for the Truth and Reconciliation Committee (TRC). The SACC was one of its strongest proponents arguing that its efforts at establishing truth, reconciliation, confession, and restitution could help lead to healing within the nation.[74] Churches were also involved in civic education campaigns concerning the TRC's structure and they provided pastoral care for both the victims and perpetrators of atrocities committed under the apartheid regime.

But religious organizations have also expressed dissatisfaction with the ANC-led government when it has violated principles of democracy. On July 25, 1994, the leadership of the SACC met Minister of Defense Joe Modise and Deputy Ronnie Kasrils to discuss concerns about the arms trade and industry. The organization argued that South Africa should not be an agent of arms proliferation.[75] Religious organizations continue to express their dissatisfaction with the state's arms industry when they publish the following statements:

> The continuing violence, potential for civil war and accompanying militarization threaten our vulnerable democratic institutions and require the establishment of a moral basis for our security. This does not depend on the strength of our defence forces and our armaments industry. This industry sucks billions of rands from development and diverts sorely needed funding from housing, clean water, education, health, land reform, environment and population control. Whatever reasons may be given for such an armaments industry, they are morally unacceptable.[76]

Religious associations have also tried to hold the government accountable when political leaders are unfairly dismissed. In 1996, Deputy-Minister of Environment Affairs and Tourism Bantu Holomisa was removed from office because of a lack of discipline within ANC ranks related to his testimony of corruption against Public Enterprises Minister Stella Sigcau before the TRC. ANC leaders subsequently asserted that ANC members had to clear their testimony with ANC leaders before appearing before the TRC.[77] The SACC, along with other organizations, chided the ANC for this statement. Malcolm Damon, public policy liaison coordinator for the SACC, explained the ANC's response in these words: "We criticized the ANC for saying Holomisa and others in the ANC had to clear their stories with the party before going to the TRC. The ANC told us to retract our statement, apologize, and follow the ANC's view. We refused and stood by our original position."[78]

The SACC's most recent effort to hold the government accountable is its criticism of GEAR, the government's macroeconomic growth, employment, and redistribution strategy. Church leaders are suspicious of economic plans that seem to be more committed to privatization and investment opportunities than meeting the poor's needs. In July 1998, at the SACC's tri-annual national conference, delegates like Beyers Naude pointed out that the government's growth strategy had serious weaknesses. He argued that "although GEAR is a 'party political issue,' when it affects fundamental Christian beliefs about the church's obligation to the poor, the church has no option but to intervene."[79] Another delegate, Professor Takatso Mofokeng, stated that when the government pursued economic goals that were contrary to societal reconstruction, churches "should go back to the trenches, because it seems that is the language the government understands. . . . People should demand what they are entitled to and use the methodology that works. GEAR didn't come up for referendum. If people are not happy about it they must stand up against it."[80] Malcolm Damon reiterates Professor Mofokeng's perspective that part of GEAR's problem relates to its creation by a hierarchically organized party:

The government's macro-economic policy wasn't constructed well. The RDP was constructed after three drafts and much input from all societal sectors. The GNU approved it. GEAR was technical and secretive. COSATU and the SACP only heard of it when it was soon to be released! The ANC didn't want any public debate on it.[81]

Damon also laments the neoliberal bias of GEAR when he notes, "It's a Structural Adjustment Program for South Africa. The government bought into the globalization project which doesn't necessarily help the poor." The government, over time, will have to respond to criticisms by church-based groups like the SACC.

In sum, religious organizations in South Africa support the state's overall programs, but they have also maintained their autonomy on policy formulation through their commitment to "critical solidarity." Despite their valuable watchdog role, religious organizations like the SACC and SACBC face significant problems related to the lack of a stable financial base, the movement of top leaders into the government, and the difficulty of engaging with and providing moral leadership within a pluralist, democratic society.[82] Because of changes in leadership and the drain on resources, religious organizations have recognized that they cannot deliver and perform in the same way that they did in the apartheid years. But as the times have changed so has their goal orientation, and religious organizations like the SACC and SACBC are taking great efforts to respond to these issues so they can remain as viable institutions in the new South Africa.

Lessons for South Africa

As indicated through the examination of religious associations in South Africa and Zimbabwe, civil society organs are crucial instruments for democratic change and consolidation because they can function as continuous instruments of political participation and mobilization. Although civil society organs can be captured by hegemonic, oppressive interests, they can also undermine the legitimacy of regimes with authoritarian tendencies (Zimbabwe) and articulate the interests of people while holding governments accountable (South Africa).

State-civil society relations in South Africa and Zimbabwe reflect their unique histories of colonialism and independence, class interests, and international linkages. In Zimbabwe, civil society is presently vibrant and diverse but also restrained and state resistant. The genesis of associational life began during the liberation struggle, but the liberation struggle defined its goals and purposes. Immediately after Zimbabwe received independence, the goals of civil society were subsumed under the state's interests of unity, class reversal, and redistribution enterprises. As the state sought more control over society, civil society became more resistant to the state.

The situation of civil society in South Africa owes to a tantalizing democratic experiment that involved widespread negotiations where certain organs of civil society were asked to take part in the restructuring of the country.

The associational life that existed throughout South Africa during apartheid formed the basis of South Africa's present civil society arrangement. Civil society organs are willing to work with the new government in its efforts at nation-building at the same time as they are willing to critically reflect upon the government's mistakes.

What lessons can South Africa learn from Zimbabwe's experience? Granted, South Africa's experience differs from Zimbabwe's as is evident in the goals of their nationalist movements, the type of transition and negotiated settlement, and economic bases that affect state-civil society relations. In terms of the role that civil society can play in the consolidation process, South Africa must avoid the Zimbabwean situation of a semiauthoritarian, weak state's trying to control society. Instead, South Africa must establish a strong, transparent, autonomous state, that is, one able to deliver public goods equitably and openly in the interests of all its citizens and one that coexists with an inclusive, autonomous civil society that holds the government accountable. What are some of the factors that can strengthen state-civil society relations in ways that can most effectively consolidate an authentic democracy?

Healthy state-civil society arrangements can be encouraged through the establishment of fundamental freedoms that encourage and protect the activity of civil society. Those rights important for an independent, vigorous civil society would include the right to equality before the law, the right to free speech, the right to assemble, and the freedom to associate—basic civil and political rights enshrined in a constitution—which would create a discrete, non-threatening environment for civil society. Unlike the Zimbabwean constitution that contains flaws related to its "neocolonial" nature, South Africa's constitution was drafted within the South African constituent assembly, awarding it more legitimacy, and it is premised on values that include human dignity, equality, nonracialism, justice, and reconciliation. It contains a detailed bill of rights that includes political, civil, and socioeconomic rights that create a context that can democratize and empower society.[83] Political leaders also established six independent institutions to ensure governmental and institutional accountability in areas like human rights, proper state conduct, and gender equality. These institutions have been generally respected by the government and help create an environment that encourages an autonomous civil society.

Related to a rights-based culture would be the passage of just acts and the establishment of fair and effective political structures. Zimbabwe's constitution contains electoral structures that benefit a strong executive or the dominant party such as the Electoral Supervisory Committee's lack of autonomy, a "winner-take-all" electoral system, and the presidential appointment of twenty Members of Parliament (MP). The Presidential Powers (Temporary Measures) Act, the Labor Relations Amendment Act, and the variety of media controls also inhibit the activities of opposition parties and civil society. For purposes of time, I cannot address the electoral and structural advantages awarded to dominant parties in South Africa, advantages that may or may not hurt democracy's consolidation, but I can point to some worrisome trends within the ruling government that send the wrong signal to civil society.

The ANC-led government has shown tendencies toward "in-bred authoritarian rule," for example, readily dismissing or demoting members who are outspoken (for example, Bantu Holomisa, Winnie Mandela, Patrick "Terror" Lekota, and Pallo Jordon) as a means "to consolidate central authority and clampdown on internal dissent."[84] The ANC also maintains an upper hand over its MPs through a tightly controlled parliamentary caucus and limits on the ability of MPs to freely question their own ministers.[85] More troubling are the ANC messages that suggest that civil society organizations must limit criticisms of the government during the era of nation-building. Although Mandela's speech at Mafikeng in 1997 will only be understood in hindsight for its true significance, Mandela pointedly criticized foreign-funded NGOs (non-governmental organizations) and the media for working against the government. Regarding the media, he said "the bulk of the mass media in our country has set itself up as a force opposed to the ANC" and "the media uses the democratic order as an instrument to protect the legacy of racism."[86] These opinions and other actions, for example, the HRC's (Human Rights Commission) recent investigation into racism by newspapers, can be viewed as a step backward for creating a tolerant, independent, democratic environment.

The new government instead must embrace laws and actions that lead to a healthy political environment and full participation within its organizations. The proposed Open Democracy Bill, which promotes citizen involvement in policy making by guaranteeing access to government-held information, would facilitate this process, but the bill has been delayed on numerous occasions. The overall effect of these actions indicates the ANC's uncomfortable position as a political party that must share power within a liberal democratic system in which it has the majority of power. In former Secretary-General of the ANC Cheryl Carolus's words, "We are still too defensive about the fact that we (had) democratically won a substantial majority which proportionally gives us a substantial majority on all parliamentary structures."[87]

Third, the new government must experience sustained economic growth at the same time as it is involved in redistributive efforts that meet the needs of black South Africans. "More than a quarter of the 9.1 million people working in South Africa earn 90 US dollars or less a month. . . . About 34 percent of the economically active population are unemployed and the highest group is black women at 52.4 percent."[88] The ANC has made considerable progress in areas like electrification and water supply, but a recent survey revealed that "53 percent of South Africans live below the poverty datum line. A staggering nine million live in shacks while 12 million have no electricity."[89] South Africa must tackle these disparities at the same time that its neoliberal macroeconomic strategy (GEAR) will make austerity demands. How will the ANC leaders negotiate differences within the alliance concerning the government's economic strategy? Can it steer a middle course between the demands of international investors and ANC alliance members, and how will it attain economic growth with equity?

Above all, the South African citizenry must engage in an extended debate about the proper role of and relationship among the state, government, and civil society, a debate that did not really occur in Zimbabwe after independence because societal groups voluntarily gave their loyalty to the government after independence. Zimbabweans did not explore in detail the proper role of state and societal institutions in promoting justice for all citizens because the government and an interventionist state were assumed to carry out these responsibilities.

South Africans, on the other hand, have embraced this debate, although it is centered mainly among academics. Mark Swilling, a former University of Witwatersrand faculty member, argued in the early 1990s that state leaders must encourage a vibrant civil society where groups can engage in voluntary, even autonomous, activity constrained by the law and oriented toward grassroots, local self-government.[90] "Associational socialism," he argued, allows for the possibility of voluntary organizations negotiating with state leaders, business leaders, and other power players on behalf of their constituency.

Individuals like Blade Nzimande and Mpume Sikhosana criticize these views because they ignore the reality of the South African situation and civil society.[91] Nzimande and Sikhosana argue that state and civil society cannot be viewed independently; they are interdependent entities. Civil society does not ensure democracy; in fact, it usually represents bourgeois or elite interests that conflict with true democracy. Civil society may not be necessary for the democratic process of consolidation because it diminishes the state's role in constructing socialism. These individuals go so far as to place their hope in "organs of people's power" or social movements rather than civil society in an effort to establish a more socialist democracy.

On the other side of neo-Marxist approaches (Nzimande) and revisionist perspectives (Swilling) are more liberal views. Steve Friedman and Maxine Reitzes fear that the concept of civil society can easily become a shroud for the hegemonic aspirations of the left, or even the elite in power (that is, the ANC), who will capture civil society and stifle its pluralism and autonomy. Left-leaning national leaders have assumed that civil society institutions oriented toward liberation epitomize the essence of participatory, grassroots democracy that can bring about development, societal change, accountability, and transparency in the economic sector, and so forth. Thus, civil society institutions need to be incorporated or co-opted into the state. But this, Friedman and Reitzes argue, neglects the fact that liberation-oriented civil society institutions are not homogenous in their interests, nor do they represent the interests of all South Africans. A strong, limited, and autonomous state committed to a free market is needed in South Africa that includes leaders who will guarantee the rights of all peoples against a domineering civil society, allow for the autonomy of civil society, and encourage a truly representative democracy.[92]

While the neoliberal perspective holds too closely to a western notion of state-civil society relations that accepts the separation of societal spheres for the sake of individualism and the promotion of freedom above equality, it carefully warns South Africans of the danger of co-opted civil society organs. It is much easier for civil society organizations to resist authoritarianism and align oneself with a liberation movement than to build democracy with a liberation-oriented party that assumes civil society's help in rebuilding society. The latter phase demands a reassessment of state-civil society relations for all groups involved. Civil society's role in a new democracy *must* be one where the former culture of resistance to the state is replaced by a "shared culture of civic responsibility." At the same time, however, civil society organizations must "maintain their distance from the state" to avoid the dangers associated with collaboration.[93] An autonomous civil society is needed particularly in an atmosphere in which the government is looking for "civil society allies." Let us return again to a brief examination of religious organizations in South Africa to understand the complexity of unfolding state-civil society relations in a new South Africa.

Paralleling Zimbabwe's history, South African churches have been encouraged by political leaders to be part of the nation-building tasks of the new democracy. In June 1997, Nelson Mandela said, "The transformation of our country requires the greatest possible cooperation between religious and political bodies, critically and wisely serving our people together. Neither political nor religious objectives can be achieved in isolation. They are held in a creative tension with common commitments. We are partners in the building of society."[94] While Mandela's call for church cooperation in efforts at nation-building can be applauded because political leaders appear to recognize that religion can be the catalyst for efforts at building social capital and reconciliation, a more curious trend emerging from the government is the subtle message that prophetic churches should also support the ANC's efforts at nation-building. The coordinator of the ANC's Commission for Religious Affairs, Rev. Cedric Mayson, writes to religious and political leaders committed to apartheid's overthrow saying, "Our people were committed to the liberation struggle and today we are free. Let us join hands to win the transformation struggle too."[95] To Mayson, there appear to be only two options for church leaders today: They either oppose the new government or support it. But can there be a third way? He goes on to chide those who oppose the new political regime (right-wingers) for they are on the wrong side.[96] The expectation that church leaders should support, not criticize, the government's transformation policies seems to be substantiated when one observes Mandela's unhappiness at remarks made by the archbishop of Cape Town, the Most Reverend Njongonkulu Ndungance, when he criticized the government for not heeding the poor enough.[97] Time will tell if the government continues to send signals to religious organizations that joining the nation-building process means supporting the ANC, but what can be said is that religious organizations like the SACC and SACBC, because of their support for critical engagement, have replaced their strategy of resistance, adopted during the liberation struggle, with a strategy of reconstruction that is able to maintain a critical distance from the government. Religious organizations have adopted a relatively healthy strategy of state-civil society relations at this point, but their role in building a strong civil society should not stop here.

Churches and religious leaders can also help nurture the moral values upon which democracy can flourish. A culture of tolerance, civility, and accommodation of diverse ethnic groups needs to be established in South Africa. The examination of South Africa's historic state-civil society relations (divided) shows that a civil society constructed along ethnic, particularistic lines damages a country's political future and democratic prospects. But an inclusive civil society can be established in South Africa if the overt prejudice and distrust of other "people groups" is attenuated and if an appreciation of other cultures is encouraged. These attitudes can be fostered through the work and outcome of civic education campaigns, church programs committed to reconciliation efforts, and even special commissions like the Truth and Reconciliation Commission. Religious organizations and churches have the skills, resources, and legitimacy to nurture values like honesty and discipline, as well as a general respect for democratic institutions. Moreover, a sustained ethical and/or theological reflection on significant political and societal issues by religious organizations can offer unique perspectives on state-societal relations.[98]

Of course, it is easy to prescribe the conditions and preconditions needed for a healthy civil society, for example, an inclusive legal framework, a culture of rights and duties, a tradition of political tolerance, and a legitimate government, and it is easy to suggest how the South African governmental and political apparatus should respond, but the actual attainment of a strong, diverse civil society and a strong, autonomous state is an enormously difficult and tiresome task. Moreover, the prospects for a democracy committed to pluralism in South Africa will take a considerable amount of effort. Democratic consolidation is a far-off dream related to the problems of political division, a fragile economy, and a fledgling civil society, but if the new government can cultivate the seeds of its strength and learn from the experiences of other nation-states like Zimbabwe, which has already traveled the difficult road of regime transformation, it will go a long way toward reaping a democratic harvest.

Notes

Reprinted with permission from the *Journal of Modern African Studies* 37, no. 4 (December 1999), 643-668. The state-civil society literature in the first section of this chapter appears in my book, *State, Civil Society, and Apartheid in South Africa: An Examination of Dutch Reformed Church-State Relations* (London: Macmillian Press, 1999).

1. The stage of a democratic transition features "the drafting of methods or rules for resolving political conflicts peacefully." This stage ends "when a new democracy has promulgated a new constitution and held free elections for political leaders with little barrier

to mass participation" (Shin, 144, see below). Democratic consolidation is a process that involves the maintenance of democratic electoral arrangements and democratic procedures over time without reversal. There are different ways to measure democratic consolidation, ranging from a "two-election" test to the grounding of a civic culture. For an exploration of the phases of democratic transition and consolidation, see Doh Chull Shin, "On the Third Wave of Democratization," *World Politics* 47 (1994): 135-70, or Michael Bratton and Nicolas van de Walle, *Democratic Experiments in Africa: Regime Transitions in Comparative Perspective* (Cambridge: Cambridge University Press, 1997).

2. A regime refers to the formal rules and organization of national political power. A regime determines the relationship that national authorities and institutions have to society through the specifics of competition and participation. Regime change, then, refers to changes in regime type, from authoritarianism to democracy, from democracy to one-party rule, and so forth.

3. These questions are based, in part, on Georgina Waylen's "Women and Democratization: Conceptualizing Gender Relations in Transition Politics," *World Politics* 46 (1994): 326-29.

4. Samuel Huntington, *The Third Wave: Democratization in the Late Twentieth Century* (Norman: University of Oklahoma Press, 1991). Space does not permit a detailed examination of democratization debates, but further analysis of democratization literature would include the following works: Larry Diamond, Juan J. Linz, and Seymour Martin Lipset, eds., *Democracy in Developing Countries: Africa*, vol. 2 (Boulder, Colo.: Lynne Rienner, 1988); Guillermo O'Donnell and Philippe Schmitter, *Transitions from Authoritarian Rule: Tentative Conclusions about Uncertain Democracies* (Baltimore: Johns Hopkins University Press, 1986); and Dietrich Rueschemeyer, Evelyn Huber Stephens, and John D. Stephens, *Capitalist Development and Democracy* (Chicago: University of Chicago Press, 1991).

5. Eboe Hutchful, "The Civil Society Debate in Africa," *International Journal* 51 (1995-96): 54.

6. The original work of philosophers like John Locke, Thomas Paine, and Karl Marx need to be consulted for further insights, but excellent secondary sources on the philosophical foundation of civil society include Robert Fine and Shirin Rai, eds., "Civil Society: Democratic Perspectives," *Democratization* 4 (1997): 1-168; John Keane, ed., *Civil Society and the State: New European Perspectives* (London: Verso, 1988); John Keane, *Democracy and Civil Society: On the Predicaments of European Socialism, the Prospects for Democracy, and the Problem of Controlling Social and Political Power* (London: Verso, 1988); Steven M. DeLue, *Political Thinking, Political Theory, and Civil Society* (Boston: Allyn and Bacon, 1997); and Adam Seligman, *The Idea of Civil Society* (New York: Free Press, 1992).

7. To explore the ongoing debates about civil society, see Hutchful, "The Civil Society Debate," 54-77.

8. Larry Diamond, "Civil Society and Democratic Consolidation: Building a Culture of Democracy in a New South Africa," in *The Bold Experiment: South Africa's New Democracy*, ed. Hermann Giliomee, Lawrence Schlemmer with Sarita Hauptfleisch (Halfway House, South Africa: Southern Book Publishers, 1994), 48.

9. Daryl Glaser, "South Africa and the Limits of Civil Society," *Journal of Southern African Studies* 23 (1997): 5.

10. Larry Diamond, "Toward Democratic Consolidation," *Journal of Democracy* 5 (1994): 4-17; John W. Harbeson, Donald Rothchild, and Naomi Chazan, eds., *Civil Society and the State in Africa* (Boulder, Colo.: Lynne Rienner, 1994); O'Donnell and Schmitter,

Transitions from Authoritarian Rule. One of the more recent perspectives on civil society's role in consolidating democracy in South Africa is Larry Diamond, "Civil Society and Democratic Consolidation," in *The Bold Experiment*, 48-80.

11. Diamond, "Toward Democratic Consolidation," 5.

12. Michael Bratton, "Beyond the State: Civil Society and Associational Life in Africa," *World Politics* 41 (1989): 407-30.

13. Pierre du Toit, *State Building and Democracy in Southern Africa: A Comparative Study of Botswana, South Africa, and Zimbabwe* (Pretoria: HSRC Publishers, 1995), 34-35.

14. Michael Bratton, "Micro-Democracy? The Merger of Farmer Unions in Zimbabwe," *African Studies Review* 37, no. 1 (1994): 13. At times, scholars use associational life and civil society interchangeably. Others define civil society more precisely as that part of associational life that is engaged in rule-setting activities related to the political order.

15. Bratton, "Micro-Democracy?" 32.

16. E. Gyimah-Boadi, "Civil Society in Africa," *Journal of Democracy* 7 (1996): 118. John Makumbe, a political scientist at the University of Zimbabwe, also notes the weak nature of civil society in Africa due to financial, environmental, and external reasons. See "Is There a Civil Society in Africa?" *International Affairs* 74 (1998): 305-17.

17. Peter Lewis, "Political Transitions and the Dilemma of Civil Society in Africa," *Journal of International Affairs* 46 (1992): 31-54.

18. Neo-Marxist scholars counter the claims of mainstream scholarship on different grounds—pointing to its ideological and substantive flaws. They argue that liberals uphold an undifferentiated, bourgeois notion of civil society, an ethnocentric understanding of liberal democracy, and a limited, noninterventionist idea of the state. Because the concept "civil society" has significant analytical and conceptual flaws, it would be better to use the concepts of gender or class to understand political change. See Chris Allen, "Who Needs Civil Society?" *Review of African Political Economy*, no. 73 (1997): 329-37, or Lloyd Sachikonye, ed., *Democracy, Civil Society, and the State* (Harare, Zimbabwe: SAPES, 1995).

19. Joel Migdal, *Strong Societies and Weak States: State-Society Relations and State Capabilities in the Third World* (Princeton: Princeton University Press, 1988), 19.

20. Kjeld E. Brodsgaard, "Civil Society and Democratization in China," in *From Leninism to Freedom*, ed. Margaret Nugent, (Boulder, Colo.: Westview Press, 1992), 47-66.

21. Colin Stoneman and Lionel Cliffe, *Zimbabwe: Politics, Economics, and Society* (London: Pinter Publications, 1989), 17.

22. For further insights into the similarities in political history and democratization in Zimbabwe and South Africa, see Tracy Kuperus, "Comparing Democratization Efforts in Zimbabwe and South Africa" (paper presented to the Stanford-Berkeley African Studies Symposium, April 1996).

23. Pierre du Toit explores the undemocratic nature of Zimbabwe's weak state in *State-Building and Democracy in Southern Africa*, chapters 5 and 6. He also examines the democratic future of Zimbabwe based on state-society relations.

24. Steven Friedman, "An Unlikely Utopia: State and Civil Society in South Africa," *Politikon* 19 (1991): 8.

25. Patrick Fitzgerald, "Democracy and Civil Society in South Africa," *Review of the African Political Economy* 49 (1990): 94-110; Mark Swilling, "Political Transition, Development and the Role of Civil Society," *Africa Insight* 20 (1990): 151-60.

26. Khehla Shubane, "Civil Society in Apartheid and Post-Apartheid South Africa," *Theoria* 79 (1992): 35.

27. Although a significant amount of South African and Zimbabwean state-civil society interactions incorporate informal associational networks and the formation of social capital, most scholars assume a more formal, institutional understanding of civil society. My focus on religious associations will adopt this latter perspective as well.

28. Margaret Dongo, "Civil Society, the Opposition Movement, and the Constitution," *Social Change and Development* 45 (August 1998): 23.

29. Virginia Curtin Knight, "Growing Opposition in Zimbabwe," *Issue* 20 (1991): 23-30; Masipula Sithole, "Is Zimbabwe Poised on a Liberal Path?" *Issue* 21 (1993): 35-43.

30. See Masipula Sithole, "Zimbabwe's Eroding Authoritarianism," *Journal of Democracy* 8 (1997): 138; and Christine Sylvester, "Whither Opposition in Zimbabwe?" *The Journal of Modern African Studies* 33 (1995): 403-23.

31. "Presidential Elections: An Assured Victory," *SAPEM* (1996): 5.

32. John Makumbe, "Electoral Procedures and Processes in Zimbabwe," in *The State and Constitutionalism*, ed. Owen Sichone (Harare: SAPES Books, 1998), 67.

33. The label of a dominant one-party state accurately describes Zimbabwe's regime, but ZANU-PF was unable to institutionalize or legalize the one-party state in 1990.

34. Dr. Welshman Ncube, interview by author, notes, Harare, Zimbabwe, 22 July 1996.

35. Per Nordlund, *Organising the Political Agora: Domination and Democratisation in Zambia and Zimbabwe* (Uppsala, South Africa.: Reprocentralen HSC, 1996), 206-208. See also Sithole, "Zimbabwe's Eroding Authoritarianism," 127-41.

36. Mike Auret, interview by author, notes, Harare, Zimbabwe, 22 July 1996.

37. Lewis Machipisa, "Zim Unionists Accuse Mugabe of 'Dictatorial' Behavior," www.mg.co.za/mg/news/98dec1/ 1dec-zimbabwe/html (December 1998).

38. Donald McNeil, "Zimbabwe's President Defies Order to Free Two Journalists," *New York Times*, 8 February 1999, A3.

39. For information related to these events, see Patrick Bond, "Behind the Protests," *Southern Africa Report* 13 (1988): 19-21; Ibbo Mandaza, "A Country in Crisis?" *SAPEM* (August-15 September 1997): 4-7; Iden Wetherell, "Mugabe under Siege: Ending the Plunder?" *Southern Africa Report* 13 (1998): 16-18.

40. Sara Rich, "The State of NGOs in Zimbabwe: Honeymoon Over?" *Southern Africa Report* 12 (1997): 17-20.

41. John Makumbe, interview by author, notes, Harare, Zimbabwe, 10 August 1998.

42. Adam Habib, "The Transition to Democracy in South Africa: Developing a Dynamic Model," *Transformation* 27 (1995): 50-73; Willem Van Vuuren, "Transition Politics and the Prospects of Democratic Consolidation in South Africa," *Politikon* 22 (1995): 5-23.

43. Steven Friedman, interview by author, notes, Johannesburg, South Africa, 4 August 1998.

44. Kimberly Lanegran, "South Africa's Civic Association Movement: ANC's Ally or Society's 'Watchdog'? Shifting Social Movement-Political Party Relations," *African Studies Review* 38 (1995): 101-26.

45. Tracy Kuperus, *State, Civil Society, and Apartheid*.

46. Paul Gifford, "Introduction: Democratisation and the Churches," in *The Christian Churches and the Democratisation of Africa*, ed. Paul Gifford (Leiden: Brill, 1995), 1-3.

47. E. Gyimah-Boadi, "Civil Society in Africa," *Journal of Democracy* 7 (1996): 119-20.

48. Carl Hallencreutz, "Church and State in Zimbabwe and South Africa," in *Religion and Politics in Southern Africa*, ed. Carl Hallencreutz and Mai Palmberg, (Uppsala: Scandinavian Press, 1991), 159-68.

49. Hallencreutz, "Church and State in Zimbabwe and South Africa," 162.

50. Zimbabwe Council of Churches, *The Church and Her Mission*, Report 1, n.d.

51. Carl Hallencreutz, "A Council in Crossfire: ZCC 1964-1980" and "Ecumenical Challenges in Independent Zimbabwe: ZCC 1980-1985," in *Church and State in Zimbabwe*, vol. 3, ed. Carl Hallencreutz and Ambrose Moyo (Gweru, Zimbabwe: Mambo Press, 1988), 51-113, 251-311.

52. P. Gundani, "The Catholic Church and National Development in Independent Zimbabwe," and P. Mutume, "The Priorities of the Zimbabwe Catholic Bishops' Conference since Independence," in *Church and State in Zimbabwe*, 215-311, 461-75.

53. David Maxwell, "The Church and Democratisation in Africa: The Case of Zimbabwe," in *The Christian Churches and the Democratisation of Africa*, 113.

54. Maxwell, "The Church and Democratisation," 114-119.

55. Catholic Commission for Justice and Peace, "Justice Is Our Concern," *Report*, 12-13, n.d.

56. See Justice, Peace, and Reconciliation Programme, Zimbabwean Council of Churches, *Church Monitoring for Peace Report*, and the *1995 Annual Report of the Catholic Commission for Justice and Peace in Zimbabwe*. See also Diana Auret, *Reaching for Justice: The Catholic Commission for Justice and Peace, 1972-1992* (Gweru: Mambo Press, 1992), 204-20.

57. Iden Wetherell, "The Matabeleland Report: A Lot to Hide," *Southern Africa Report* 12 (June 1997): 21. Interestingly, the Catholic Bishops' Conference terminated its partnership with CCJP in August 1997 because of the Matabeleland Report. The Conference felt CCJP acted hastily in publishing the report as Mugabe had not yet responded to it.

58. "Focus on the NCA," *Social Change and Development* 45 (1998): 16-18. See also *Agenda*, issue no. 2, published by the NCA with sponsorship from the Fredrich Ebert Stiftung, Zimbabwe.

59. "A Constitution Is Bigger than a Ruling Party," *Social Change and Development* 45 (1998): 1.

60. Farai Dzirutwe, "Does the Church Have a Role in Politics?" *The Sunday Mail*, 26 July 1998, 11.

61. "And Now to the Notebook," *The Zimbabwean Independent*, 9 August 1998, 23.

62. John De Gruchy, *The Church Struggle in South Africa* (Grand Rapids, Mich.: Eerdmans, 1986), 120.

63. David Chidester, *Religions of South Africa* (London: Routledge, 1992), 246. Black theology, among other things, embraced the concept of dynamic communalism, reaffirmed one's blackness, and actively resisted white liberalism, cheap reconciliation, and socioeconomic injustices. See Alan Boesak, *Farewell to Innocence* (Maryknoll, N.Y.: Orbis, 1977); B. Goba, *An Agenda for Black Theology* (Johannesburg: Skotaville Publishers, 1988); Itumelang Mosala and Buti Thagale, eds., *The Unquestionable Right to Be Free* (Maryknoll, N.Y.: Orbis, 1986).

64. Daryl M. Balia, *Christian Resistance to Apartheid* (Johannesburg: Skotaville Publishers, 1989); Peter Walshe, *Prophetic Christianity and the Liberation Movement in South Africa* (Pietermaritzburg: Cluster Publications, 1995).

65. Walshe, *Prophetic Christianity*, 114.

66. Walshe, *Prophetic Christianity*, 115.

67. Walshe, *Prophetic Christianity*, 121.

68. Charles Villa-Vicencio, "Beyond Liberation Theology," *Challenge* 12 (February 1993): 24. See also, Charles Villa-Vicencio, *A Theology of Reconstruction* (Cambridge: Cambridge University Press, 1992).

69. Some religious leaders criticize "theologies of reconstruction" because they have moved too quickly to embrace a "new order" of freedom and liberation. The vast majority of South Africans have not experienced liberation and justice; thus, the idea that there is a "contextual basis for a change of attitude" is questionable. See Tinyiko Sam Maluleke, "A Critical Look at Some New Theologies," *Challenge* 41 (April-May 1997): 28.

70. Albert Nolan, "Reconstructing and Developing the Churches," *Challenge* 30 (June-July 1995): 21.

71. Charles Villa-Vicencio, "Freedom Is Forever Unfinished: The Incomplete Theological Agenda," in *Being the Church in South Africa Today*, ed. B. Pityana and Charles Villa-Vicencio (Johannesburg: SACC, 1995), 61.

72. "Catholic Parliamentary Liaison," *Challenge* 41 (April-May 1997): 23.

73. The Employment Equity Bill, Briefing Paper 7, SACBC Parliamentary Liaison Office, February 1998; Submission to the Portfolio Committee on Labour on the Employment Equity Bill, SACBC Parliamentary Liaison Office, July 1998; Employment Equity Bill, SACC Legislative Submission, July 1998.

74. Brigalia Hlope Bam, "The Church in South Africa," in *Being in the Church in South Africa Today*, 48-50.

75. "Arms Trade: SACC Meets Minister," *South African News Update* 3, no. 31 (1994): 5.

76. WCC-SACC Conference of Churches, Reconstructing and Renewing the Church in South Africa, *Report*, March 19-23, 1995.

77. Gaye Davis, "Holomisa Refused Mandela's Appeal," *Weekly Mail and Guardian*, 2-8 August 1996, 4.

78. Malcolm Damon, interview by author, notes, Cape Town, South Africa, 31 July 1996.

79. Wonder Hlongwa, "Churches Go to War against GEAR," *Electronic Mail and Guardian*, www.mg.co.za/mg/ news/9jul-gear.html.

80. "Mbeki's Blues," *Southern Africa Report* 13 (August 1998): 3.

81. Malcolm Damon, interview by author, notes, Cape Town, South Africa, 12 August 1998.

82. Peter Walshe, *Prophetic Christianity and the Liberation Movement in South Africa* (Pietermaritzburg: Cluster Publications, 1995), 143. See also Barney Pityana and Charles Villa-Vicencio, *Being the Church in South Africa Today* (Johannesburg: South African Council of Churches Publishers, 1995).

83. Nicholas Haysom, Firoz Cachalia, and Edwin Molahlehi, "Civil Society and Fundamental Freedoms," *Report Commissioned by the Independent Study into an Enabling Environment for NGOs*, July 1993, 32-33.

84. Gaye Davis, "Authoritarian Leadership Alarms ANC Politicians," *Weekly Mail*, 10 October 1996, 4.

85. Sean Jacobs, "Parliament's Post-Election Performance," in *Pulse*, ed. Wilmot James and Moira Levy (Cape Town: IDASA, 1998), 9.

86. "An Enemy under Every Bed," *Electronic Mail and Guardian*, 19 December 1997, http://www.mg.co.za/mg/news/97dec2/19dec-enemy.html.

87. Jacobs, "Parliament's Post-Election Performance," 10.

88. "Census Reveals Racial Disparities," *Electronic Mail and Guardian*, 21 October 1998, http://www.mg.co.za/mg/ news/98oct2/21 oc-census.html.

89. T. Dumbutshena, "South Africa: A Dream Deferred?" *SAPEM* 11 (May 1998): 5.

90. Mark Swilling, "The Case for Associational Socialism," *Works in Progress* 76 (1991): 20-23.

91. See Blade Nzimande and Mpume Sikhosana, "Civil Society and Democracy," *African Communist* 1 (1992): 37-51, and "'Civil Society': A Theoretical Survey and Critique of Some South African Conceptions," in *Democracy, Civil Society and the State*, ed. Lloyd Sachikonye (Harare: SAPES Books, 1995), 20-45.

92. Steve Friedman and Maxine Reitzes, "Democratic Selections: Civil Society and Development in South Africa's New Democracy," in *Transformation in South Africa? Policy Debates in the 1990s*, ed. Ernest Maganya and Rachel Houghton (Johannesburg: Institute for African Alternatives, 1996), 230-50. See also Jannie Gagiano and Pierre du Toit, "Consolidating Democracy in South Africa: The Role of Civil Society," in *Consolidating Democracy: What Role for Civil Society in South Africa?* ed. Hennie Kotzé (Stellenbosch: Centre for International and Comparative Politics, 1996).

93. Diamond, "Civil Society and Democratic Consolidation," 67-68.

94. Cedric Mayson, "The President's Appeal to Religious Leaders," *Challenge* 45 (December 1997/January 1998): 20. See also "Mandela's Challenge to the Church," *Challenge* 12 (February 1993): 21.

95. Cedric Mayson, "The President's Appeal to Religious Leaders," 21.

96. Cedric Mayson, "Finding Faith Power Again," *Challenge* 49 (August-September 1998): 20.

97. "Newsbriefs," *Challenge* 47 (April-May 1998): 12.

98. See John De Gruchy, *Christianity and Democracy* (Cape Town: David Philip, 1995); Martin Prozesky, "Religious Justice at Last?" *Journal of Theology for Southern Africa* 92 (1995): 11-21; J. Skillen, "Confessing Christ in Politics: How?" in *Christianity and Democracy in South Africa*, ed. (Potchefstroom: Institute for Reformational Studies, 1996), 150-78.

Chapter Six

The Church Partitioned or the Church Reconciled? South Africa's Theological and Historical Dilemma

H. Russel Botman

Doing Reconciling History

THE LATE FRANK WRIGHT, political scientist and historian, claimed that historians should also be reconcilers because history has a reconciling role. Despite the fact that history often seems to manifest itself in oppositional terms, pitching nation against nation, religion against religion, race against race, its most crucial challenge is reconciliation. He particularly urged historians to assist the cause of reconciliation in Northern Ireland by attempting to reconcile the "two opposed national histories" of Protestants and Catholics.[1] This task, he believed, would require the uncovering of stories that are only important when they are of service to some preexisting reconciling purpose. Whenever we dig into history, we should clarify purpose, and just purpose should be a reconciling one.

Frank Wright's work should be fairly congenial with historians and theologians doing their work in religious and theological contexts. Christians in particular have some understanding of their calling to be "ambassadors of reconciliation" in a divided and violent world. You either become part of the history of antagonisms or you make a commitment to the endeavor of reconciling history. The notion of "reconciling history" denotes the political and human purpose of such academic work, on the one hand, as well as a challenge to an academy skilled in oppositional kinds of historical work, on the other.

I see the challenge of reconciling history as crucial to the quest for Africanization. If we are all to associate our identities with our place and purpose in Africa and South Africa, if we are all to learn the art of building "one nation from many cultures" without succumbing to new forms of domination and oppression, then reconciliation has to become a challenge to the academy in general and to history in particular. I am not a historian. However, I have been trained by theologians who instilled in me an understanding that nothing academic has a future if it does not consider history. This chapter is, therefore, an attempt to look back at an oppositional past with the purpose of serving the future reconciliation of South Africa and one of its church families.

Historical Invocations of Reconciliation

This chapter is interested in the occurrence of the theme of reconciliation as it has become an instrument of dealing with the intricacies of difference and unity in the apartheid and postapartheid context. It investigates a number of theological texts that have emerged within the South African context that are of particular significance in the examination of reconciliation as a theme in the context of racial realities. My study of some of the major theological documents of the 1960s, 1970s, 1980s, and 1990s has been quite revealing. In this section, I offer some of my findings as they relate to such historical texts.

Obviously, this chapter does not allow for a broad focus on every single text. I have therefore selected the major texts of the period. These include the Cottesloe Statement in 1960, Human Relations in Light of the Scriptures in 1974, the Draft Confession of Belhar in 1982, the Kairos Document in 1985, the Church and Society document of the Dutch Reformed Church in 1990, the Story of the Dutch Reformed Church's Journey with Apartheid: 1960-1994, and the Joint Resolution between the World Alliance of Reformed Churches and the Dutch Reformed Church in 1998.

The Cottesloe Statement in 1960

The massacre at Sharpeville in March 1960 was a major turning point in the history of South Africa. Sixty people were massacred by the apartheid government. After the Sharpeville massacre the political situation became more intense and caused a deepening of the conflict. The crisis led to the banning of the African National Congress and the Pan African Congress; the exile of many revolutionaries; and the imprisonment of leaders, among them people like Nelson Mandela. Many of them were Christians. Sharpeville inevitably led the armed struggle. In December 1960, the World Council of Churches (WCC) held a conference at Cottesloe, South Africa. The Cottesloe meeting became the watershed conference that caused the Dutch Reformed Church (DRC) to leave the WCC.

The conference issued a statement that has two references to reconciliation. The first is used in the context of the relationship among churches. The second calls for the ministry of reconciliation in Christ. Although the churches held divergent views on many theological matters, they were united in these two issues. However, both of these references, one using reconciliation in an ecclesiocentric fashion and the other in a Christocentric way, are not theologically further developed in the statement. The serious theological development would come in a subsequent statement issued by the South African Council of Churches (SACC). Thus, the Cottesloe Statement led to the emergence of the *Message to the People of South Africa* issued by the South African Council of Churches in 1968.

The *Message to the People of South Africa* defines apartheid as a false faith and a novel gospel built on the theory of separation. Apartheid is also branded as a false salvation. Over against apartheid, the statement proclaims the lordship of Christ. It refers to attempts to justify apartheid through the use of Scripture, especially by using the idea of an order of creation. The statement then insists that any political scheme claiming to be Christian has to be based on the reconciliation already achieved in Christ. It develops the idea of reconciliation by focussing on its ecclesiological implications. The policy of separation, when enforced over churches, means the destruction of the church since it is based on the reconciling work of Christ. Supporting separation would therefore mean distrust in the gospel of Christ.

These were the beginnings of what would later become the most serious historical judgment on the dehumanizing system of apartheid.

Human Relations in Light of the Scripture in 1974

The year 1974 would see the birth of the DRC's first theological proposition for a theology of racial separation in their policy document, "Human Relations and the South African Scene in the Light of Scripture." This text provides an understanding to the DRC's theological justification of apartheid. It represents the DRC's official response to the existence of a possible faith relationship between apartheid and a church-centered and Christ-centered understanding of reconciliation. It constitutes the DRC's response to the claim that apartheid is a false faith.

"Human Relations and the South African Scene in the Light of Scripture" claims that it merely represents an attempt by the church to listen anew to what the Word of God had to say on race relations in a plural society. The document assumes that the Bible is normative on all aspects of race relations. There was no need for an explanation of the meaning of "a reformed scientific understanding of Scripture." The meaning was clearly obvious to all Reformed-minded people in the DRC at the time. They had just gone through a strenuous debate between the young Barthians and the senior Kuyperians. They had heard that Kuyperians regarded Barth as suspect because they disagreed with what they understood to be his views on Scripture. They knew the seniors regarded Barth's views on the authority and inspiration of Scripture as less than orthodox or Reformed.[2] They agreed that the mother of all questions is the question of race relations and that the mother of all books, the Bible, speaks with authority on issues of Babel. They had heard that many papers presented at Afrikaner people's congresses and symposia (e.g., 1961 at Stellenbosch) confirmed that Kuyper's "common grace" and "Pro Rege I, II, and III" are valuable resources to South African Reformed theology. By 1974, the majority opinion of the DRC was convinced that the biblical metaphor of the tower of Babel, in Genesis 11, and creation theology, allegedly designed by Kuyper, would serve as adequate cornerstones of a theology of race that would not contradict the idea of separateness.

The real root of apartheid is indeed in the Dutch Reformed Church's mission policy (1935). However, several sources show the influence of Abraham Kuyper on the theology and life of the Dutch Reformed Church, South Africa, and its people.[3] The DRC started by taking Kuyper's creation theology and developing it into a grand natural theological foundation for racial separation. The long-standing struggle between the Barthians and the Kuyperians in the Dutch Reformed Church centered on the issue of creation theology. Jaap Durand, a Barthian himself, makes the following poignant statement regarding this power struggle:

> Unfortunately, Barth's theological influence . . . was negative as far as the three most crucial decades in the development of Afrikaner Reformed theology are concerned. During this period, from the beginning of the 1930s to the end of the 1950s, Barthian theology had such a formidable opponent in Kuyperianism that it was never able to obtain a firm foothold in the field of Afrikaner theological thinking. . . . It was only as late as the 1960s, and particularly the early 1970s, that the Barthian resistance to a creation theology began to take hold among young Afrikaner theologians and new thoughts with a definite Barthian flavor made significant inroads into the debates on church and society.[4]

F. Deist, through his studies of the way Scripture was interpreted in the history of the Dutch Reformed Church between 1840 and 1990, described the period 1935-1950 as the "neo-Calvinist period of the Dutch Reformed Church."[5] Although the Afrikaner ambitiously wanted to develop an "Afrikaner Calvinism" free from Princeton and the Free University, the principles in their political theology remained Kuyperian. The reference to the notions of sphere sovereignty and "common grace," the attack on "the revolutionary spirit" of "humanism," the usages of sphere sovereignty, and the centrality of a systemic life and worldview that is Dutch and Reformed are distinct signs of the Kuyperian influence. There is enough evidence of a neo-Calvinist influence that started around 1930. According to Durand, a Barthian resistance later began to take hold among young Afrikaner theologians in the early 1970s. Their foothold was unfortunately not strong enough to resist the acceptance of the theological justification of apartheid.

Kuyper's theology played a significant role in the thinking of the Dutch Reformed Church at the time of its formulation of a theological justification of apartheid. The official DRC policy booklet, "Human Relations and the South African Scene in Light of Scripture," was released in 1974 after approval by the General Synod meeting in Cape Town. Kuyper's notion of sphere sovereignty played a fundamental role in the formulations of this document. The state had a reconciling responsibility. It was charged with the responsibility to reconcile and regulate the legal interests of the various groups in society in order to preserve justice and public order, and to combat evil. However, the state is limited in this responsibility. The "golden rule" of sovereignty for each institution in its own sphere of justice and of love should be sufficiently preserved to keep the state from revolutionary chaos, political absolutism, and tyranny.

This 1974 document also has very distinct references to reconciliation as it impacts on the responsibility of the church in society. The church, it declared, is responsible to preach the kingdom's prophetic message of reconciliation and healing. This responsibility included the need to denounce sin and to seek the correction of sinful structures in society. In a certain sense, the DRC, therefore, acknowledged the existence of structural sins. However, it lacked theological tools to draw confessional conclusions from such a position. It continued saying that the church should not merely be concerned about public opinion that could not be justified according to Scripture but fulfill its prophetic responsibility in this case.

However, in its teaching of social justice and Christian relations in Southern Africa, the church has to account for actual, practical situations without accepting such situations as normative. In searching for reconciliation, the church has to consider the created unity and diversity of the human race. Unity expresses a common cultural heritage among all people. Although there is an increase in the common cultural heritage of people living in the same country, such commonalities are largely material. Deeper, and more intrinsic, cultural inheritance concerns philosophy of life, worldview, norms, and values. Such intrinsic cultural heritage is highly conservative and shows only minor changes in the lives of subsequent generations. The intrinsic cultural possessions establish the identity of a people, not the "superficial" cultural similarities. This identity determines the rightful place and understanding of diversity. Such diversity had to be maintained in the interest of peace and equitable order in South Africa. The subsequent existence of separate Dutch Reformed Church "affiliations" for the various population groups is recognized as being in accordance with such diversity prescribed by the Bible. However, these church affiliations are essentially based on their common belief, their attachment to the same God and Word, and their acceptance of the same Reformed confessions.

Reconciliation, although invoked, was thus interpreted in terms of sphere sovereignty and racial separation based on a particular understanding of creation and the story of Babel (Gen. 11). It is clear that this text upheld the notion of people's being objectively reconciled in Christ but concretely separated from each other. The distinction between intrinsic and extrinsic cultural heritage serves the purpose of limiting reconciliation as belonging to the realm of extrinsic or superficial cultural similarities. The notion of reconciliation has political meaning only insofar as it means that the state is responsible for reconciliation, that is, to use its power to oppose what the text calls revolutionary chaos.

The Draft Confession of Belhar in 1982

The further deepening of the conceptualization of the notion of reconciliation happened in one of the so-called daughter churches of the Dutch Reformed

Church, the Dutch Reformed Mission Church (DRMC). This church placed reconciliation at the theological center of its critique against apartheid. It subsequently developed the understanding of reconciliation beyond ecclesiological divisions and connected it directly to the notion of justice. This identification of the theological center of apartheid was born in a classroom in which I was a participant supervised by Jaap J. F. Durand in 1978. After hard deliberation, the class concluded that the theological problem of the system of apartheid could be described in the following terms: "Apartheid, being a system of oppression and injustice, is sinful and antithetical to the gospel because it is based on the fundamental irreconcilability of human beings, thus rendering ineffective the reconciling and uniting power of our Lord Jesus Christ" (Synodical decision 1978, DRMC). It dawned on the Dutch Reformed Mission Church, meeting in the same year, that if this was the case, the church was indeed faced with a different gospel, an adversarial gospel, a gospel against reconciliation. At this point, which is in fact the very point of departure of the logic of apartheid, the heart of the gospel was at stake. In Ottawa, Canada, the World Alliance of Reformed Churches had its general council in 1982. The General Council received Allan Boesak, one of the delegates of the Dutch Reformed Mission Church, and subsequently declared that the theological justification of apartheid represents a *status confessionis*, is essentially sinful, and that its theology is a heresy. The Dutch Reformed Mission Church, at its meeting later in the same year, took that same stance and concluded that the theological justification of apartheid is a heresy and its endurance an idolatry.

The advent of the text of the Confession of Belhar[6] of the Dutch Reformed Mission Church in South Africa confronted the community with the idea of the following of Christ, that is, discipleship.[7] The Confession of Belhar states that in a situation of enmity and injustice, God is revealed in a special way as the God of justice, standing with those against whom the injustice is being done, and God calls the church to stand where God is standing. As such it represents the most poignant contextual confession of our times. The fact that it was the first confession of faith drafted and adopted by a church within the Dutch Reformed tradition since the seventeenth century is sufficiently significant in itself. Nevertheless, its true epistemological significance stems from the fact that it made ethical commitment central to faith, confession, and the unity of the church.[8] The Confession of Belhar is a witness to the fact that this church understood its political and ecclesiastical task as a matter of faithfulness in following Jesus of Nazareth. In this way, reconciliation was inextricably linked to the biblical notion of justice, and specifically to the struggle for justice.

It then goes further, stating that the God of justice who stands with the oppressed against the oppression, is the God of reconciliation. God's option for justice is indeed God's reconciling work on earth. As central as its doctrine of God is its doctrine of reconciliation. It describes reconciliation as a divine gift and a human task. The first two paragraphs point distinctly to these two areas. These paragraphs constitute a series of reconciliation affirmations, stated as divine tasks for the church. Significantly, it starts by saying that reconciliation is a task of the church. Jesus entrusted this responsibility to the church in particular. The church is what it is, namely salt of the earth, light of the world, and peacemaker, because it was made a witness of reconciliation. This gift came into being through the life-giving Word and Spirit of God that conquered all forms of irreconcilability, enmity, and bitterness. It allows God's people to live in a new obedience that creates new life-creating options in the world and society.

The final three paragraphs identify the concrete obstacles presented by the system of apartheid. In the first place, apartheid opposes the credibility of the witness to reconciliation. While claiming a Christian foundation, apartheid incompatibly manifested forced division, promoted hatred, and established enmity based on racism. Second, it presupposed the irreconcilability of people as it affirmed racial prejudice, fear, selfishness, and heresy. Therefore, the Confession of Belhar rejected any doctrine or ideology that sanctions the forced division of people on the basis of their race and color. Apartheid, it subsequently concludes, dis-empowered the biblical calling to reconciliation in the context of South Africa.

The Confession of Belhar took the matter of reconciliation beyond the responsibility of the state and focussed it ecclesiologically on the theology of the church as a matter of justice. It thus disclosed the political and economic dimensions of the doctrine of reconciliation over and against the political and economic dimensions of the theology of apartheid.

The Kairos Document in 1985

Besides the discussion within the Dutch Reformed community in South Africa, the judgment of the Kairos movement on Afrikaner Calvinism and the theology of the DRC as state theology received international attention. The Kairos movement is that brand of contextual theology that arose in South Africa from the flames of black townships in 1985 after the declaration of a state of emergency by the then president, P. W. Botha. His draconian laws unleashed the worst repression on black people in many centers of South Africa. The "flames of the township" united contextual theologians of all persuasions—African theology, black theology, Confession church theology, feminist theology, and liberation theology—in dealing with the challenge to church-state relations in South Africa under the apartheid regime. The document was signed by 153 Christians, including a significant number of Reformed theologians. It has succeeded in drawing attention to the existence of three types of theologies defining church-state relations and its related public discourses in South Africa. First, there was the legitimizing state theology, second, the middle-of-the road church theology, and finally, the proposal of an active prophetic theology. In a certain sense, the Kairos Document accused neo-Calvinism in the Dutch Reformed Church of being a state theology. State theology, it maintained, was indeed a public theology, but at heart a theology of the oppressive status quo in South Africa. The document was welcomed nationally and internationally as a fresh approach to questions of unity and diversity as they relate to reconciliation. The Kairos Document maintained that the conflict in South Africa was between an oppressor and the oppressed. In opposition they represented irreconcilable causes or interests. It was in the interest of the oppressors that superficial political reforms took place to serve them. Against this viewpoint the document calls the regime the enemy of God and an enemy of the people.

Joe Slovo's proposal of the sunset-clause (1992) challenged this strict understanding of reconcilability. The African National Congress and the South African Communist Party subsequently adopted the so-called sunset-clause as a policy position. The sunset-clause is a pragmatic, political acceptance that the revolution against the Pretoria regime could not be taken to its conclusion. The "enemy" was politically overcome but not militarily destroyed. Negotiations with a greater willingness to compromise were eventually accepted as the correct response in view of these conditions.

The main theological criticisms levelled against the Kairos Document reveal that its understanding of reconciliation lacked a future vision of how nations are formed, as well as the Christological depth that all the other documents seemed to insist upon. The messianic language used to justify the proposal for a prophetic theology of direct action was also criticized. José Miquez Bonino, the Argentinean professor of theology of the University of Buenos Aires, questioned the wisdom of the Kairos theologians in addressing the struggle in eschatological language: The God of the enemy is not only an idol, it is Satan, the anti-Christ. He made the following crucial statement:

> Those of us who have confronted repressive and reactionary regimes who have used this theological discourse to justify the violation of all human laws and values (and this is not far from the experience of our sisters and brothers in South Africa) know what it can mean to a nation. The Church has also a long experience in this demonizing of historical struggles.[9]

Bonino sees a direct relationship between the antagonisms bred by an unjust system, the questionable justifications for the antagonisms, and the impact they would have on the future nation-building process.

Clifford Green criticized what he called the weak Christological center of the Kairos Document. He referred to the position of the Barmen Declaration of the German Christians who opposed Hitler. Christology was used to combat idolatry. The highest obedience belongs to Christ. He said that a stronger Christological emphasis would have clarified the point that God is not revealed anywhere else but in Jesus Christ. This would have given new strength to the document's argument on the issues of power and reconciliation. Green addresses with great concern the problem of the doctrine of reconciliation of the Kairos Document. He expresses appreciation for the way in which the document describes the dynamics of repentance and new life, which are the two sides of the Christian doctrine of reconciliation. However, since it lacks the Christological concentration, he found the statements on reconciliation in the document less than adequate. He heard "through first hand reports" that Archbishop Desmond Tutu did not sign the document because he found its theology of reconciliation "less than biblical." Green adamantly maintains that what is "biblical" should be more sharply focussed on what is "Christological." Ironically, Tutu would later become the chairperson of the Truth and Reconciliation Commission of South Africa.

The narrow interest-based notion of theological irreconcilability in the Kairos Document was challenged by political leaders and the African National Congress by a contextual approach to the political, ideological, military, and economic realities that make for reconciliation. Reconciliation meant that the light has to negotiate with the forces of the darkness to bring the sunrise.

The Church and Society Document in 1990

A critical encounter between Dutch Reformed Church theologians, E. P. J. Kleynhans, F. E. O'Brien Geldenhuys, C. W. H. Boshoff, J. A. Heynes, A. B. du Toit, P. A. Verhoef, W. D. Jonker, and N. J. Smith with theologians of the Swiss Protestant Federation in April 1979 led to a decision by the General Synod in 1982 to revise the document "Human Relations and the South African Scene in Light of the Scripture." The product of the process is the document "Church and Society" (C&S) first adopted in 1986 as official policy of the DRC, subsequently revised and reissued in 1990.

"Church and Society" is silent on the idea of reconciliation in its description of the prophetic task of the church. Instead, it insists that reconciliation between God and human beings and among human beings is rooted in the priestly (over and against the prophetic) function of the church. This means that reconciliation could not be construed as a calling that requires a sociopolitical critique (par. 2.2.3). In this sense the church is also described as a "reconciling community" (par. 2.7). What this means is explained in nonpolitical terms. Three points are demarcated, each of them carrying the same basic meaning. Saying that the church is a reconciling community demands from it a particular style of conduct. First, the church should always act peacefully and lovingly. Second, it should never be confrontational and should not promote confrontation in resolving their conflicts. Third, the church should not be driven by self-justification. It should listen to others, accept others, talk with others, and acknowledge its own guilt. The extent to which these statements mean a new understanding of reconciliation becomes clear only from a further reading of the document.

The Dutch Reformed Church's document, "Church and Society," argues that the actual theological problem of South Africa is the unique composition of the South African society out of different groups and peoples and a variety of languages and cultures. With regard to this premise, there is no difference between C&S 1990 and the 1974 policy document of the DRC, "Human Relations and the South African Scene in Light of the Scripture." This central historical problem thus places the church of Jesus Christ before great and exceptional challenges concerning the kingdom of God. The Dutch Reformed Church then sums up its historical wrestling with this central theological problem, saying that during the many years of its existence in South Africa, it endeavored to understand which demands these circumstances, that is, the reality of diversity, pose to the ministry of the gospel. The next time C&S 1990 refers to those long years of theological agonizing, it addresses the question of apartheid in paragraph 279: "The Dutch Reformed Church realises that the ideal and policy of apartheid took form and shape over a long period in our history." This should be read with paragraph 3: "Knowing what has been done in this respect in the past, however faulty and full of shortcomings it may have been, the Dutch Reformed Church is nevertheless convinced that everything was not without significance, but was of service to the Kingdom of God." Here the system of apartheid is not being understood as an evil. Instead, the DRC contended that it is "unreasonable to brand as wrong and bad everything that took place within the political structure of apartheid" (par. 280).

What then was regarded as reasonable judgment against apartheid in the mind of the DRC? It was at the time reasonable to say that a legitimate cultural issue (par. 281) in later years began to function as an oppressive system (par. 284). Of course, this management fault was unacceptable in the light of Scripture and the Christian conscience (par. 285). "Church and Society" 1990 then continues: "Any system which in practices functions in this way . . . must be rejected as sinful" (par. 285).

Immediately after the final paragraph of C&S 1990 was adopted by the DRC, a member of Synod posed a very necessary question that received a very revealing reply:

> Question: "Does the final adoption of this revised document "Church and Society" mean that the political model of partitioning is sinful?"

To this the Synod answered as follows:

> Sin is not vested in an issue (saak), but in the attitude of a person's heart and his actions. The test to establish if the support for the political model of partitioning is sinful and unacceptable to the Christian conscience, is whether in reality by forced division of people it unjustly advantages one group over and against the other and in so doing violates the Biblical principles of human dignity, love and justice."[10]

This clearly shows that the DRC's rejection of apartheid at the time was an ethical position that fed on a dispositional ethics, that is, ethics defined by the attitudes of people. What is especially revealing about this response of synod is that it refers to paragraph 282 of C&S 1990, which in fact carries the following acknowledgement: "The Dutch Reformed Church however acknowledges that for too long it has adjudged the policy of apartheid . . . too abstractly and theoretically, and therefore too uncritically." It is true that the DRC already "rejects racism in all its forms as contrary to the Word of God" (par. 110) in C&S 1990. However, apartheid was not then regarded as racism per se. Instead, apartheid was described, in the first place, as an extension of rightful love of one's own people and one's own cultural values (par. 272 and par. 279). This means "that a sincere love of one's own people," that is, one's own race, "aimed at creating and preserving one's own culture must be clearly distinguished from racism" (par. 111). In fact, the document declares, "there were honest and noble development [sic] of the other people's cultural traditions" (par. 279). Theologically, this means that, in the orthodox sense of the word, apartheid is a legitimate cultural phenomenon. Only in the second instance, that is in its practical appearance, should it be rejected as sinful (par. 285). There is thus nothing inherently wrong with apartheid as a doctrine. Certainly, its subsequent practice and the ideological attitudes that became part of it represented its downfall.

This undoubtedly revealed that the DRC was, at least in this instance, in silent agreement with the Conservative Party of South Africa, which viewed partitioning as a legitimate model of cultural protection for the Afrikaner. Herein lies the great tragedy of the DRC: They did not understand then that a *status confessionis* was as much a rejection of "an intimate bond" of church and state as it wanted to be of an uncritically close tie between church and people that adulterated the very notion of reconciliation. Therefore, the World Alliance of Reformed Churches regarded nonracial church unity as an essential part of the journey away from apartheid.

Tragically, the DRC's concept of church, developed out of the so-called legitimate love for one's own race, was vexed by the insistence that "there is an intimate bond between the Dutch Reformed Church and the Afrikaner people" (par. 271). Time and again they painstakingly stated that "people" refers to a group with the same cultural identity. The notions of intrinsic and extrinsic cultural heritage continues to undermine the renewal of the notion of reconciliation.

Story of the Dutch Reformed Church's Journey with Apartheid: 1960-1994

In 1997 the DRC issued a historical overview and interpretation of its journey with apartheid. It is called "The Story of the Dutch Reformed Church's Journey with Apartheid: 1960-1994." In this document, they speak of the General Synod of 1994 as the "Synod of Reconciliation." As evidence they refer to the presence of President Nelson Mandela at the Synod, his conciliatory address to Synod, Synod's decision to study and support the Reconstruction and Development Program of government, and the visits of two Afrikaners who suffered horrendous treatment from the DRC because of their opposition to apartheid, namely Professor B. J. K. Marais and Beyers Naudé. Synod also acknowledged that it often dealt with nonconformists in an uncharitable and inappropriate way. The document also refers to the decision to give the church unity processes greater momentum.

Looking back at the journey with apartheid, the document reaffirms the good intentions of those who justified apartheid biblically. Unfortunately, it continues, the policy of apartheid was allowed to degenerate to the point where it was forcefully applied against the will of the majority. The people's innate human dignity was not fully recognized. The church, the document states, unfortunately viewed apartheid far too theoretically. Having said that, the document goes on to utter a series of disclaimers. Although the DRC, in a certain sense, took the lead with apartheid, the National Party is held solely responsible for the degeneration. The concept was in itself not wrong because separate states exist in many parts of the world, such as Lesotho and Swaziland. With regard to ecclesiastical apartheid, it was not wrong to bring the Word of God to people in their own languages and cultural contexts.

The DRC also apologized for its silence or muted responses when people suffered under the system of apartheid. The document concludes with a reference to the church's vision for reconciliation. In the interest of reconciliation, the DRC will spread the message of reconciliation within its own structures, will call its people to lasting reconciliation, contribute to combating poverty and illiteracy, and promote job creation, among other things.

The DRC now clearly broadened its understanding of reconciliation without rooting it where it belongs, in the division of churches. The church still does not see a contradiction between the doctrine of reconciliation and the division of peoples based on their race. Clearly, racism is rejected and the forced division of races is seen as sinful. Division itself is still a theologically justifiable option where it does not infringe on the rights of others.

The Joint Resolution between the WARC and the DRC

It took another decision for the DRC to return to the crucial issue of reconciliation. At its General Synod, held in October 1998, the DRC had to accept a joint resolution with the World Alliance of Reformed Churches, which the Alliance endorsed in Debrecen, at its meeting in August 1997. This document is of extreme importance since it moved the Dutch Reformed Church to an unequivocal rejection of apartheid as a matter of *status confessionis*, its theological justification a travesty of the gospel, and its persistent disobedience to the Word of God a heresy. After many years of refusing to speak these words, the Synod has taken the ultimate step against apartheid. Furthermore, the rejection refers not only to the effects and operation of apartheid, but also to its fundamental nature. Apartheid is being rejected as sinful by nature. Together with the WARC the DRC further commits itself to reconciliation. The term *reconciliation* is used in two ways in this document. On the one hand, it speaks of reconciliation as a process, while, on the other hand, it calls the mere acceptance of the resolution an act of reconciliation.[11]

Based on this document, one could say that the Dutch Reformed Church has ended its long journey with apartheid, at least on paper. It has underscored the many texts that claimed that reconciliation requires the rejection of apartheid. However, we should remember that the Dutch Reformed Church has chosen to reject the Confession of Belhar and its understanding of reconciliation. The bone of contention in the Dutch Reformed Church is the way in which the Confession of Belhar defines reconciliation in relation to justice. We may now have a decision against apartheid and even a commitment for reconciliation. This does not imply a commitment to justice as defined from below, as the Confession of Belhar confesses.

Conclusion

This leaves us with a serious problem. How are we to promote reconciliation on such a limited basis? What is the future responsibility of the Dutch Reformed Church? Beyond the need for more concrete confessions of complicity, the church should enter the realm of reconciling histories.

Frank Wright was aware of the limitations of reconciling histories, that is, a reading of the past done for the purpose of reconciliation.

> First, it can never prove the histories generated by antagonism "wrong." It will at most demonstrate how pessimistic judgments about the other, born of real experiences, turn into righteous causes. Secondly, what counts as attempts to create a new world will depend upon the type of world the antagonism is generating. Such history is therefore at a series of tangents to the antagonism and, as story, makes no sense without it. Thirdly, it only makes any cumulative sense because it is of service to reconciling purpose now. Otherwise, from a purely academic point of view, it will look like meandering. The only freedom we have of looking at our past is to choose a different angle of vision, to look in the past for the things which we believe have healing power in the present.[12]

I have attempted to show how pessimistic judgments about the other turned into the dehumanizing "cause of apartheid." I have shown how it was given "righteous" trappings in the development of a heresy. We now see how the antagonism was shaped in proximity to the notion of reconciliation. However, reconciliation was never a cause of the Dutch Reformed Church until recently. I have also shown decisions that place the church in a reconciling stance.

Any attempt to generate our new social world and our new faith communities will be tangential on the kinds of antagonisms already generated among the people. The church has built oppositional relationships, masquerading antagonistic history as truth. It is now challenged to take the other cause, the cause of reconciliation as historical responsibility. The recent decisions of the Dutch Reformed Church seem to say that the theological basis that once constituted a righteous cause for the antagonisms has been removed. Wherever it continues to exist, it can no longer feed on the theological justification provided by the Dutch Reformed Church. The question is whether the Dutch Reformed Church is willing to commit itself to a reconciling history. This will require an equally uncompromising commitment to reconciliation as a purpose for looking at their past and reconstructing the stories for future generations.

A notion of reconciliation merely born out of the cause of a people and the interest of its identity is not enough. The Bible also connects the church and the gift and task of reconciliation to a "people," namely the poor people. It is through the poor as theological interlocuter that reconciliation finds its actual roots in the biblical notion of justice. Where the claim for cultural identity receives a central place in the quest for reconciliation, especially when it is the identity of the privileged community that is at stake, then the reconciliation one may find is not rooted in justice. It is a different matter when oppressed minorities or African Americans claim their right to assert their cultural identity. Such an insistence is in itself an act for justice because issues of identity and justice coincide.

However, when a church simply uses the notion of cultural identity to further the interest of its own ethnic communities, protecting their privileges and remaking the apartheid's volks-church into a postapartheid cultural church, it is not the reconciliation of justice and nonracialism. For this to happen we may have to wait, work, and pray a while longer. So be it, for the gift of reconciliation is the most important task of the church in South Africa.

Instead of a continued commitment to Afrikanerization, the Dutch Reformed Church could join hands with the Uniting Reformed Church to Africanize the church so that it can more vividly represent the continent of its birth and not just the histories of its oppositions. This will be reconciliation, contextualization, and a step closer to justice for the poor people of South Africa.

Notes

1. Wright's article "Reconciling the Histories of Protestant and Catholic in Northern Ireland" has been republished in *Reconciling Memories*, ed. A. D. Falconer and J. Leichty (Dublin: Columbia Press, 1998), 128-48.

2. J. J. F. Durand, "Church and State in South Africa: Karl Barth vs. Abraham Kuyper," in *On Reading Karl Barth in South Africa*, ed. C. Villa-Vilchlio (Grand Rapids: Eerdmans, 1988), 122.

3. J. De Gruchy, *Bonhoeffer and South Africa* (Grand Rapids: Eerdmans, 1984); J. De Gruchy, *Liberating Reformed Theology: A South African Contribution to an Ecumenical Debate* (Grand Rapids: Eerdmans, 1991); D. J. Smit, "Reformed Theology in South Africa—A Story of Many Stories," *Acta Theologia*, 12, no. 1 (1992): 88-110; P. J. Strauss, "Abraham Kuyper, Apartheid, and Reformed Churches in South Africa in Their Support of Apartheid," *Theological Forum* 23, no. 1(1995): 4-27.

4. Durand, "Church and State in South Africa," 122.

5. F. Deist, *Evvaring, rede en Metode in Skrifuitteg* (Pretoria: RGN, 1994), 155.

6. G. D. Cloete and D. J. Smit, eds., *Moment of Truth* (Grand Rapids: Eerdmans, 1984), 7-10.

7. The Confession of Belhar is the result of the declaration of a *status confessionis* (D. J. Smit, "Wat beteken Status Confessionis?" in *Moment of Truth*, 14-38.) with regard to the theological justification of apartheid by the Dutch Reformed Church. C. Loff, "The History of a Heresy," in *Apartheid Is a History*, ed. J. W. De Gruchy and C. Villa-Vicencio (Cape Town: David Phillip, 1983), 6, is of the opinion that the only difference between the Belgic Confession (NGB) and the Heidelberg Catechism (HK) on the one hand and the Confession of Belhar on the other, is that the latter deals with only one

confessional issue, namely the way the Dutch Reformed Mission Church understands the concept of church (ecclesiology). My reading finds that theology (the contextual question of God) as it relates to a Christologically understood notion of reconciliation (i.e., reconciliation in the context of the question of Jesus Christ) forms the central matter of the Confession of Belhar. Indeed, this Christological focus is not unrelated to the issue of church unity, but the latter does not form the center. The actual dynamic of the Confession of Belhar is the establishment of a direct connection between the reconciling, uniting, and liberating acts of God and the praxis of the believers (see also D. J. Smit, "op 'n Besondere wyse God van die moodlyende, die arme en die veronregte," in *Moment of Truth*, 141-57). Durand argues ("'n Bellydenis-was dit werklik nodig?" in *Moment of Truth*, 39) for the confession in the midst of the ecumenical debate that calls for the subjugation of the word *confession* to the confessional deed. He believed that the heretical nature of the context of South Africa at the time required a confessional word that could result in deeds. De Gruchy, who regarded the Confession of Belhar as the result of Black theology, goes further by stating that the significance of the Confession of Belhar stems from the fact that ethical commitment becomes the center of faith and confession ("From Cottesloe to the Road to Damascus," in *Listening to South African Voices: Critical Reflection on Contemporary Theological Documents*, ed. G. Loots [Cape Town: Woordkor, 1990], 13-14.) It is my understanding that Belhar must be heard as a herald of the deed (praxis) and not as affirmation of an orthodoxy. The final word of the confession is not about "the right belief." The ultimate language of Belhar is the language of "obedience" and the "following of Jesus of Nazareth" (discipleship): "We believe that, in obedience to Jesus Christ, its only Head, the Church is called to confess and to do all these things, even though the authorities and human laws might forbid them and punishment and suffering be the consequence."

8. See also J. W. De Gruchy, "From Cottesloe to the Road to Damascus: Confessing Landmarks in the Struggle against Apartheid," in *Listening to South African Voices: Critical Reflection on Contemporary Theological Documents. Proceedings of the Annual Meeting of the Theological Society of Southern Africa Held at the University of Port Elizabeth, 29-31 August 1990*, ed. G. Loots (Johannesburg: Woordkor, 1990), 13-14; D. J. Smit, " . . . In a special way the God of the poor . . . ," in *Moment of Truth: The Confession of the Dutch Reformed Mission Church, 1982*, ed. G. D. Cloete and D. J. Smit (Grand Rapids, Mich.: Eerdmans, 1984), 53-65 .

9. J. M. Bonino, "The Challenge to the Church: A Comment on the Kairoi Document," in *PCR Information*, World Council of Churches (Geneva: WCC, 1985)

10. *Acts*, DRC, 1990, 604.

11. Proceedings of the twenty-third General Council of the World Alliance of Reformed Churches, 1997, 246-247.

12. F. Wright, "Reconciling the Histories of Protestant and Catholic in Northern Ireland," in *Reconciling Memories*, Falconer and Keichty, eds., 147-148.

Chapter Seven

Christian Scholarship for Reconciliation? The Free University of Amsterdam and Potchefstroom University for Christian Higher Education

M. Elaine Botha

Common Roots—Different Fruits?

Although the P. U. and F. U. have basic principles in common, it became evident earlier that, in the application of these principles, fundamental differences in viewpoints arise between our universities regarding the task and function of a Christian university (Free University, 1975).

THIS QUOTE SUCCINCTLY formulates the question central to this chapter. How do these viewpoints differ and how did these differences come about? How does reconciliation fit into these differing viewpoints concerning the task and function of a Christian university? One could argue that the presence of institutions for Christian higher education in war-torn, or strife-ridden countries, or countries inhabited by peoples with apparently irreconcilable historical conflicts ought to be one that not only signifies reconciliation, but also actively contributes to the actual processes of reconciliation between groups. The judgment whether this is feasible and actually the case depends on the definition of the task of the university and higher education in general, and the concept of its relationship to society and societal conflict. It also depends on what is regarded as "reconciliation" in a specific concrete situation. The definitions of these variables determines to what extent their functioning in specific cultural situations is actually comparable.

The theme of this chapter deals with the question of whether the two models of Christian scholarship pursued by the two institutions actually contributed to societal reconciliation—reconciliation within racial and ethnic tensions as they have become apparent in South Africa. This narrows the focus of reconciliation to a societal and political focus, which in turn shapes the question of whether a university as an academic community can or ought to in any way contribute to or become involved in the resolution of such tension. Moreover the scope of reconciliation is much wider than this narrow sociopolitical focus. But it does beg the question concerning the relationship among the academy, scholarship, teaching, education, and reconciliation. This in turn entails answers to questions such as: What is the nature of a university? What is the nature of academic scholarship? How does this internal and intrinsic task of the university relate to external societal and political situations and forces? Only when these issues have been clarified can questions such as the contribution of the Free University of Amsterdam in the Netherlands (established in 1880) and the Potchefstroom University for Christian Higher Education in Potchefstroom, South Africa (established 1869), to the resolution of racial and ethnic tension and conflict be pursued. Pivotal to these questions is the self-understanding of the identity and vision of these two institutions. The puzzling question of why the ideal of Christian scholarship changed so fundamentally over time and became so diluted in the case of both institutions remains open to diverse interpretations. Two hypotheses could be explored: The Free University was never actually able to overcome its positivist legacy and instrumental view of science, and ultimately chose religious commitment via social engagement and service to the policies of the World Council of Churches. Potchefstroom University never fully overcame the intrinsic dualism of the "Christian national" ideals of its founders. "Christian" was interpreted in the Calvinistic sense of the word, but the domain of the "national" life always seemed to have remained an autonomous area claimed only by the people, nation, or state.

In both cases, a mediating notion between Scripture and the knowledge of the world, that of the Reformed principles, or the Christian-historical principles, was postulated. The way they were understood contributed to either the disillusionment with the feasibility of Christian scholarship or led to an insufficiently radical reformation of scholarship. Yet, the postulation of Reformed principles revealed an understanding that the influence and role of Scripture and the knowledge of God's revelation in creation was mediated by a view or perspective of some kind. This notion was later articulated in the tradition of reformational philosophy that argued that the relevance of Scripture to scholarship becomes apparent via the mediation of a theoretically articulated worldview, that is, a philosophy. Both approaches in which some form of Reformed principles were postulated approximated this understanding but were inadequate. Moreover, in both cases the pursuit of these Christian-historical principles derailed the quest for a Christian academic witness that could contribute to actual societal and political reconciliation. This became manifest not only in the implicit understanding of the relationship between the university and society, but also in its intrinsic understanding of the nature of scholarship. In the final instance, I would like to argue that the intrinsic calling of the academy is to demonstrate its Christian commitment to the poor and guilt-laden by bringing about justice in shalom through the typical structural task of the university: the academic endeavor, that is, education, teaching, and research. Only a university able to produce, explore, and teach "theories pregnant with shalom" can actually contribute to reconciliation.[1] Whether this is accomplished is very closely related to its understanding of self-identity.

Both the Free University of Amsterdam and the Potchefstroom University for Christian Higher Education in South Africa stem from a rich Reformed and Calvinistic legacy that confesses the integrality of faith and action. Both institutions claim to represent an understanding of the gospel that is world embracing and world affirmative.[2] In the history of both institutions there was a conscious and deliberate move away from dualistic or pietistic understandings of Christian presence in society. The Free University developed along the general lines of Reformed Calvinism and consciously shied away from the pietism of the reveille. Potchefstroom University developed from the embryonic beginnings of a theological seminary for the Gereformeerde Kerk that broke away from the Nederduitse Gereformeerde Kerk (NGK) in South Africa because of the pietism and purported Arminianism of the NGK. So both institutions shared an understanding of the nature of creation, sin, redemption, and grace that entailed that higher education and scholarship requires the recognition and embodiment of the claim of the lordship of Jesus Christ over all aspects of human life. It stands to reason that even though these two institutions shared historical, and to some extent even cultural, roots, their self-understanding and articulation of identity evolved differently. So did their respective implementation of fundamental notions concerning the nature of Christian scholarship and the relationship of school to society.

Notions of academic self-understanding and identity are central to a university's concept of its task and role as academic institution and its role in society. Not only were Holland and South Africa very different breeding grounds for Christianity and for the development of education and scholarship in the late nineteenth century, but a fundamental shift in their respective understanding and articulation of self-identity took place that influenced their positioning toward societal issues of racial conflict, ethnic tension, and reconciliation. In both cases, this self-understanding was closely related to philosophical and ideological shifts in the surrounding culture and specifically in reformulations of the nature of Christian witness amidst societal tensions. But the shifts were also mediated by their typical understanding of the nature of scientific endeavor. The test case for their respective views on reconciliation was the question of the relationship of the academy to the South African political system of apartheid. This came to a head in the late 1960s and early 1970s and culminated in a parting of ways at the International Conference in Christian Higher Education held at Potchefstroom in 1975.

I have deliberately restricted this comparative analysis to the period between 1975 and 1995. The reason for this is quite simple. The International Conference on Christian Higher Education that took place at Potchefstroom in 1975 could be seen as a historical watershed in the relationship between the two institutions, but it also represents a watershed in their respective self-understandings as institutions of Christian higher learning. Before we take a closer look at this historical watershed, some reflections on the relationship between academia and politics are necessary.

No Politically or Religiously Neutral University

A dominant strand in the Reformed tradition in higher learning is that no single dimension of human life can be seen as religiously neutral.[3] This tradition argues that this claim holds as much for the nature of theorizing[4] and scholarship as it does for the nature of education and societal structures.[5] This in turn entails that in the interrelationship of the university and politics there is no possibility of arguing for a politically neutral university. This does not imply that there are no boundaries between politics and the university, or that these boundaries are not normative. But it does imply that a university always implicitly or explicitly positions itself toward the political system or practice within which it is placed.

In the literature that deals with the interrelationship of academia and politics, two positions are juxtaposed—on the one hand, the notion of the neutral or apolitical university and, on the other hand, the recognition of the inevitable political involvement of the university. The following quote from Wallerstein points to the latter position: "It is a political act for the university to support the government in its normal functions. It is a political act for the university to be indifferent to the government. It is a political act for the university to oppose the government. However it acts in its relation to the government, the university is engaged in politics."[6] Juxtaposed to this position is that of Philip M. Hauser who argues that the university is essentially apolitical and called to fulfil a unique apolitical task.[7] Hauser develops his position in conjunction with the Weberian thesis concerning the value-neutrality of scholarship. This does not exclude the possibility that students and faculty members can participate in active politics or in advisory political roles in their capacity as citizens, but within the context of the university itself the student or faculty member is called to be a "political eunuch."[8]

These positions warrant discussion, but within the context of this chapter it is the tacit political involvement of the university that requires illumination. The so-called apolitical character of the university becomes highly questionable when it appears that the university uncritically supports, actively or tacitly, a questionable political policy that sustains its own existence. I argue that a university as an institution of higher learning cannot escape making choices concerning politics as it cannot escape its inevitable religious or confessional choices. These choices are obviously made in the process of fulfilling its typical task, that is, scholarship, research, and teaching (for example, the "relevance" of university curricula).[9] But the point being made here is the fact that institutions of higher learning need to make explicit their positions vis-à-vis political systems and ideologies within which they are called to operate. The unmasking of the idols and idolatry of the surrounding society is part of the intrinsic task of scholarship and teaching. This brings us to the question: To what extent did these two institutions accomplish this?

The Free University

Both the Free University of Amsterdam and the so-called Vereniging voor Wetenschappelijke Onderwijs op Gereformeerde Grondslag (The Association for Scientific Education on Reformed Basis) date from the turbulent and creative 1870s. These were times in the Netherlands during which Christian organizations and institutions were spawned in practically every aspect of Dutch culture—education, politics, journalism, culture, and social issues. The Dutch Calvinist newspaper *De Standaard* (1872), the establishment of *Patrimonium* (1878), and the establishment of national electoral associations for the AntiRevolutionary Party are examples of movements in the area of Christian education that came into existence during this period of time. It was a time that heralded the development of manifold organizations in which the age-old struggle of faith and unbelief came to a new and more pronounced expression. The founders of the Free University of Amsterdam were convinced that it was the task of the university to disclose a view of the world and of humankind based on the message of the gospel. Obviously, the establishment of the Free University cannot be isolated from the historical ecclesiastical developments in the Netherlands of the late nineteenth century.

Prior to this event, the Netherlands had its first Christian university established in Leiden in 1575. As the nature of Dutch society secularized, the relationship between the University of Leiden and church and religion eroded. These trends also characterized other Dutch universities that were influenced by the spirits of rationalism and empiricism. It was the religious reveille of the nineteenth century in Holland and the ecclesiastical developments in the circle of the Dutch Reformed churches during that time that formed the cultural background to the establishment of the association that brought the Free University into existence. It availed itself of the opportunity created by the Wet op hoger onderwijs (Law on Higher Education) of 1876 that formally made it possible to establish universities on the basis of special religious considerations.[10] The Reformed Christian founders of the Free University of Amsterdam believed that the spirit of the age, with its theological liberalism and state absolutism, needed to be countered by an act of faith that would point to the freedom of humankind to serve God and the freedom from all state prescription in academic education. They were convinced that the biblical message would be mediated via the uncovering of the creational ordinances (gereformeerde beginselen, literally "reformed principles") or structures, and this message would then be relayed via the academic endeavor to a world in which the signs of chaos and relativism are ever present.[11] They regarded the academic search on the basis of their faith for these differentiated creational structures as the primary task of the university. This task came to expression in their formulation of the well-known Kuyperian principle of sphere sovereignty. These principles would provide guidelines for personal and societal action and behavior.[12] They would also provide the bridge to the renewal of society, and they were the key to the resolution of the question at the heart of Christian scholarship: What is the internal relationship between God's Word and the various areas of academic endeavor?[13] The seemingly elusive nature of these principles is one of the many factors that gradually led to a radical rethinking of the articulation of the confessional basis of the Free University.[14] A brief historical note about the origin and evolution of this notion is necessary.

The notion of Reformed principles (gereformeerde beginselen) is invoked by Kuyper as an explanation, mechanism, and/or articulation of the way the university and scholarship are related and bound to God's revelation in Scripture and in nature.[15] Kuyper's grounds for this claim are based on article 2 of the *Netherlands Confession of Faith*, which bases the knowledge of God on two means: His creation (described by the well-known book metaphor) and Scripture. The potentially diverse interpretations of Scripture would be laid to rest when the Reformed principles were chosen as a common frame of reference. These Reformed principles would function as a hermeneutical key to the articulation of the understanding of Scripture concerning humankind, world, and society. They would function both as the distinguishing traits or identity of the Free University and the spiritually unifying factors in the coherence of presuppositions required by both research and teaching.[16] Kuyper's complicated view of the place of Scripture in Reformed principles gave rise to a certain tension. Scripture had two purposes, Kuyper argued. The first is to disclose the way of reconciliation. This happens primarily through the church and as such relates only indirectly to the academy. Second, Scripture enables us to understand the book of nature, which is the domain of science.[17] It is this historical view of the relationship between the Reformed principles and the identity of the Free University of Amsterdam that is called into question by developments in the early 1960s and 1970s. The Reformed principles were to form the basis (grondslag) of the pursuit of research, scholarship, and teaching at the Free University. Operating in this fashion, the university was called to oppose the threats of naturalism and contribute to the re-Christianization of culture and the conservation of orthodoxy.[18]

The enigmatic question as to what these Reformed principles actually were surfaces in every commemoration of the history of the Free University.[19] It seemed to have been a bone of contention from the very beginning.[20] The emphases in the articulation of the nature of the principles vary from time to time: At times Christian and Reformed (principles) are equated, at other times the emphasis is on the *Calvinistic* nature of the Christian principles (in contrast to general Christian or Protestant). Fabius, on the other hand, interprets these principles as par excellence, the national or historical Calvinism referring to the lifestyle developed in Holland during the course of the sixteenth and seventeenth centuries.[21]

The question also surfaced in the conflict between Kuyper and De Saponin Lehman in the period immediately before Lehman was required to leave the Free University in 1896. The fundamental issue at stake was the question of whether these principles could be identified and were of such a nature that their historical appearance would provide a system for diverse facets of Reformed life. De Saponin Lehman did not think this was the case; moreover, he believed that facts were facts and did not differ when they were being seen from a Reformed perspective.[22] By 1927, a special committee appointed by the directors and curators of the Free University came to the conclusion that these principles had not yet been found![23] Van Deursen's analysis of the mirror image of the Free University represented in four publications dealing with its history shows that the expectation that these principles would be realized and concretely worked out was a matter of faith and prayer.[24] When they were eventually embodied in the philosophical system of Herman Dooyeweerd and D. th Vollenhoven, it was seen as an answer to prayer.[25] Roelink, however, states: "But, now concerning the principle ([begin*sel]*. This word has stood as a wicked fairy at the cradle of the Association and the Free University established by the Association and have accompanied both through a whole century . . . vexatiously accompanied both until today."[26] The historians of the Free University emphasized the close relationship between the academy and the Reformed community's supporting the work of the Free University in the course of these historical developments. This community was historically bound to and guided by these same Reformed principles as the Free University was.

The elaboration of these Reformed principles in the philosophy of Herman Dooyeweerd requires a passing comment. Where Kuyper and the founders of the Free University saw the encyclopaedia of the disciplines develop from the embryonic cells of a Christian worldview, Dooyeweerd and Vollenhoven clearly distinguished between "structure" and "direction."[27] This entailed the recognition that science and the university as societal structures have their own structural principles or laws that characterize their existence and that the influence of faith and worldview comes to expression in the direction in which these structures are given concrete shape and form. The knowledge of the disciplines is not inferred from, or developed out of, kernels already contained in the Reformed principles.[28]

In the 1960s and 1970s a growing sense of unrest was experienced by the academic staff of the Free University. The university had developed to encompass all the traditional university faculties, with the consequence that more and more teaching faculty were appointed but were not comfortable with the basis and principles of the Free University, or they simply lacked adequate training in and exposure to the Reformed tradition. Within the university, a growing pluriformity of Protestant orthodoxy was occurring that was making it more difficult to accomplish the development of a university on a broad Reformed basis. A number of other factors contributed to the fact that the Free University chose a new route to relate religious commitment to the surrounding culture: internal disillusionment with the purported elusive character of the Reformed principles on which to base scholarship and teaching, a gradual dilution of the originally required confessional commitment of academics, a growing sense of the need of ecumenism in the face of growing confessional pluralism, and a new political understanding of the calling of the university amid the brokenness and suffering of society. In 1971, these developments came to a climax in the replacement of the Reformed principles with a differently formulated goal (doelstelling),[29] which was to articulate that biblical revelation has significance for humankind and for society.[30] The changes in the basis of the Free University represented a definite move toward an instrumentalist view of science in the service of evangelical goals and purposes.[31]

In his analysis of four publications commemorating different historical phases of the Free University, Van Deursen points out two recurring issues: the Reformed principles and the relationship to the Reformed community (achterban).[32] The common denominator between these two issues was the fact that they were radically opposed to plurality or pluriformity, yet, plurality is exactly what the change in the articulation of the basis of the Free University accomplishes and recognizes. When the content of what this change entails is unpacked, it becomes apparent that Christian commitment needs to relate to poverty, injustice, racial tension, suffering, anxiety, war, guilt, environmental issues, and death.[33] Does this represent a fundamental shift in the Free University's understanding of the range and implications of faith? This is a difficult question to answer. Undoubtedly the shift in emphasis from the Reformed principles to the relevance of scholarship and the academy to concrete societal issues represents a new approach. The formative claims of Reformed principles have been replaced by an emphasis on engagement in concrete issues of reconciliation. A major shift in the policies of the Free University occurred in 1993 when the Free University ceased to require that faculty and staff applying for positions formally agree with the Christian goals of the university.[34]

The establishment in 1993 of a steering group with the mandate to investigate values and norms in teaching and research at the Free University marks another important phase in the development of the university's understanding of Christian scholarship. The goal of this project was formulated as follows:

> (To educate) students to become academics who will function in a responsible way in society, who will apply their academic knowledge within the context of broader knowledge of society and conscious of values (in the sense of life views and human rights) that play an implicit role. This would entail making these values explicit and testing these values.[35] (free translation)

Because teaching is a culturally determined activity, it is a value-laden form of communication. Teaching and scholarship assume that there is a common commitment to search for truth. Central to this project is the training and education of students for responsible decision making. The final report does not give a very optimistic picture. Professors in many of the faculties were unsure as to the way in which these values were to be embodied in their disciplines and teaching. Others felt they did not have adequate time and resources to devote to these matters. Some were not very enamoured with the idea that there would be some external intervention or involvement in their discussions about values in their disciplines.[36] In an interview with Professor E. Boeker, the idea of service to society and the implementation of values is quite clear, but the notion of "serving God," he claims, "is not fruitful discussion within the context of the task of a university.[37] These developments are self-evident. They constitute a clear shift from the initial idea of the Reformed principles, for though 'reconciliation' is still a valuable pursuit, it has been emptied of its Christian content." Certainly an argument on the basis of what Caper would have called common grace is required here, but this will have to suffice for now.

The development of the Free University's understanding of reconciliation is a litmus test of its sensitivity to theological, philosophical, cultural, and political changes in its surrounding culture. Philosophical movements such as neo-Marxism and later postmodernism also influenced these changes profoundly. The test case in which these views concerning reconciliation were to be tried and tested was the relationship to a Reformed university shaped in the crucible of the same historical tradition, the Potchefstroom University for Christian Higher Education in South Africa.

Potchefstroom University for Christian Higher Education

Perhaps the most intriguing question concerning the role of Potchefstroom University is why this institution, which so courageously positioned itself in the struggle against neutrality in scholarship and education and for the propagation of the lordship of Jesus Christ in all areas of life, did not in a similar fashion speak out prophetically and critically against the obvious injustice of the South African apartheid system. Potchefstroom always had so-called dissenting voices, who were willing to take a stand against the discrimination and injustice of the political system, but the question here is why the university as an institution did not speak out against or oppose government policies that clearly contravened the most basic message of the gospel. Perhaps even more dubitable is the fact that the philosophical and theological justification of apartheid was hardly questioned by generations of academics and students at Potchefstroom University. One of the most well-known academic defenders of racial segregation was the Potchefstroom Calvinistic philosopher, H. G. Stoker. What is especially puzzling is the fact that he was an ardent defender of the postulate that all knowledge is fundamentally determined by religious convictions. He introduced and elaborated Dutch neo-Calvinism, particularly the philosophy of Herman Dooyeweerd, to South Africa. Although he was an avid opponent of the neutrality postulate in scholarship and science, he was not consistent in drawing the consequences of these convictions through to national and political life. Perhaps this is not a fair statement. His application of Calvinistic convictions to issues of culture, nationality, and politics led him to argue that separate development as a political system was justified. His philosophical defense of apartheid and his views on the nature of Christian scholarship were influential in the shaping of the policies and educational practices of Potchefstroom University.

Potchefstroom University's interpretation of its Christian character in the course of its history strongly reflected the dominant political-ideological views of the surrounding culture. These views, strengthened by Stoker's views on the nature of the university, scholarship, and academic freedom, contributed to the university's lack of prophetic-critical distance to the dominant political system. The history of Potchefstroom University, as that of most other universities, clearly shows a correlation between the changes in the historical, political, and cultural situation and its views concerning its identity, self-understanding, and specifically its interpretation of what the notion of Christian actually implies. When British imperialism was the enemy of most Afrikaans-language universities in South Africa, Potchefstroom University's understanding of Christian was deeply colored by Afrikaner nationalistic and cultural overtones. When the struggle focused on exemption from the so-called conscience clause, which prohibited enquiry concerning the religious convictions of professors and the struggle for independence, it was these focal points that colored the way in which the "Christian" character was understood.[38] The early seventies confronted Potchefstroom with a new challenge, one that would once again force the university to rethink its interpretation of its mission. This came to a head when the Free University of Amsterdam and other kindred universities posed the critical question concerning the sociocritical task of the university within the context of a discriminatory political system. Later developments under the influence of postmodernism and more specifically the radical political shift in South Africa with its challenges of multiculturalism and reconstruction have posed a whole new set of questions that require Christian reflection. Because of the role of the Calvinistic philosopher H. G. Stoker in molding the identity and self-understanding of Potchefstroom University, I would like to highlight some aspects of his views.

H. G. Stoker: Academic Freedom, University Freedom, and Apartheid

In Stoker's ceaseless struggle to establish Christian scholarship, a strong, prophetic-critical dimension was ever present. His magisterial contribution to the academy was the constant emphasis on the radically religious determination of knowledge and thought. This certainly made him one of the strongest crusaders for the recognition of Potchefstroom as an independent university with a unique calling. Although Stoker wrote much on the struggle of Potchefstroom to be recognized as a Christian university, one does not find many publications in which he explicitly deals with the relationship between the university and the wider society. Like many of his contemporaries, Stoker was deeply rooted in the cultural struggle of the existence of the Afrikaner people, a fact that obviously made him less critical of the political system of apartheid that was the outcome of a fierce struggle for the recognition of the cultural and racial identity of the Afrikaners and all other groups destined to share a common territory in South Africa.

To the question of whether racial segregation in any way diminishes academic freedom, Stoker declared, "I give my personal view, which is, as far as

I can see, fundamentally in agreement with the South African Government's policy of apartheid."[39] This article is devoted to the question of whether the prohibition of Bantu students at white or European universities could be seen to be in contravention of academic freedom. In his response to this question he operates with the contrast between European and Bantu racial groups. But the term *racial* is consistently followed by *national*.

Stoker argued that apartheid emphasizes the relationship between human societal groups and that it accepts the primary principle of the universal equality and freedom of all human beings primarily in respect of racial groups.[40] Racial groups, he claims, have their own individuality and lifestyle and apartheid wants to protect all races in order to elevate them to their highest level of development according to their own nature. When this has taken place, existing discriminatory measures ought to be abolished.[41] The unfortunate fact that many of the Bantu race have already reached such a level of development, he claims, is an "unhappy victim of a transitional phase of Bantu development."[42] This "puberty phase," he says, requires adjustments from both the "parent" and the "child." This racial crisis has been brought about by the acceleration of economic integration of the urban Bantu and the Europeans. This is a crisis that will force South Africa to make a choice between integration and differentiation. There is no middle ground between apartheid and integration because integration inevitably leads to assimilation.[43]

In his attempt to answer the question concerning academic freedom, Stoker introduces the distinction between "academic" freedom and "university" freedom. The former is intrinsic to the university, the latter relates to the way the university ought to be free to serve its own racial group. He says: "the ideal of a policy of integration, namely that a university should not serve only a section of the country, but that it should have a multiracial character, and be a cross-section of the racial composition of South Africa, appears to be unacceptable."[44] Stoker summarizes his own position by concluding that the South African government has a good case for the establishment of separate non-European universities. When he discusses the important question of whether the prohibition of Bantu students at European universities might not be a transgression of university freedom, he argues that the criterion for access to European universities should be based on a number of conditions. Three of these conditions are: has the pattern of apartheid been realized, has the danger of integration and assimilation been thwarted, and has the national or racial character of the university been protected? He reproaches the so-called open universities for the fact that their entry requirements are not based on academic grounds but on the pretheoretical principles of liberalism.[45] Once the pattern of racial differentiation has been established and the Bantu people have reached a certain level of development he sees no objection to the fact that a graduate student may, as an exception, be allowed to study at a European university under the guidance of a competent academic.

Stoker's views and philosophical undergirding of apartheid and racial separation were as important to Potchefstroom University as Caper's views were to the establishment and development of the Free University's understanding of a Christian presence and witness in academia and society. Obviously his views were time and context bound. The ease with which he exchanged racial and national qualifications reveals how closely these notions were linked in his thought. Here there are few indications of his earlier, clear distinctions among state, people, and nation.[46] The contours of a Eurocentric elitist philosophy of culture dominate his analysis. He reproaches liberalism for its uncritical assumption of pretheoretical tenets, but fails to recognize that his own position is as bound to pretheoretical notions as the position he criticizes. Why this detour? Stoker's thought is but a more sophisticated articulation of the views basic to the policies and direction of Potchefstroom University virtually from its inception. The crucial question is, of course, to what extent this line of thinking could in any way be construed as an attempt at articulating a Christian view of racial and ethnic reconciliation. To us, this question is far-fetched, perhaps even ludicrous. To the proponents of the line of thinking represented by Stoker, apartheid, racial segregation, and differentiation were the only avenues that would ultimately lead to any form of reconciliation. The term reconciliation hardly figures in the writings of Stoker except as a philosophical or religious term, usually in the triad of creation, fall, and redemption. When these notions are analyzed by Stoker he argues for the Christianizing of all of human life, but always with the recurring qualification: Although this claim is a "total" one, it acquires a typically differentiated national and ethnic (volk) form.[47] This view of the total claims of a Christian world and life view forms an integral part of his articulation of the diversity of callings of humankind to obey God in wider circles of obedience. In his "Hoe is ons roeping wêreldwyd?" ("What Is Our Worldwide Calling?") he clearly states that the "racial problem and racial policy" is part of the ecumenical task of humanity.[48] He says,

> Our whole racial problem and policy is ecumenical. With the differentiated development of each racial group we are confronted with the ecumenical question of the organized unity of the population of our Republic without the sacrifice of the diversity of races and peoples and all that goes with it. Must the child not already learn at school what his attitude towards other people, ethnic groups ("volke") or racial groups in our country ought to be?[49]

In Stoker's thought, the relationship between the calling to serve and obey God in all areas of human life, including the academy, is inextricably related to the central notions of a "people" and a "nation." This vignette of Stoker's views is a close-up of the philosophical undercurrent that surfaced so often in the historical development of Potchefstroom University for Christian Higher Education (PU for CHE).

The PU for CHE: Politically Neutral?

From its inception, Potchefstroom University's self-understanding as a Christian institution was inextricably tied to its national or "Christian-historical character." This surfaced time and again in the inaugural and other addresses of the rectors (that is, presidents) of the university. When analyzed, practically every historical appeal to the Christian principles or Christian-historical principles reveals the close relationship between the principles and the culture, history, traditions, and language of the Afrikaner people.[50] This comes to expression very clearly in the following quote from H. G. Stoker:

> The P.U.C. for C.H.E thus far the only Christian university in our country where Christian scholarship is done and where students are formed "in Thy light . . ." to become leaders of the people the only 100% Afrikaans university in our country stands for the same principles that our Calvinistic Afrikaans people stand for. And for this reason it is not pretentious to state that the P.U.C. for C.H.E may in the deepest sense of the word principially call itself:
>
> > Our Afrikaans peoples' university
> > May the Afrikaner people come to realize this.[51]

The qualification "historical" carries the same ambivalence already found in the concept as it was originally conceived in the tradition of Groen van Prinsterer; it refers both to the heritage of the Christian tradition in general and the specific national historical heritage. A couple of quotes make the case in point. The first rector of the university, Professor Ferdinand Postma, stated unambiguously:

> Education must be national. The principle out of which the PUC has lived is national consciousness, national loyalty and love of the nation. The youth must be educated in the steadfast faith in the God given calling of the Afrikaner people. This is the national principle of the P.U.C.[52]

A later rector, J. Chris Coetzee, said:

> But the university has a calling towards the people of the country as a whole and also another important calling. It must take care of the preservation and transmission of the national culture; it must therefore make provision for the teaching and guidance with respect to the most significant aspects of the national culture. Every university must have a national character and every Christian university should have a Christian-national character.[53]

Note also the views of Professor H. J. J. Bingle:

> The university supplies people "mense" to the nation "volk" and the church; it contributes and creatively builds the culture and the Reformed doctrine and life. These issues can only be served when the spiritual leaders lead the people in a correct world and life view. In this connection the responsibility of the PU for CHE is very important so that the beacons of the people "volk" are not displaced and it truly remains Christian-national.[54]

Perhaps the most succinct expression of this notion is the well-known adage formulated by Professor Tjaart van der Walt: The PU for CHE is a Christian university that is "onvoorwaardelik Christelik . . . onbeskaamd Afrikaans . . ." ("unconditionally Christian . . . unashamedly Afrikaans . . .").[55]

When changes were considered for the Private Act of the University in 1992, a new language clause that protects the Afrikaans language but allows for education in English was introduced. So there was a minor shift, yet the main emphasis is still the strong, historical Christian character of the university: "The new language clause affirms both the cultural character of the university and its attitude towards service irrespective of language. The time for cultural exclusivity has finally passed."[56] As was the case with the Reformed principles in the history of the Free University of Amsterdam, these Christian historical principles are seldom clearly defined, except in the explication of the close relationship of Christian convictions to the history, culture, and language of the Afrikaner people. Its practical application became apparent predominantly in the restrictions and conditions for student access to the university, the conditions set for teaching faculty and staff, and in the development of a curriculum that claimed to embody the basic tenets of a Calvinistic understanding of an encompassing Christian life and worldview. It was this very close relationship between the university and the cultural and historical identity of the Afrikaner people that made it practically impossible for the university to take a stand on the political injustices of the day. To justify the position of the university, Professor H. J. J. Bingle, rector at the time when the historic meeting of Institutions for Christian Higher Education took place at Potchefstroom in 1975, argued that a university is only called to criticize policies of the government to the extent that government impinges on the limited task of the university.[57]

The Christian-historical character of the university comes to expression in three foci: (1) the relationship to the cultural heritage of the Afrikaner people; (2) the very close relationship to the political aspirations of the Afrikaner; and (3) the strong emphasis on a world-embracing and world-formative understanding of the impact of the gospel. Yet, it would be untrue to state that the university was actually apolitical in the sense argued by some. Not only was there a very clear tacit political involvement with the political system of the day, but during one phase of its history the university and many of its faculty and staff were more than willing to become very radically involved in overt political protest. H. G. Stoker, J. A. L. Taljaard, J. H. Coetzee, and others found their way to internment camps during the period of the Second World War because of their very vocal opposition to involvement in the war and their sympathies with the Ossewa Brandwag.[58]

In the 1970s, a small group of faculty, staff, and students were involved in the 1976 Koinonia declaration, which criticized government policies and practice in a number of areas. This constant stream (trickle?) of criticism gradually acquired the label "The Voice of Potchefstroom" in the media. To some extent, the explicit witness in the area of racial tension and political injustice was held hostage by the close relationship to the supporting, cultural community and the fear that alienation from this community would inevitably lead to diminished enrollment and support. It is this issue of critical academic engagement and prophetic political witness in a multicultural society that constitutes the watershed in the relationship between the Free University and

Potchefstroom University in the early 1970s. Many factors played a role in this process of alienation. One of the decisive factors being the policy, which controlled student access and admission to the university, as part and parcel of government policy since 1948. It was only from 1972 that graduate students and from 1984 that undergraduate students of color were allowed entry to the university on a selective basis. In 1984, these students were allowed access to classes but were not to mingle socially or share residences. What was interesting about the university board resolution of 1984 was the fact that it echoed the type of language used by Stoker in 1957 in which the university could allow students of color to be educated but without any social mingling. It was only in 1990 that students of color were awarded full access both to classes and residences. The reasons for this reluctance was the fact that assimilation and integration was seen to be a threat to the national and cultural heritage of the university and a threat to its relationship with the supporting constituency who remained far removed from accepting such fundamental changes.

Potchefstroom University claimed that it saw its relationship to the political system as an apolitical one. But its administration of the entry requirements and its control of student access to the university represented policy decisions that implicitly harbored a very strong bias toward the uncritical implicit subscription to government policies.[59] It was this situation that in 1975 led to the inevitable clash of views on what a Christian university's task in society ought to be.

Alienation

The inclusion of Dr. C. F. Beyers Naudé, director of the Christian Institute of South Africa, in the delegation of the Free University of Amsterdam to the First International Conference of Institutions for Christian Higher Education held at Potchefstroom from September 9-13, 1975, brought the radically different interpretations of the nature of Christian education to a head. In the correspondence and dialogue about this matter, it became apparent that sharing basic principles from the Reformed tradition certainly did not imply that these two institutions shared a common vision concerning justice and reconciliation. The Free University believed that the task of a Christian university was prophetic Christian witness in situations of injustice and racial tension. Potchefstroom University believed that science and scholarship were primarily an in-house academic affair in which it was of primary importance to attempt to relate the Bible and Christian worldview to scholarship. Involvement in political issues outside of academia was regarded as a political affair, not to impinge on or intrude in university affairs. The fact that such a position concerning racial matters, injustice, and discrimination actually sanctioned the status quo was an argument not considered by the authorities of the university.[60] The reason for this was simple. The status quo was the preservation of their own cultural and historical identity and this identity was conflated with their Christian identity.

In turn, Potchefstroom University reproached the Free University for choosing the way of secularization because it had dropped the so-called grondslagartikel (basis of principles) and had chosen a sociocritical involvement in societal ills. They saw the act of including Beyers Naude in their delegation as a political act that had very little to do with the actual substance of Christian scholarship. It is interesting that in the important paper by Stoker read at this conference that this critical role of the university is not even given a passing note.[61] It was the vague nature and lack of articulation of the Christian historical principles and Calvinistic character of Potchefstroom that gave the Free University the most difficulties. Was it neo-Calvinism along the lines of Abraham Kuyper or naar een eigen Zuid-Afrikaansche Calvinistische traditie (according to a particular South African tradition). The Free University had left this baggage far behind. It had chosen ecumenical and critical political engagement of all research and teaching in the task of the advancement of justice in the modern world. "Our point of departure is no longer apologetical, many of us being open to listening to those who have different views. Our thinking is directed towards finding a new common identity, while accepting the plurality of a modern university as a positive factor."[62]

The conflict between the Free University and Potchefstroom University resulted in the unilateral breaking of this relationship by Potchefstroom University in 1974, which also led to the alienation of Potchefstroom from the international community of Institutions for Christian Higher Education until 1992.[63] The developments surrounding the publication of the Koinonia Document exacerbated this isolation of Potchefstroom in the international community. The critical issue was whether a university had the right to put pressure on its faculty, staff, and students to conform to its policies regarding political issues. An interesting element of historical irony surfaced in this whole episode. The leadership of Potchefstroom University seemed to find it acceptable that their forebearers had broken rank with the ecclesiastical and political establishment of 1869 and 1940, but totally unacceptable that people from their own fold would be willing to distance themselves from the political system of apartheid in which the university was entrenched.

A Question of Principle?

The puzzling question of why the traditional ideal of Christian scholarship changed considerably over time in the case of both institutions remains unanswered. They shared the same roots. Their views, policies, and practice, as well as their views on the nature of Christian scholarship reflect the local historical color and character of each. Yet, somewhere along the line of historical development the content of their understanding of the nature of science and theorizing diverged. One can only hypothesize why this was the case. Perhaps the challenge of developing the notion of Reformed principles as a bridge between Scripture and academia is actually not feasible in the way it was originally envisaged by the founders of the Free University. Some suggest that the Free University never was able to overcome its positivist legacy and instrumental view of science.[64] Is this the reason why it ultimately chose religious commitment via social engagement and service to the policies of the World Council of Churches? Was the elusive and evasive character of the so-called gereformeerde beginselen (Reformed principles) the source of the derailment?

Did Potchefstroom University ever fully overcome the intrinsic dualism of the Christian national ideals of its founders? *Christian* was theoretically and dogmatically interpreted in the Calvinistic sense of the word, but the domain of the national life always seemed to have remained an autonomous (neutral?) area claimed only by the people, nation, or state.

The ultimate question is: To what extent are both institutions as centers for higher learning called and able to actually contribute to reconciliation? Our argument has come full circle; it depends on one's definition of reconciliation. It depends on one's view of the nature of the academy. When the academy is called to demonstrate its Christian commitment through justice in shalom, this has to become apparent through its service to the poor and suffering and the conflict and guilt-laden. However, this has to be accomplished through the typical structural task of the university, the academic endeavor. Only a university able to produce and explore theories "pregnant with shalom" can actually contribute to reconciliation.

Notes

1. Calvin Seerveld, "A Cloud of Witnesses and a New Generation," *Vanguard-Supplement* (November-December 1978).

2. Harry Brinkman, *Identiteit van de Vrije Universiteit. Beschouwingen bij de opening van de cursus 1992-1993 aan de Vrije Universiteit* (Amsterdam: Vrije Universiteit, 1992), 7. See also M. Elaine Botha, "Christelike universiteit en politiek in 'n apartheid- en post apartheid bedeling," *Koers* 60, no. 1 (March 1995): 121-148.

3. M. Elaine Botha, "School in Society," in *The Responsibility of Christian Institutions of Higher Education to Justice in the International Economic Order* (Grand Rapids: CRC Publications, 1978), 43-66.

4. Roy A. Clouser, *The Myth of Religious Neutrality: An Essay on the Hidden Role of Religious Belief in Theories* (Notre Dame: University of Notre Dame Press, 1991).

5. It is not clear whether this line of argument is shared by H. J. Brinkman, *Identiteit van de Vrije Universiteit*, who claims in his rendering of one of the many "small narratives" about the university that universities do not (cannot?) have goals (doelstellings) in the same fashion that an individual has goals. Probably his claim is the negation of the "religious commitment" of societal structures such as universities. Whether this also entails the rejection of the idea of a (God-given) structure is not clear from this article.

6. I. Wallerstein, *University in Turmoil: The Politics of Change* (New York: Atheneum, 1969), 11.

7. Philip M. Hauser, "Political Actionism in the University," *Daedalus* 104 (Winter 1975): 270.

8. Hauser, "Political Actionism in the University," 265-272.

9. Wallerstein, *University in Turmoil: The Politics of Change*, 145.

10. J. Roelink, *Een blinkend spoor, 1879-1979: Beeld van een eeuw geschiedenis der vereniging voor wetenschappelijk onderwijs op gereformeerde grondslag* (Kampen: Kok, 1979), 25-43.

11. J. P. Verhoogt, S. Griffioen, and R. Fernhout, eds., *Vinden en Zoeken: Het bijzondere van de Vrije Universiteit* (Kampen: Kok, 1997).

12. Verhoogt, Griffioen, and Fernhout, *Vinden en Zoeken*, 4.

13. See also A. J. Van Dijk, "Wetenschap en Beginsel," *Beweging 79* 43, no. 2 (April 1979): 31.

14. W. J. Wieringa, "De Vrije Universiteit als bijzondere instelling," in *Wetenschap en rekenschap, 1880-1980: Een eeuw wetenschapsbeoefening en wetenschapsbeschouwing aan de Vrije Universiteit* (Kampen: Kok, 1980), 11-43. See also A. Van Deursen, "De Vrije Universiteit in eigen spiegel," in *Vinden en zoeken*.

15. Abraham Kuyper, *Band aan het woord: Antwoord op de vraag "Hoe is eene Universiteit aan het woord van God te binden?"* (Amsterdam: Hoveker en Wormser, 1899). See also R. Fernhout, "Hoe is een universiteit aan het Woord van God te binden? Kuypers antwoord en de huidige situatie aan de Vrije Universiteit," in *Vinden en zoeken*, 9.

16. Abraham Kuyper, *Scholastica II: Om het zoeken of om het vinden? Of Het doel van echte studie* (Amsterdam: Hoveker and Wormser, 1900).

17. Fernhout, "Hoe is een christelijk universiteit aan het Woord van God te binden?" 13.

18. Wieringa, "De Vrije Universiteit als bijzondere instelling," 11-43.

19. Van Deursen, "De Vrije Universiteit in eigen spiegel," 28-29. See also J. Roelink, *Vijfenzeventig jaar Vrije Universiteit, 1880-1955. Gedenboek bij het vijf en zeventig-jarig bestaan der Vrije Universiteit te Amsterdam* (Kampen: Kok, 1956); Roelink, *Een blinkend spoor, 1879-1979*, 19-21.

20. Roelink, *Vijfenzeventig jaar Vrije Universiteit, 1880-1955*; Roelink, *Een blinkend spoor*, 1879-1979, 19-21.

21. Reference in: Roelink, *Een blinkend spoor, 1879-1979*, 17: "het Gereformeerde, het Calvinistische, of het bij uitnemendheid nationale."

22. Roelink, *Vijfenzeentig jaar Vrije Universiteit, 1880-1955*, 111.

23. This so-called expressionist understanding of the development of Christian scholarship (i.e., the idea that science develops from certain "basic principles") proved historically inaccurate. Brinkman, *Identiteit van de Vrije Universiteit*, 10; Nicholas Wolterstorff, "The Project of a Christian University in a Postmodern Culture," Inaugural address, Free University of Amsterdam, 1988.

24. Van Deursen, "De Vrije Universiteit in eigen spiegel," 34-35.

25. Van Deursen, "De Vrije Universiteit in eigen spiegel," 34-36.

26. "Maar nu het beginsel. Dat woord heeft als een boze fee aan de wieg der Vereniging en de van haar uitgaande VU gestaan en beide een eeuw begeleid. Kwellend begeleid, tot vandaag toe." Roelink, *Een blinkend spoor, 1879-1979*, 10.

27. Sander Griffioen, "Cultuuromslag aan de V.U.," in *Vinden en zoeken*, 72.

28. Sander Griffioen, "Cultuuromslag aan de V.U.," 72.

29. Van Deursen, "De Vrije Universiteit in eigen spiegel," 38.

30. Wieringa, "De Vrije Universiteit als bijzondere instelling," 43. See also Brinkman, *Identiteit van de Vrije Universiteit*, 3.

31. Van Dijk, "Wetenschap en Beginsel," 28-36.

32. Van Deursen, "De Vrije Universiteit in eigen spiegel," 41.

33. Brinkman, *Identiteit van de Vrije Universiteit*, 7.

34. Martine Zuidweg, "Faculteiten worstelen met doelstelling," *Ad Valvas*, 21 March 1996, 5.

35. R. Boschhuizen and B. Goudzwaard, *Van Waarden Weten: De plaats van waarden in het VU-onderwijs* (Amsterdam: Vrije Universiteit, 1995), 6.

36. Boschhuizen and Goudzwaard, *Van Waarden Weten*, 36-38. See also Zuidweg, "Faculteiten worstelen met doelstelling," 5.

37. "Faculteiten worstelen met doelstelling," *Ad Valvas*, 21 March 1996, 6.

38. Clause 25 of law no. 12 of 1916. See C. J. Reinecke, "Rektorale inhuldigingsrede: Die PU vir CHO: Verankerd in sy beginsels en gerig op die toekoms," *Koers* 54, no. 4 (1989): 121-148.

39. H. G. Stoker, "At the Crossroads: Apartheid and University Freedom in South Africa," 1967, originally published as *Oorsprong en Rigting*, vol. 1 (Cape Town: Tafelberg Publishers, 1967), 210-11.

40. Stoker, "At the Crossroads," 213.

41. Stoker, "At the Crossroads," 213.

42. Stoker, "At the Crossroads," 214.

43. Stoker, "At the Crossroads," 216.

44. Stoker, "At the Crossroads," 218.

45. Stoker, "At the Crossroads," 221.

46. H. G. Stoker, *Beginsels en Metodes in die wetenskap* (Potchefstroom: Pro Rege Pers, 1961), 172.

47. Stoker, *Oorsprong en Rigting*, 42-82.

48. H. G. Stoker, *Hoe is ons roeping wereldwyd?* (Potchefstroom: Pro Rege Pers, 1963).

49. "Ons hele rasseprobleem en rassebeleid is ekumenies van aard. Met die gedifferensieerde ontwikkeling van elke rassegroep kom ons voor die ekumeniese vraag te staan van 'n georganiseerde eenheid van die bevolking van ons Republiek sonder prysgawe van die verskeidenheid van rasse en volke en alles wat daarmee saamhang. Moet die kind nie reeds op skool leer wat—ekumenies gesien—sy holding tot ander mense, volke en rasse in ons land behoort te wees nie?" Stoker, *Hoe is ons roeping wereldwyd*, 20.

50. One could oppose such an analysis on the grounds of methodological objections. Obviously a careful analysis of official policy statements of the university would be better grounds for such conclusions, but for the purposes of this chapter an analysis of the trends in these addresses will have to suffice.

51. "Die P.U.K. ver C.H.O.—tot dusver die enigste Christelike universiteit in ons land, waar die Christelike wetenskap beoefen word en die studente in U lig gevorm word tot volksleiers (en daarby die enigste 100% Afr. Univ. van ons land)—staan air dieslfde beginsels waarvoor ons Calvinisties-Afrikaanse volk staan, waarvoor die Voortrekker gestaan het, en daarom is dit seker nie aanmatigend om te se dat die P.U.K. air C.H.O. sig prinsipieel in die diepste sin van die woord mag noem: Ons Afrikaanse volksuniversiteit Mag die Afrikaanse volk dit leer besef!" (Stoker archives, undated document: "Waarom 'n Christlike universiteit?") "P.U.C." is the abbreviation used for Potchefstroom University College. This designation changed when the university received its charter as an independent university, no longer associated with the University of South Africa.

52. "Die onderwys moet nasionaal wees. Die beginsel waaruit die PUK geleef het, is die van nasiebewustheid, nasiegetrouheid en nasieliefde. Die jeug moet opgevoed word in die onwrikbare geloof in die Godgegewe taak en roeping van die Afrikaanse volk. Dis die nasionale beginsel van die P.U.K." (Puk asiekomitee pamphlet, 21 May 1984).

53. "Maar die universiteit het teenoor die volk en die land as 'n geheel ook nog 'n ander belangrike roeping. Dit moet ook sorg dra vir die behoud en oordrag van die nasionale kultuur; dit moet dus voorsiening maak vir die onderrig en leiding ten opsigte van die belangrikste aspekte van die nasionale kultuur. Elke univeristeit moet 'n nasionale karakter dra en elke Christelike universiteit 'n Christelik-nasionale karakter." Chris J. Coetzee, "Die Christelike Universiteit. Intreerede as Rektor van die Potchefstroomse Universiteit vir Christelike Hoer Onderwys gehou op 19 Februarie 1954," *Koers* (April 1954): 1-34.

54. "Hy (die universiteit red.) lewer mense aan volk en kerk; hy bou dus aan die naionale kultur skeppend en aan die Gereformeerde leer en lewe. En hierdie sake kan alleen gedien word as die geestelike leiers die volk reg voorgaan in beskouing oor wereld en lewe. Groot is die verantwoordelikheid van die P.U. vir C.H.O. in hierdie verband sodat die bakens van die volk nie versit sal word nie en dat hy inderdaad Christelik-Nasionaal sal bly." H. J. J. Bingle, "Enkele aspekte van vryheid en verantwoordelikheid van die universiteit," *Koers* (January-February 1964): 481-89.

55. Tjaart van der Walt, "Koers hou in die stroomversnelling." Rectoral address, Potchefstroom University for Christian Higher Education, 10 February 1978. Wetenskaplike Bydraes van die PU vir CHO, Reeks H: Inougurele Redes, nr. 41. Potchefstroomse Universiteit, 10-11.

56. "Die nuwe taalklousule bevestig daarenteen egter sowel die kulturele karakter van die universiteit as sy ingesteldheid tot diens-lewering ongeag taal." "Die tyd vir kulturele eksklusiwiteit is finaal verby." C. J. Reinecke, "National Development and Higher Education: The South African Experience," in *Conference Proceedings on Education and Human Resource Development in the Pacific Basin, 20-24 April 1992* (Taichung, Taiwan: Tunghai University, 1992), 18-19.

57. Vrije Universiteit, 1976. Verslag van een samenspreking tussen delegaties van de Vrije Universiteit en de Potchefstroomse Universiteit vir Christelike Hoer Onderwys, Amsterdam.

58. In all fairness it needs to be recognized that Hennie Coetzee continued this line of critical opposition to unjust government policies in a later political phase through his editorial work on the journal *Woord en Daad*.

59. Marthina E. Botha, "Moet 'n universiteit 'n bepaalde kultuur dra?" *Woord en daad* 25, no. 276 (August 1985): 19-20.

60. Botha, "School in Society," 49, 53.

61. H. G. Stoker, "Our Christian Calling of Doing Science," in *Institute for the Advancement of Calvinism. Christian Higher Education. The Contemporary Challenge. Proceedings of the First International Conference of Reformed Institutions for Christian Scholarship*, Potchefstroom, September 9-13, 1975.

62. Free University, *Memorandum on the Relationship between the Free University and the Potchefstroom University for Christian Higher Education: An Exchange of Views on Apartheid* (Amsterdam: Free University, 1975).

63. PU for CHE: Minutes of the Board, 20 November 1974, art. 4.12.3.

64. Van Dijk, "Wetenschap en Beginsel," 33. That positivism actually influenced many faculty at the Free University is also acknowledged by other authors. C. C. Jonker, "Natuurkunde en Scheikunde," in *Wetenschap en Rekenschap, 1880-1980*, 252. It would be unfair and also unjustified to generalize that positivism characterized the legacy and approach of all faculties of the Free University. The opposite is argued by C. Sanders and L. K. A. Eisenga, "De psychologie aan de Vrije Universiteit," in *Wetenschap en Rekenschap, 1880-1980*, 484-527.

Chapter Eight

South Africa's Bill of Rights: Reconciliation and a Just Society

Lourens M. du Plessis

A COUNTRY'S CONSTITUTION both helps tell and make its history. As Martin Heidegger said, "History as happening is an acting and being acted upon which pass through the present, which are determined from out of the future and which take over the past. It is precisely the *present* that vanishes in happening."[1] Concentrating on (but not restricting myself to) the Bill of Rights in South Africa's constitution, I want to show that this constitution, as a hallmark of reconciliation, seeks to take over an unjust past (by overtaking its grim consequences) and that it anticipates the advent of an optimally just society. In doing so, the constitution simultaneously narrates and authors the story of a just South Africa.[2] Read South Africa's constitution and it is clear, even without reading between the lines, that its framers meant to predicate it on certain values. This chapter deals with how the constitution seeks to lend "operational" credibility to the values whose meaningfulness it proclaims and whose achievement it promises.

On reading the preamble to the constitution, those with pastoral inclinations will rejoice. It preaches reconciliation! The preamble reminisces the rather extraordinary postamble to the transitional constitution agreed on in the last gasps of the Kempton Park negotiations. The postamble laid the foundation for what later became the truth and reconciliation process.[3] The 1996 preamble recognizes "the injustices of our past," honors "those who suffered for justice and freedom in our land," and respects "those who have worked to build and develop our country." Believing "that South Africa belongs to all who live in it, united in our diversity" the constitution, "as the supreme law of the Republic," is said to be adopted to:

Heal the divisions of our past and establish a society based on democratic values. social justice and fundamental human rights;

Lay the foundations for a democratic and open society in which government is based on the will of the people and every citizen is equally protected by law;

Improve the quality of life of all citizens and free the potential of each person; and

Build a united and democratic South Africa able to take its rightful place as a sovereign state in the family of nations.

The constitution apparently endeavors to restore the collective *dignity* of the South African state and its people. Emphasis on human dignity elsewhere in the constitution (and in the Bill of Rights in particular) confirms this impression. Section 1(a) of the constitution lists "[h]uman dignity, the achievement of equality and advancement of human rights and freedoms" as values on which "the Republic of South Africa" as "one sovereign democratic state" is founded. According to section 7(1), the Bill of Rights affirms the democratic values of human dignity, equality, and freedom. These provisions all afford human dignity a centrality in the transitional constitution.

The dialectic of freedom and equality in sections 35(1), the interpretation clause, and 33(1)(a)(ii), the limitation clause, of the 1993 constitution were central in understanding its Bill of Rights and helped constrain an interpretative overemphasis of either of these elements.[4] References to freedom and equality, apart from occurring in the foundational value statements in sections 1(a) and 7(1), have remained in the comparable interpretation and limitation provisions of the final 1996 constitution in sections 39(1)(a) and 36(1) respectively. However, in all four instances human dignity has been added as a guiding value in addition to and preceding equality and freedom. "Dignity enriched" concepts of freedom and equality thus constitute the perennial freedom—equality dialectic in the 1996 constitution—and this may well enhance the helpfulness of this dialectic as an interpretive aid.

Christians will probably welcome the final Constitution's decided emphasis on human dignity. Freedom and equality are Christian values, too, but, politically speaking, they are but means to ends rather than ends in themselves. Neither pure *libertarianism* nor undiluted *egalitarianism* seem to be *the Christian* option: freedom and equality must both pursue a higher purpose, such as the realization of human dignity, to fully recognize humans' creation in the image of God. This is particularly true in a society that endeavors to overcome an era where an oppressive regime held the humanness of most of its citizens in contempt.

The Bill of Rights and the Advent of an Optimally Just Society

A constitution is only an eloquently formulated catalogue of values. It also promises to imbue society with the values it enshrines. With trepidation a society imbued with such values is referred to as "an optimally just society," appreciating full well that the *just society* is ultimately unachievable. The actualization of the rights entrenched in our Bill of Rights augurs the advent of an optimally just society.

Section 1(c) of South Africa's constitution states that the Republic of South Africa is a "sovereign democratic state" founded on, among others, the "[s]upremacy of the constitution and the rule of law." Section 2 gives legal effect to this expectation: "[t]his constitution is the supreme law of the Republic; law or conduct inconsistent with it is invalid, and the duties imposed by it must be performed." This *tangible recognition of the constitution as effectual, supreme law*, is the *fons et origo* of active checks and balances on state power. It effectuates the prime object of the constitution and the Bill of Rights, namely to stem the power of government, thus tying in with the Christian quest for *government constrained by higher norms and values* rooted in the conviction that no mortal ruler should have absolute power.[5] But South Africa's Bill of Rights does not simply fend off profusions of state authority vis-à-vis "subordinates." Section 7(2) also imposes a positive duty on the state to "respect, *protect, promote* and *fulfill* the rights" (italics mine*)* enshrined in the Bill of Rights. The Bill of Rights is, in other words, not just laissez-faire or abstentionist in nature.

Purist libertarians might object that requiring the state to promote rights opens the door to public interference in the private sphere too widely. Thus perceived, the state's duty to fulfill rights is a nightmare! However, the Bill of Rights clearly sets itself the objective of alleviating the plight of society's marginalized and disadvantaged people. It deliberately chooses an egalitarian strategy of modest state intervention to this end. This explains the explicit (albeit cautious) inclusion of socioeconomic (or second generation) rights in the Bill of Rights, namely the rights "to have access to" adequate housing (section 26) as well as to health care, food, water, and social security (section 27). The latter entitlements, however, have not been included at the expense of duly entrenched classical, first generation freedom rights.

A legal system is rooted in foundational norms that express the sense of fair play of the community it serves. They shepherd the application of more specific, issue-directed "black letter" legal rules. Examples of such norms are:

- *nullum crimen sine lege*—without a law prescribing the punishment, no charge is possible; and *nulla crimen sine culpa*—without blame, no crime is possible in criminal law, and
- *audi et alteram partem*—hear the other side; and *nemo iudex in re sua*—no one is fit to be the judge in his/her own cause (in other words, the rules of natural justice) in the adjudication of justiciable disputes.

South Africa's Bill of Rights caters to these foundational norms in various ways, especially in section 35 that meticulously itemizes various constitutional requirements for due process in criminal trials. However, in the quest of refraining from too detailed a discussion of legally technical issues, I merely mention this. The discussion of the standards for a just society under the next heading is of more general interest.

I previously acceded to the ultimate unattainableness of *the just society*. However, we all entertain certain expectations of an *optimally* just society. These expectations, oversimplified as they may be, are starting points for discussion. I proffer eight of them (there can, of course, be more) as axioms, and then show how South Africa's Bill of Rights promises to actualize them.

First, members of society feel themselves physically and mentally secure, satisfied that the legal order lends effective safeguards against threats to and actual violations of (1) life and limb; (2) physical, mental, and spiritual integrity; and (3) material possessions.

This standard of justice is a fundamental prerequisite for a just society. Rights cannot be safeguarded if these rudiments of human existence are left unattended. In the new South Africa, where crime is rife and the ability of law enforcement agencies to contain it is suspect, we realize this all too well. The previously mentioned section 7(2) of the constitution that enjoins the state to *respect* and *protect* the rights in the Bill of Rights musters constitutional forces to shield these basic rights. It is, in other words, the state's *constitutional responsibility* to ward off all threats to our survival as humans. This entails a duty to remove from society, to punish, and to attempt to rehabilitate wrongdoers who violate this basic security of the people.[6]

The entrenchment of the rights to human dignity (section 10); life (section 11), freedom, and security of the person (section 12); as well as the prohibition of slavery, servitude, and forced labor (section 13) is thus a source of proactive, basic guarantees in this enriched signification. However, not only guarantees of physical security are rudimental. The entrenchment of, for example, the rights to privacy (section 14); freedom of conscience, religion, thought, belief, and opinion (section 15[1]); citizenship (section 20); a healthy environment (section 24[a]), and the protection of property (section 25) fall in this category too.

Second, the distinctiveness and autonomy of all facets of human life are recognized, respected, and protected.

The law is not to prescribe what art is good, what religion is correct, or which business principles are best, but it must procure a framework within which art, religion, and business can be practiced *in security*. Or, put another way, "[L]aw defines the basic structure within which the pursuit of all other activities takes place."[7] This standard of justice is embodied in the Bill of Rights, as a principle of *sphere autonomy*, by entrenching the rights to:

- control of one's own person (section 12[2]);
- personal privacy (section 14);
- individual freedom of conscience, religion, thought, belief, and opinion (section 15[1]);
- individual freedom of expression (section 16[1]);

- freedom of movement and residence (section 21);
- freedom of trade, occupation, and profession (section 22); and
- the use of a language and participation in a cultural life of one's own choice (section 30).

The protection of private property (section 25) constitutes a further recognition of sphere autonomy. So, too, do the philological fetters on the horizontal operation of the Bill of Rights in section 8(2), where any particular provision of chapter 2 is said to bind natural and juristic persons *only* "*if, and to the extent that it is applicable*" (italics mine).[8] Given this restraint, section 9(4), which proscribes unfair "private" or "horizontal" discrimination and authorizes legislation to prevent or prohibit such discrimination, could, from a purist libertarian perspective, be controversial. However, this particular provision shows that sphere autonomy and the rights associated with it are, like all other entitlements entrenched in the Bill of Rights, not unbounded.

Third, the state recognizes the autonomy of the institutions of, as well as groups within, civil society and vouches for their freedom and authority to, within reasonable limits, manage their own affairs.

The state's exercise of power in civil society must thus be legally restrained. The state can, however, help demarcate the operating space of such institutions (and balance the interests of different groups) vis-à-vis one another, provide legal means for settling intra- and interinstitutional, as well as group disputes, and invoke legal mechanisms to these ends. In principle, however, the state's interest in the business of the institutions and groups within civil society is *finite*.

This standard of justice has been incorporated in the Bill of Rights as, primarily, a principle of *institutional autonomy*,[9] guaranteeing the rights to:

- privacy of one's home and communications (section 14[a] and 14[d]);
- institutional freedom of religion, in other words, the freedom of religious organizations and groups (section 15[1]);
- institutional freedom of expression such as freedom of the press and other media (section 16[1][a]) as well as academic freedom and the freedom of scientific research associated with institutions of higher learning (section 16[1][d]);
- freedom of association (section 18);
- form, participate in the activities of, recruit members, and campaign for a political party (section 18); and
- freedom of trade, occupation, and profession as entitlements of bodies corporate or of associations to engage in and/or regulate the affairs of a particular trade, occupation, and profession (section 22).

The recognition in sections 23(2)-(6) of trade unions and employers' organizations as principal role players who chisel labor relations connotes further compliance with the principle of institutional autonomy. The philological fetters on the horizontal operation of the Bill of Rights in section 8(2) also pertain to this principle, while the section 9(4) prohibition of private discrimination is as disputable (and yet explicable) in respect of institutional autonomy as it is with regard to sphere autonomy.

Secondarily, the South African constitution caters generously to the "group rights" to "form, join and maintain cultural religious and linguistic associations and other organs of civil society" (section 31[1][b]) but does so in somewhat restrained terms. "Persons belonging to a cultural, religious or linguistic community *may not be denied the right*, with other members of that community" (italics mine) to do what section 31(1)(b) sanctions. Section 31 probably aims to protect the rights of linguistic, cultural, and religious *minorities*. Section 235 of the constitution strengthens this perception, stating that the right of the South African people as a whole to self-determination does not preclude recognition of the notion of the right of self-determination of any community sharing a common cultural and language heritage. Sections 31 and 235 were included in the constitution at the behest of the Freedom Front, a right-wing, predominantly white and Afrikaans-speaking political party that made separatist demands for an independent state for Afrikaner people (a volkstaat). This party has in the meantime dispensed with its claims to full independence, but it still maintains that the right to cultural and linguistic self-determination can find territorial expression—a likelihood that section 235 indeed envisages.

The constitution makers furthermore regarded (minority) group protection as important enough to warrant the establishment of a Commission for the Promotion and Protection of the Rights of Cultural, Religious, and Linguistic Communities (section 185). The commission must promote respect, peace, friendship, humanity, tolerance, and national unity among communities on the basis of nondiscrimination and free association (sections 185[1] [a] and [b]).

Fourth, there is equal treatment for all and all are equal before the law. The law precludes discrimination.

Equality does not simply mean *exactly the same* treatment for all in all circumstances. *Differential treatment* in certain circumstances and for certain purposes is allowable. Some criteria for differentiation, such as race, ethnic origin, sex, gender, class, religion, and descent are, however, so profoundly suspect that differential treatment based on any of them for almost any purpose, is held to be *discriminatory per se*. This is what section 9(3) of the constitution in effect says, and it mentions seventeen such suspect criteria of differentiation by name.

Equality is not a simple concept, and contemporary reflections highlight a need to distinguish between *formal* and *substantive* equality. I propose reliance on a model of equality that proceeds beyond this distinction but endorses its purpose.[10] Formal equality is said to express the fact "that all persons are equal bearers of rights within a just social order" while substantive equality requires an examination of "the actual social and economic conditions of groups and individuals" in addition.[11]

Schematically the proposed model looks as follows:

ABSTRACT RATIONALITY+ CONCRETE EXISTENTIALITY

(1) NUMERICAL EQUALITY: Similarity of things

(2) GEOMETRICAL EQUALITY: Individual talentedness recognized and individual effort and performance encouraged

(3) SUBSTANTIVE EQUALITY: Sameness of people as human beings that outweighs their differences as individuals

(4) CORRECTIVE EQUALITY: Restrains the strong and protects the weak

Harmonizing and restoring the relationship between (1) – (4):
EMPOWERING EQUALITY

CONCRETE EXISTENTIALITY+ ABSTRACT RATIONALITY

Numerical or *arithmetical equality* denotes a similarity of "nonhuman" objects and seeks to procure an equilibrium of performance and counter-performance when objects of value are exchanged. Numerical equality furthermore seeks to balance injury and indemnification when damage is recompensed. This form of equality hinges on impersonal similarity and it is consequently an example of *formal equality*. It is not mentioned anywhere in the South African constitution by the name, but it is implicit in the notion of equality before the law (section 9[1]) predicated on *a rationally defensible equilibrium*. Equality before the law, however, also entails more than this version of equivalence, as will be shown in substantive equality below.

Geometrical equality assumes that people are different and hence recognizes individual talent and encourages individual effort, thus rewarding individuals accordingly. It establishes a relationship between A and B, the substance of which is said to be *merit*, judged chiefly by A's and B's real or expected *output* at any given point in time. It is mostly this notion of equality that prompts the assertion that personal merit ought to be decisive to determine individual entitlement. Such merit cannot, however, be considered in isolation from disparities beyond the individual's control that have been impeding the unfolding of her or his talents, thus causing her or his efforts and performance to compare unfavorably to those of others who are free from such impediments. Geometrical equality is, in other words, too *formal* a manifestation of equality to determine by itself what someone is entitled to. It does not sufficiently account for disparate input beyond individuals' control. It is a sound standard nevertheless where such disparities are absent or have been eliminated.

The equality clause in the constitution (section 9) does not mention geometrical equality by name, though the prohibition of *unfair discrimination* (sections 9[3] and 9[5]) implies it. Such discrimination involves differential treatment that disregards personal merit and that is premised on a suspect criterion instead. Differential treatment postulated on personal attributes and aptitude is occasionally recognized in the constitution. For instance:

- the right to vote in elections in section 19(3)(a) is subject to an age restriction of eighteen years (section 46[1][c]);
- public servants, unrehabilitated insolvents, someone of unsound mind, and certain categories of criminal offenders (section 47 [1][a], [c], [d], and [e]) do not have the section 19(3)(b) right to stand for and be a member of the National Assembly; and
- a judicial officer must be an "appropriately qualified woman or man who is a fit and proper person" (section 174[1]).

Substantive equality demands that people be treated *exactly the same*, irrespective of individual differences, in situations where their essential similarity as human beings outweighs their variant merits as individuals. Equality as such constitutes the substance of such a relationship between A and B. The distinctive, individual qualities of A and B are not denied, but substantive equality celebrates human dignity by focusing on the human attributes that they invariably share.

Equality before the law (section 9[1]) is an example of substantive equality. Diké, the goddess of justice, who metes out appropriate treatment in contentious proceedings, is blindfolded. What A and B get does not depend on who each one is or what social status they enjoy. They have to be treated the same in similar circumstances.

Political equality, as an equal entitlement to political rights and the guarantee of equal participation in political processes (section 19 read with section 9), is in essence substantive equality also. It is, however, other than equality before the law, limitable with reference to personal attributes, as was shown in geometrical equality above.

Though the demand for substantive equality is unconditional, its realization can be thwarted due to other manifestations of (severe) inequality. Litigants, such as one who can and one who cannot afford a legal representative, are not equals before a court of law and only intervention by some authority can level the playing field.

Corrective or *curative equality* redresses the deficiencies of other forms of equality that in spite of noble intentions, sometimes fail to prevent a distortion of apportionments and entitlements through normal legal channels. Some differentiations that seem quite in order in terms of the logic of a particular form of equality (such as geometrical equality) may actually disadvantage some, thereby thwarting the realization of their full potential. Previously, it was, for instance, argued that *merit* for purposes of *geometrical equality* has to be determined (also) in the light of disparities beyond an individual's control that impede the unfolding of her or his talents. It was remarked that such disparities can even hamper equality before the law. Corrective equality fosters an awareness of the effect of these disparities, calls for intervention to redress them, and thereby seeks to overcome and undo the effects of historically entrenched distortions in the system.

Corrective or curative equality is more commonly known as *affirmative action*. The Afrikaans term *regstellende aksie*, however, says more accurately what corrective equality actually does. As will be argued shortly, "affirmative action" could also be used in a broader sense.

Section 9(2) of South Africa's constitution authorizes *measures* (presumably both legislative and administrative) "designed to protect or advance persons, or categories of persons, disadvantaged by unfair discrimination." This authorization is premised on the assumption that "[e]quality includes the full and equal enjoyment of rights and freedoms." This means that corrective equality is quite a normal form of equality and not an exception to the rule of, for instance, geometrical equality. Section 25(6)-(9) provides for the restoration of property rights to those previously dispossessed of their property by virtue of racially discriminatory measures. This is another example of corrective equality, as is the injunction in section 174(2) that when judicial officers are appointed, "[t]he need for the judiciary to reflect broadly the racial and gender composition of South Africa" must be considered.

In the different types of equality just discussed, *concrete existentiality* and *abstract rationality* are inversely proportionate. The principally rational manifestations of equality, such as numerical and geometrical, will remain, but rational abstractions are ill-fitted to cater to the exigencies of the concrete human existence, if not counterbalanced by preponderantly existential forms of equality, such as substantive and corrective. Contrarily, more concrete and existential manifestations of equality, altogether unrestrained by rationales for more abstract manifestations of equality (such as merit or the equilibrium of performance and counterperformance), are arbitrary hits-or-misses. The art of equal treatment lies in the harmonious integration of the various manifestations of equality. *Empowering equality* seeks proactively to effect, to restore (where necessary), and to maintain this integration.

The various manifestations of equality just discussed are contingent upon and supplement one another. As argued above, the implementation of geometrical equality based on merit can, for instance, remain but a hollow gesture in the absence of corrective equality. By the same token, however, corrective equality that completely loses sight of merit and thus isolates itself from geometrical equality, could be humiliating if invoked out of mere pity, thereby lacking any rational justification.

Empowering equality is action, *affirmative* action. It affirms the fullness and integrity of equality. This is why it empowers. The constitution does not explicitly outline a procedure that may be called empowering equality. It cannot. Empowering equality is accomplished through the judicious and thus congruous realization of the various manifestations of equality for which the constitution explicitly provides. The best that a constitution can do is to make sufficient provision for all the various manifestations of equality—which the South African Constitution does. Section 9(2) makes it clear that corrective equality is congruous with other manifestations of equality. This is a good example of an affirmation of the fullness and integrity of the notion of equality that stands the accomplishment of empowering equality in good stead.

Of even greater significance in this regard is the constitution's repeated affirmation, in sections 1, 7, 36(1), the limitation clause, and 39(1)(a), the interpretation clause, of the integration and harmonization of human dignity, *equality*, and freedom for the interpretation and application of the constitution in life's concrete situations. The accomplishment of empowering equality is equity driven; it seeks a congruous actualization of the various manifestations of equality in the light of the demands of each particular situation. The notions of human dignity and freedom are well suited to guide this process. They shepherd equality toward concrete, human existentiality lest it absconds into the labyrinths of abstract rationality.

Fifth, the legal system operates with reasonable certainty, and those to whom it applies are reasonably able to determine what it provides.

Section 2 of the constitution is a profoundly consequential rendition of legal certainty unbeknown to South Africans before April 27, 1994. As discussed above, it proclaims the constitution's status as supreme law and provides for the nullity of law or conduct inconsistent with it.

The injunction in section 33(1) that administrative action be *lawful* requires adherence to legal precepts and prescribed procedures in the day-to-day performance of executive functions. This makes for predictable state action, which, in turn, advances legal certainty.

Access to adjudication, entrenched as a right in section 34, also procures legal certainty because it facilitates the resolution of justiciable disputes. Access to legal advice and representation in matters requiring proficient assistance seeks to achieve a similar outcome (prior to or without adjudication). This latter entitlement is guaranteed, in so many words, for detained and accused persons.

Sixth, those in authority play by the cardinal rules of the game, thus engendering widespread esteem for law and order.

This is what *legality* as a standard of justice entails. Legality and *legitimacy* are distinct. The latter refers to the de facto popular acceptance of and support for a rule or an institution. Legality, on the other hand, calls for deference to rules and institutions *because* they are believed to make sense. Legitimacy is thus likely to beget legality, while the nonobservance of legality will probably impair popular respect for a rule or an institution and thereby subvert its legitimacy.

Legality is most noticeably expressed by the notion of *due process of law* that inspirits the rights of arrested, detained, and accused persons (in section 35) and rules out the arbitrary expropriation of (private) property (in section 25).

Seventh, there is provision for the impartial settlement of disputes.

Adjudicators are independent referees who have to apply the rules of the game in a nonpartisan way. This standard of justice is closely linked to the foundational norms of due process. Adjudicators are not only the traditional courts of law, but also all state and state-recognized agencies and administrative bodies that settle disputes. Section 34 thus provides not only for a right of access to *courts* (in the traditional sense), but, where appropriate, also to any other impartial tribunal or forum. Section 35, conversely, guarantees a fair *criminal trial* before *an ordinary* court. Chapter 8 of the constitution, which deals with courts and administrative justice, furthermore provides in principle for institutions to settle disputes and fleshes out the rudiments of their jurisdiction and powers.

Eighth, there is popular participation in establishing and maintaining legal institutions and legal processes that are accessible to the populace.

This standard of justice pertains to people's right to elect those who make laws as well as to the openness and user-friendliness of legal processes. Lawmaking and adjudication processes must also be open to public scrutiny.

Section 1(d) of the constitution elevates popular participation in (accountable) government to one of the basic values on which the (new) Republic of South Africa is founded. This value is enshrined in the Bill of Rights, too, not only because section 19 comprehensively protects rights relevant to the participation in political processes, but also because the rights to freedom of belief and opinion (section 15[1]); freedom of expression (section 16[1]), and assembly, demonstration, picket, and petition (section 17) are entrenched.

Only an informed populace can participate in day-to-day government. The Bill of Rights empowers South Africans to insist on the provision of relevant information. Section 32(1) guarantees a right of access to information held by the state or another person where such information is required for the exercise or protection of any rights. The right to just administrative action in section 33 moreover includes a right to written reasons for conduct that adversely affects rights.

No provision in the constitution explicitly vouches for the openness of adjudication processes in general. Section 35, however, explicitly provides for open and public *criminal* processes. An accused person, for instance, has the right to a *public* trial before an *ordinary court* (section 35[3][c]). (S)he also has a right of appeal and review (section 35[3][o]), which means that (s)he can have the outcome of a criminal process *openly* scrutinized in a higher forum.

It is quite controversial as to what extent the populace should be allowed a say in appointing the judiciary.[12] The South African constitution provides for some (albeit indirect) popular participation in the appointment of judges. Of the twenty-four members of the Judicial Service Commission (the body that plays a vital role in the appointment of judges of the Constitutional Court as well as the Supreme Court of Appeal and high courts (sections 174[3], [4], and [6]) at least fifteen are politicians or political appointments, assumedly representative of the "popular will," namely:

- the cabinet member responsible for the administration of justice;
- six persons designated by the National Assembly from among its members;
- four permanent delegates to the National Council of Provinces; and
- four persons designated by the president of the Republic of South Africa as head of the national executive, after consultation with the leaders of all the parties in the National Assembly (sections 178[1] [d], [h], [I], and [j]).

Conclusion

The mere fact that one can glean attributes of the optimally just society from the text of a constitution such as South Africa's final constitution does not by itself guarantee an actually just dispensation. The constitution nevertheless obligates deference to certain precepts and principles of justice with adequate force and with a sense of purpose sufficiently clear to render this highest law of the land the most vital stanchion in the scaffolding of a legally just South Africa. This is a modest but meaningful beginning. It is now up to the organs of state, and to the people, who will (by realizing the constitution) add the brickwork (and eventually do the finishing touches) to the building of a just society, thereby aiding the fulfilment of the promises presently held out by the appearance of the scaffolding.

Notes

1. Martin Heidegger, *An Introduction to Metaphysics* (New York: Anchor Books, 1961), 36.
2. Constitution of the Republic of South Africa, Act 200 of 1993.
3. This process was initiated by virtue of the Promotion of National Unity and Reconciliation Act 34 of 1995.

4. Lourens M. du Plessis, "The Genesis of a Bill of Rights in a Divided Society: Observations on the Ideological Dialectic Reflected in the Chapter on Fundamental Rights in South Africa's Transitional Constitution," *Jahrbuch für Recht und Ethik* 3 (1995): 353-74.

5. See also Lourens du Plessis, "A Christian Assessment of Aspects of the Bill of Rights in South Africa's Final Constitution," *Journal of Theology for Southern Africa* 96 (November 1996): 59-74.

6. See also in this regard *Matinkinca v. Council of State, Ciskei,* 1994 (4) S.A. 472 (Ck.).

7. John Rawls, *A Theory of Justice* (Cambridge: Harvard University Press, 1971), 236.

8. "Taking into account the nature of the right and the nature of any duty imposed by the right" (section 8[2]).

9. Or Kuyperian Calvinism's *sphere sovereignty*; see also Abraham Kuyper, *Het Calvinisme: Zes Stone-lezingen* (Kampen: Kok, 1959), 62-88.

10. For its origins, see Lourens M. du Plessis, "Conceptualising Law and Justice (2): Just Legal Institutions in an Optimally Just Society," *Stellenbosch Law Review* 3 (1992): 357-74.

11. Catherine Albertyn and Janet Kentridge, "Introducing the Right to Equality in the Interim Constitution," *South African Journal on Human Rights* 10 (1994): 149-78.

12. For example, see also Hugh Corder, "The Appointment of Judges: Some Comparative Ideas," *Stellenbosch Law Review* 3 (1992): 207-30.

Chapter Nine

Multiculturalism: How Can the Human World Live Its Difference?

Johan Degenaar

Culture

FOR THE PURPOSE of this chapter the term *culture* can be defined as the form of life of a community viewed as a group of people who share common characteristics. The content of this form of life, or lifestyle, depends on the community involved and the characteristics ascribed to the members of the group. The community can be small, as in the case of the academic culture of a community of scholars, or it can be large, as in the case of human culture as a reference to the form of life of the human race. I propose that we look at a few examples of what the term *culture* can mean.

A common meaning of the term *culture* concerns its use in an ethnic context. Ethnic culture can be defined as the form of life of a community with a common descent, shared experience, history, and language that provide members of the community with a common sense of identity and a common way of ascribing meaning to things and events.

In the context of a national state the term *culture* refers to the form of life of a national community in which uniformity of culture is achieved by the effective imposition of a dominant ethnic culture or by a common culture brought about by the process of modernization.

Culture as the form of life of society as a whole succeeds in accommodating a variety of ethnic communities. In this context, one speaks of a democratic culture based on a constitution that protects the rights of individuals and the rights of ethnic communities.

Culture can mean a more inclusive form of life in which various national and ethnic cultures are accommodated. In this context, terms such as *European culture* and *Western culture* are used. Problems concerning notions such as Eurocentrism, Afrocentrism, and Orientalism are related to this more inclusive form of life.

Finally, culture can mean the general process of spiritual development of humanity as a whole. If this use of the term is introduced, one can distinguish between, on the one hand, culture in the singular that refers to "the core of what is common to all humanity" and, on the other hand, culture in the plural that designates the forms of life of particular communities.

By looking at only a few uses of the term *culture* it is obvious that there is not only a variety of cultures involved, but also a variety of kinds of culture. This is an important point that should constantly be kept in mind when multiculturalism is under discussion. This also applies to cases in which we limit ourselves, for example, to the coexistence of ethnic cultures in the same country.

Another point that should be kept in mind is the fact that making distinctions among various cultures and among a variety of kinds of culture, we should not assume that cultures are "self-enclosed wholes" that would entail a reification of cultures into static entities—a view that ignores the characteristic of blurred edges, the differences within cultures themselves, and the fact that change does take place in communities.

Multiculturalism

In the previous section, I analyzed the notion of culture and pointed out that one should not only distinguish among a plurality of cultures, but also among a plurality of kinds of culture. That section concerned mainly the existence of cultures. The notion of multiculturalism shifts the focus to the coexistence of cultures entailing difference that leads to tension and eventually to conflict. The conflict is caused both by the difficulties entailed in living difference and by the asymmetrical relations of power between cultures.

The term *multiculturalism* turned out to be far more controversial than I anticipated when I started my research. J. L. Comaroff states: "Multiculturalism is a complex and misleading term. Everybody in America—from right, left and center—seems to espouse the virtues of 'multiculturalism.' But they often imply different things by it; as long as the term remains inadequately examined, it may justify old forms of cultural imperialism in new guise."[1] She does, however, grant that the term can be used in a fruitful manner that allows the notion of difference to undermine cultural imperialism and careless assumptions. K. Malik also problematizes the concept and queries the widespread view that multiculturism is a good thing. He states his position as follows:

> The idea of a plural or multicultural society is, however, a deeply ambiguous one. Just as the discourse of culture has recast the concept of race in a new form, so multiculturalism represents not a means to an equal society, but an alternative to one, where equality has given way to the toleration of difference and, indeed, of inequality. From a racial viewpoint, economic, social, and technological inequalities are the natural outcome of racial differences. From the standpoint of multiculturalism, however, differences are welcomed as expressions of cultural diversity. In the final analysis both philosophies attempt to impute rational meaning to inequality.[2]

In spite of the ambiguity related to the use of the term *multiculturalism*, I propose that we take it seriously and that we negotiate a meaning that can be used appropriately. I intend to use the term *multiculturality* descriptively to designate the coexistence of cultures without judging in advance whether it entails a positive or negative state of affairs. A negative evaluation concentrates on the inequalities in multicultural societies and argues that "multiculturalism is no more than a masking rhetoric to conceal the ugly realities of inequality and ghettoisation of minorities in order to facilitate control, manipulation and discrimination."[3] One need not agree with this negative judgment that reduces multiculturalism to *merely* a "masking rhetoric to conceal the ugly realities," but this should not withhold us from addressing the serious problems of inequality and discrimination in multicultural societies.

Another possibility is to allow for a positive evaluation of multiculturalism while acknowledging the misuse of the term in certain instances. T. Turner can be cited as an example of this approach. He points out that "multiculturalism tends to become a form of identity politics, in which the concept of *culture* becomes merged with that of ethnic identity." He argues that this ideological shift is fraught with dangers, which he summarizes as follows:

> It risks essentialising the idea of culture as the property of an ethnic group or race; it risks reifying cultures as separate entities by overemphasising their boundedness and mutual distinctness; it risks overemphasising the internal homogeneity of cultures in terms that potentially legitimise repressive demands for communial conformity; and by treating cultures as badges of group identity, it tends to fetishize them in ways that put them beyond the reach of critical analysis—and thus of anthropology.[4]

Essentialism, reification, homogenization, conformism, fetishization, indeed, all these dangers should be avoided, and the critical dimension should be kept alive. But need we assume that since the term *multiculturalism* is tainted by these dangers that it should therefore be abandoned altogether? Turner argues that there are important theoretical and political possibilities attached to multiculturalism. There is "a liberating recognition of de facto heterogeneity" of cultures and an endeavor to "accommodate, rather than ignore or repress, the multiplicity of identities." Furthermore, this approach can lead to an involvement in the struggle against oppression of ethnic minorities.

If one compares these positive remarks with the negative judgment of multiculturalism, one is struck by a marked difference. The view of multiculturalism as merely a masking rhetoric, concealing discrimination and oppression, is cancelled by the view that multiculturalism is a liberating recognition of the multiplicity of cultures that can lead to an involvement in the struggle against oppression.

J. L. Kincheloe and S. R. Steinberg distinguish five forms of multiculturalism, namely, conservative, liberal, pluralist, left-essentialist, and critical.[5] Conservative multiculturalism is also referred to as monoculturalism—"the belief in the superiority of Western patriarchal culture." Although the existence of a plurality of cultures is acknowledged, the superiority of Western culture is assumed, and the aim is assimilation to a common Western standard characterized by them as "the colonialist tradition of white male supremacy."

Liberal multiculturalism also acknowledges the existence of a diversity of cultures, but the liberal view that individuals share a "natural equality and a common humanity" presupposes Eurocentric culture as the tacit norm. Because of the myth of natural equality, the liberal does not pay due attention to "the contextual specificity of difference" and the fact that power is distributed unequally. One can speak the language of natural equality while remaining ignorant of the influence of a "dominant cultural discursive power . . . on the production of subjectivity."

Pluralist multiculturalism not only focuses on difference between cultures, but also views diversity as intrinsically valuable. It emphasizes freedom from other cultures and pride in the achievements of one's own culture. To the extent that pluralist multiculturalism highlights this aspect, it has a limited view of emancipation since, according to Kincheloe and Steinberg, it "confuses psychological affirmation with political empowerment."

Essentialism in the context of cultural studies assumes that an essence or a set of unchanging properties inheres in a culture in such a way that it "transcends the forces of history, social context and power." Left-essentialist multiculturalism romanticizes the essence of its own culture and claims "oppression privilege" and moral superiority among members of the culture. This essentialized notion of the identity of a culture, which excludes morally committed outsiders, is not conducive to democracy since it "concerns itself more with self-assertion than with the effort to build strategic democratic alliances for social justice."

In view of the limitations of all these forms of multiculturalism, Kincheloe and Steinberg decide that what is called for is a *critical* form of multiculturalism that concerns itself with the power of self-reflection by means of which individuals become conscious of the way in which their consciousness has been formed by being socialized within a culture and by the asymmetrical relations of power in a multicultural context. The introduction of the critical dimension enables one to respect difference while, at the same time, opposing oppression in favor of emancipation and justice. "Critical multiculturalism refuses to position the mere establishment of diversity as its final objective; instead it seeks a diversity that understands the power of difference when it is conceptualized within a larger concern with social justice."

In this section, I have looked at some of the uses of the term *multiculturalism* and at a variety of evaluations of the phenomenon of multiculturality. I propose that we concentrate on the positive use of the term in the form of critical multiculturalism for the following reasons: it exposes the authoritarian nature of monoculturalism; it criticizes forms of multiculturalism that are not self-critical with regard to their own assumptions; it gives pride of place to bringing to consciousness members of a culture, enhancing in this manner, the quality of cultural membership; while acknowledging the value of cultural diversity, it raises the issue of asymmetrical relations of power; and it answers the question of how the human world can live its difference by calling participants to work toward a coexistence characterized by a concern for social justice.

The Politics of Difference

In the previous section, I looked at multiculturalism in opposition to monoculturalism. In this section I explore insights produced by postmodern philosophy that contribute to our positive understanding of multiculturality and to possible ways for human beings to live their difference. Although there are many postmodern insights that can be discussed for this purpose, I propose that we focus on the crucial notion of difference in spite of its controversial nature as pointed out, for example, by C. Sypnowich in her article, "Some Disquiet about 'Difference.'"[6] My thoughts on the politics of difference are based on my research as published in the article entitled, "The Concept of Politics in Postmodernism."[7]

Within the strategy of deconstruction, the notion of difference has been introduced in a special way. The emphasis is placed on three aspects of difference, namely, difference, differing, and deferring—reminding us, in this manner, that understanding is historically conditioned and that we have to take into account the distinctions made in the past, those that are being made in the present and those that will be made in the future. The advantages of this way of looking at difference are the following: first, differences are linked with processes of differentiation; second, by introducing the historical dimension, no component of differentiation is a self-enclosed static unit unaffected by change in time; third, each component is always involved in a dynamic set of relationships; and fourth, we should be wary of differences that fossilize into binary oppositions imposing hierarchical and discriminatory structures on our thinking. This is an important insight: We not only speak a language, but a language also speaks us and we have consistently to remain conscious of this influence.

These remarks on the postmodern use of the word *difference* already demonstrate some aspects of a politics of difference: the emphasis placed on process, history, dynamic relationships, and the criticism of entrenched hierarchies. Another aspect is the interdependent nature of human relationships. The notion of difference entails not only that the self differs from the other, but that they are interdependent in the process of differentiation. For both participants in the relationship, it implies that the otherness of the other is a precondition of self-understanding. This relationship should not be romanticized into a harmonious state of affairs but rather viewed as a relationship of tension since difference is retained. W. E. Conolly speaks of the "antagonism of identity"—each person being only set on maintaining her or his own sovereignty—that has to be transformed into the "agonism of difference"—each person respecting while opposing the other.[8]

The politics of difference also applies to the differentiation among cultures, groups, communities, organizations, and nations. In all these cases of inevitable conflict it also applies that antagonism of identity has to be transformed into agonism of difference. Here again antagonism is not idealistically transformed into harmony but realistically into agonism. The tension of living difference is kept alive. Human dignity is not supported by the denial of difference but by the cultivation of agonistic respect between contending parties. It is clear that the politics of difference does not romanticize politics in terms of the brotherhood or sisterhood of humankind but encourages diversity and enables us to live in the same world and the same country without being friends and without being reduced to sameness.

Although my main purpose is to describe and evaluate multiculturalism, one should not isolate this phenomenon from the broader context of a pluralist concern with diversity. The following diversities come to mind: first, a plurality of cultures, whether extranational or intranational. Second, a plurality of parties reflecting a variety of ideological positions in the state; third, a plurality of associations in civil society that do not compete for the power of the state but nevertheless claim allegiance from members that can clash with the obligation to obey the state, including institutions such as the church and the academy, as well as social movements organized by feminists and ecologists; fourth, a plurality of regions claiming autonomy in opposition to the sovereignty of centralized power. In accordance with Foucault's notion of power without the king, the politics of plurality advances the idea of distribution of power.

I have looked at positive aspects of the politics of difference and demonstrated how it develops into a pluralist mind-set that does not merely acknowledge the existence of plurality but judges plurality to be a value worth pursuing. This view entails a positive approach to multiculturality. The politics of difference exposes the false universalism of the Enlightenment and the cultural imperialism it espouses. J. S. Kahn formulates the value of difference as follows:

> We live in a world characterized not just by difference, but by a consuming and erotic passion for it. Gone are the metanarratives by which modernist thinkers sought to interpret the world through simplistic Enlightenment universalisms. But gone too are the forces of modernism and cultural imperialism that have operated in the past to constitute a homogenous world after images constructed in eighteenth century European bourgeois thought, hence making it possible for those of postmodern sensitivity at the same time to fear and marvel at that difference which is thereby revealed to them. . . . Recognizing difference is, in short, an exhilaration, indeed a liberation, allowing us to expose the false universalism of the Enlightenment utopia.[9]

M. Walzer, who also opposes Enlightenment utopianism, speaks out in favor of cultural diversity, encouraging us not to run away from the difficult task of involving ourselves in the process of intercultural contact and in the never-ending negotiations of difference it entails. I have often used the following quotation from Walzer, and because of the challenging nature of his dramatic presentation I repeat it here:

Since the nature and the number of our identities will be different, even characteristically different for whole populations, a great variety of arrangements ought to be expected and welcomed. Each of them will have its usefulness and its irritations; none of them will be permanent, the negotiation of difference will never produce a final settlement. What this also means is that our common humanity will never make us members of a single universal tribe. The crucial commonality of the human race is particularism. With the end of imperial and totalitarian rule, we can at last recognise this commonality and begin the difficult negotiations it requires.[10]

Living difference consists in our discovering our common humanity, which includes not only the existence of difference, but also the ongoing negotiation of that difference.

This positive view of multiculturality in terms of celebration and negotiation of difference is an advance on the imperialism entailed by monocultural movements. It does, however, give rise to some issues that have to be taken seriously. I mention two of these issues: the one concerns context, the other democracy.

The Need for Contextualization

The question can be raised whether celebration and negotiation of difference are necessary and sufficient conditions for living difference in a just dispensation. Some writers claim that a politics of difference should be viewed as including a concern for those communities who have been excluded, marginalized, silenced, and oppressed. Others criticize the tendency to romanticize and essentialize difference with the result that the social context of differentiation is not sufficiently taken into account. These writers argue that the principle of the negotiation of difference has to be supplemented by the notion of empowerment of the oppressed. In this manner, a concern for social justice is introduced—a concern expressed by Sypnowich as follows: "If we recognize that some differences are the fruits of injustice, then justice may require the elimination of difference, or at least the difference that difference makes."[11] This approach introduces the important issue of "the different status of different differences."

R. Jenkins is an example of those writers who argue in favor of a politics of difference that need not be supplemented since it is viewed as including social concerns. He states:

The key to this new discourse of 'pluralism' is a celebration of *difference* as the site of resistance to Eurocentric and androcentric meta-narratives of history and progress; as a bulwark against fundamentalist images of the world; as an assertion of the rights to autonomous (co-)existence of peripheralized, marginalized, minority-ized peoples; as the inspiration for ethics and politics of representation and diversity which challenge the centralization, the homogenization, the integration, and the domination of—it will come as no surprise after *that* list—the nation or more particularly the nation-state.[12]

Contrarily, T. Turner argues that the emphasis on difference tends to obscure the fact that difference also operates in terms of relations of power. By introducing the principle of contextualization one is capable of a critical analysis of the role that power plays in multicultural situations. Because of contradictory tendencies within multiculturalism (as pointed out above), Turner distinguishes between *critical* multiculturalism and *difference* multiculturalism. The positive form he describes as follows: "Critical multiculturalism seeks to use cultural diversity as a basis for challenging, revising, and relativizing basic notions and principles common to dominant and minority cultures alike, so as to construct a more vital, open, and democratic common culture." In contrast to this, difference multiculturalism turns difference into a fetish and reduces culture to "a tag for ethnic identity and a license for political and intellectual separatism." This "romancing of difference" entails a form of romantic essentialism that "presupposes the abstraction of cultural phenomena from their real social and political-economic contexts." Critical multiculturism is set on placing culture within political contexts enabling pluralist discourse to contribute to a "demystified respect for actual difference."[13] This process of demystification is also possible since critical multiculturalism rejects an essentialist concept of identity in favor of a view of culture as a dynamic and interactive phenomenon.

The way in which critical multiculturalism succeeds in linking multiculturalism with transformational politics brings to our attention a shift that has taken place in the use of the term *culture*. Instead of emphasizing the form of life of a community, the focus is now placed on the transformational power attributed to culture. Turner points out that anthropologists have to choose between, "on the one hand, *encyclopedic* conceptions of cultures as more or less practico-inert arrays of traits and, on the other, praxis-oriented notions of culture as the realisation of a collective human potential for self-production and transformation." It is in this context that one can say that the notion of culture is a site of struggle and the aim of multiculturalism should be to enhance the quality of culture as "the empowerment of the basic human capacity for self-creation (i.e., for culture, in the active sense of collective self-production) for all members and groups of society."[14]

The Need for a Democratic Culture

Another problem that a politics of difference has to take seriously concerns the nature of the culture that is presupposed as the frame of reference within which the conflict between cultures can be managed appropriately. In order to make sense of critical multiculturalism, we need to give content to the political space within which multiculturality operates and competing claims of difference can be accommodated. We have to assume that members of diverse cultures are at the same time also members of a larger society in which a rights culture prevails. The notion of rights is important for it generates the articulation of the claims of individuals and of diverse cultural groups. Rights should not be viewed in terms of an ideal of justice conceived as an ahistorical standard.

Rights and justice are constructed in historical contexts of struggle in which politically contested claims are made. Benhabib argues that "the constitution of rights must come from an 'actual dialogue situation in which moral agents communicate with each other' about their needs."[15]

Rights discourse enables participants to view the larger community as a creative site of struggle in which members of different communal cultures realize that membership of a common culture is a real possibility. In this way, cultures can live diversely in common to the extent that they experience that their interests are interpreted as claims for justice. Sypnowich formulates this point as follows: "The universalism of rights thus makes it possible for diverse groups to unite around a common political ideal. While rights discourse can be used to specify and meet particular needs . . . it does so by reference to a consensus about a fulfilling or empowered life which is available to all. By protecting different interests, rights give us grounds for a commitment to an entity outside of our disparate entities."[16]

These insights based on critical multiculturalist principles clearly illustrate to what extent the politics of difference presupposes a democratic culture in order to function successfully. A democratic system should not be viewed as a state of affairs that has already been achieved, but rather as principles to which citizens commit themselves—principles such as freedom, empowerment, constitutionalism, and a bill of rights. Democracy should, furthermore, not be equated with majoritarianism and mystifications such as "the general will of the people"—notions that are destructive of multicultural values. The best way to protect us from reductionist thinking about democracy is to combine the positive aspects of liberal, plural, and social democracies. Liberal democracy contributes the notion of individual rights. Plural democracy emphasizes the political role of four pluralities, namely, a plurality of political parties, of political regions, of autonomous organizations, and of communal cultures. It proposes the principle of cultural rights in order to counter the ever-present danger of the tyranny of the majority. Social democracy calls on the state to provide the material conditions that will enable citizens to make effective use of their democratic rights and to empower them by involving them in decision-making processes.

It is clear from these three crucial aspects of democracy to what extent critical multiculturalism is dependent on a democratic culture for its proper functioning. By introducing the notion of democracy in multicultural contexts we are not solving any problems. Democracy primarily provides the frame of reference in which problems can be tackled. The difficult task is to practice democracy in each situation. A. Boraine correctly states: "There is no inevitability about democracy. It must be sought for, fought for and won in every generation."[17] I would like to reinforce this idea in the following way: Democracy must be sought for, fought for, and won in every situation. In this sense we can speak of struggle democracy or agonistic democracy, thus highlighting the inevitable *agon* or struggle that is involved in living difference and in managing it in a just manner. If we seriously want to live difference in multicultural situations, we should not be ignorant of what this ongoing struggle involves.

We must also keep in mind that agonistic democracy in multicultural set-ups does not only concern the managing of conflict in political society, but also in civil society—a fact that places an awesome responsibility on ordinary citizens. It entails, for example, the introduction of tension in all spheres of social life. The value of critical multiculturalism consists of, among other things, highlighting these issues and encouraging citizens to involve themselves in the struggle.

In the absence of universal values that can be imposed, the participants from various cultures have to negotiate common values. The negotiation of values is one of the crucial aspects of a democratic culture. This point is also made in "The Statement of Principles of Teachers for a Democratic Culture," which includes the following exposition of the concept of a democratic culture:

> What does the notion of a "democratic culture" mean and how does it relate to education? In our view, a democratic culture is one that acknowledges that criteria of value in art are not permanently fixed by tradition and authority, but are subject to constant revision. It is a culture in which terms like canon, literature, tradition, artistic value, common culture, and even truth are seen as disputed rather than given. This means not that standards for judging art and scholarship must be discarded, but that such standards should evolve out of democratic processes in which they can be thoughtfully challenged.[18]

In order to situate the politics of difference in a wider context, I intend to look at three examples of philosophers who take the challenge of multiculturalism seriously and contribute to our understanding of multiculturality. I discuss this contribution in terms of the three following themes: the politics of recognition (Charles Taylor); the politics of multicultural citizenship (Will Kymlicka); and the philosophy of self-reflective contextualization (Willie van der Merwe).

The Politics of Recognition

In "The Politics of Recognition" Charles Taylor also pays attention to tensions characteristic of multicultural situations.[19] He argues that a politics of difference should be based on a politics of equal dignity. It is the act of mutual recognition among equals that constitutes the moral quality of individuals and groups. This entails that we must "*recognize* the equal value of different cultures; that we not only let them survive, but acknowledge their *worth*."[20] A crucial question, however, concerns the nature of this recognition of the equal value of different cultures. How is it possible to understand and evaluate a culture that is different, strange, and unfamiliar? Taylor solves this problem by introducing Gadamer's notion of "the fusion of horizons" as expressed in *Wahrheit und Methode*. Although we cannot assume that we share the same final vocabulary, new vocabularies can develop in the ongoing process of intercultural contact. "The 'fusion of horizons' operates through our developing new vocabularies of comparison, by means of which we can articulate these contrasts."[21]

In his essay "Understanding and Ethnocentricity" Taylor formulates his view in terms of the notion of the language of perspicuous contrast as follows: "It will almost always be the case that the adequate language in which we can understand another society is not our language of understanding, or theirs, but rather what one could call a language of perspicuous contrast. This would be a language in which we could formulate both their way of life and ours as alternative possibilities in relation to some human constants at work in both."[22]

The notion of the language of perspicuous contrast seems to be capable of keeping differences alive, while the metaphor of the fusion of horizons suggests at least the ideal of the homogenization of cultures. Taylor also moves in this direction when he calls us to open ourselves to "comparative cultural study of the kind that must displace our horizons in the resulting fusions. What it requires above all is an admission that we are very far away from that ultimate horizon from which the relative worth of different cultures might be evident."[23] A crucial question in this regard is the following: What is the function of the notion of *ultimate* horizon in a world characterized by contingent horizons? In the light of this problem, I propose that we free ourselves from the illusion of homogeneity entailed by the notions of final vocabulary and ultimate horizon, and give priority to the notion of the language of perspicuous contrast, since it succeeds in keeping the tension entailed in difference alive.

The value of Taylor's contribution to multiculturalism is the manner in which the proposed politics of dignity produces respect for difference and leads to a politics of recognition of the worth of a plurality of cultures. This view enables him to ascribe to cultures equal rights that enable citizens to live within a cultural heritage in a multicultural society without being discriminated against because of it. The notion of cultural rights is a controversial notion that is frowned upon by liberals since liberal discourse, biased in favor of individuals, assumes that cultures can be accommodated sufficiently by allowing individuals the right of free association with the culture of their choice. On the basis of this individual right, however, the state has no obligation to help a cultural group to survive or to promote its own language, for example. The liberal state can recognize and accommodate particular cultures but cannot ascribe rights to cultures.

Although A. Gutmann criticizes Taylor in terms of liberal democracy, which she defends as being capable both of protecting universal rights and of recognizing particular cultures, she summarizes her position on the value of multiculturalism in a manner with which Taylor can concur. She writes: "Multicultural societies and communities that stand for the freedom and equality of all people rest upon mutual respect for reasonable intellectual, political, and cultural differences. Mutual respect requires a widespread willingness and ability to articulate our disagreements, to defend them before people with whom we disagree, to discern the difference between respectable and disrespectable disagreement, and to be open to changing our own minds when faced with well-reasoned criticism."[24] These virtues of mutual respect will indeed enable participants in the multicultural conflict to imbue multiculturalism with a moral quality, but a crucial question remains, namely, what language do we use in articulating our disagreements in a meaningful way for both parties?

The Politics of Multicultural Citizenship

Because of the ambiguity of the term *multiculturalism*, W. Kymlicka advises us to keep different senses of the terms *culture* and *multiculturalism* in mind.[25] He distinguishes, for example, between the following cultural groups: national minorities; ethnic groups; and new social movements such as gays, women, the poor, and the disabled. With regard to the question whether group rights should be granted to cultural groups, he argues in favor of a liberal theory that is capable of protecting the interests of cultural groups sufficiently on the basis of the rights of individuals. He states his case as follows:

> In all liberal democracies, one of the major mechanisms for accommodating cultural differences is the protection of the civil and political rights of individuals. It is impossible to overstate the importance of freedom of association, religion, speech, mobility, and political organization for protecting group difference. These rights enable individuals to form and maintain the various groups and associations which constitute civil society, to adapt these groups to changing circumstances, and to promote their views and interests to the wider population. The protection afforded by these common rights of citizenship is sufficient for many of the legitimate forms of diversity in society.[26]

What strikes one is that Kymlicka does not say that common rights of citizenship provide sufficient protection for *all* the legitimate forms of diversity but only for *many* of the forms. It therefore does not come as a surprise that he goes along with the fact that "it is increasingly accepted in many countries that some forms of cultural difference can only be accommodated through special legal or constitutional measures, above and beyond the common rights of citizenship."

In order to cope with these cases, Kymlicka introduces three forms of group-differentiated rights, namely, self-government rights, polyethnic rights, and special representation rights. He argues that these cases should all be taken seriously and treated in a variety of ways in the particular contexts in which groups lay their claims. He also reminds us that cultural groups have a history and that they are historically constituted in different ways in a society. He points out that, although the category "Hispanic" is used for an ethnic group in America, the Hispanics view themselves as Puerto Ricans, Chicanos, Cubans, Mexicans, Spaniards, or Guatemalans—all with their own histories, identities, and demands.[27] To ignore differences among cultures and differences within cultures is a refusal to admit the basic fact that each cultural group has its own history and that justice demands that each should be treated accordingly.

Kymlicka furthermore states that without introducing special measures for disadvantaged cultural groups, the liberal "talk of 'treating people as individuals' is itself just a cover for ethnic and national injustice."[28] The value of this response to the challenge of multiculturalism is that he brings to our attention that our concern for justice should not focus merely on the individual. Our task to live our differences is especially urgent today since "at present, the fate of ethnic and national groups around the world is in the hand of xenophobic nationalists, religious extremists, and military dictators,"[29]—all three being positions of power that leave no room for cultural pluralism.

The Philosophy of Self-Reflective Contextualization

In this section, I focus on the contribution of a South African philosopher who has accepted the challenge of multiculturalism. W. L. Van der Merwe has developed a theory of self-reflective contextualization, encouraging intellectuals in general and philosophers in particular to view the phenomenon of multiculturality not as a drawback but rather as the precondition for their important contribution to our understanding of intercultural contact and pluralist discourse. He acted as guest editor of a special edition of the *South African Journal of Philosophy* devoted to problems related to multiculturalism.

In his article entitled, "African Philosophy and Multiculturalism," Van der Merwe relates African philosophy to "the need for the self-reflective contextualization of philosophy in a multicultural society."[30] Pluralism is already evident in his discussion of the lack of a singular identity in African philosophy. It is merely a family name for a variety of "articulations of philosophy of and for Africa." The plurality of articulations is viewed in a positive way since "it exemplifies in a paradigmatic way the historical and cultural contingency, the contextual particularity, of philosophy." This insight enables us not to expect philosophy to operate from a transcultural and universal position but to acknowledge its limitations. Instead of claiming a universal point of reference for philosophy, we should rather aim for a self-reflective contextualization of philosophy and ascertain how it can enable us to cope with the challenges of multiculturalism.

Van der Merwe links multiculturalism to the paradoxical nature of the process of the globalization of late-modern culture. He describes it in the following way:

> This ironic logic of modernity in terms of which it realises a radical pluralisation of society and culture in the same movement in which it achieves global expansion is also what 'postmodernity' as a description of the distinctive cultural conditions of our present existence refers to. . . . The commonality of sharing increasingly the same postmodern societal context is, however, not the sharing of a homogeneous culture but a common encounter with multiculturalism as a universal feature of postmodern societies.[31]

Philosophy can contribute to our understanding of this complex situation not by claiming a universal perspective, but by self-reflectively contextualizing itself. This contextualized philosophy entails the following insights:

1. In the absence of a metanarrative, philosophy has to admit its cultural contingency and enter into dialogue with other cultures.

2. The contingency of one's philosophy and one's identity as a person are both multicultural. "One's identity is a continuous reweaving of various patterns of the cultures one is exposed to."[32]

3. An essentialist view of culture, entailing, for example, that cultures are incommensurable, must be replaced by a view that acknowledges the dynamics of culture.

4. Multiculturalism refers not only to the coexistence of various cultures, but also to cultural differences "running across various cultures and being inherent in any distinct culture."[33] The notion of cultural differences running across different cultures enables Van der Merwe to highlight the complexity of cultures and to remind us not to view cultures as self-enclosed wholes.

In the light of the complex nature of multiculturality, the task of philosophers is, at least, to interpret this complexity for the societies in which they live. Although this interpretative dialogue is of crucial importance, conflicts cannot be resolved merely in this manner. In these cases, political negotiation is inevitable and important to enable citizens to live their differences. What the nature of this modus vivendi could be I discussed in terms of agonistic democracy in the section entitled "The Need for a Democratic Culture."

Conclusion

In the light of the foregoing discussion one can state that multiculturality is indeed a challenge in a postmodern world and that critical multiculturalism provides us with a creative way of coping with this challenge. This also applies to the multicultural set-up in South Africa.

M. Singh correctly argues that the replacement of apartheid by a democratic state provides us with "the historic opportunity to fashion a new set of understandings about who we are and what we consider to be of fundamental value to us."[34] This amounts to a challenge to reconstruct national, communal, and individual identities in South Africa. These processes of identification are viewed by her to be "extremely exciting and challenging and also enormously fraught with disintegrative tensions and dangers." One of the contributions of multiculturalism to our political consciousness is that it functions as an opportunity to seriously raise the question: What does it mean to be a human being in a multicultural set-up at this stage of our history? The choice in this chapter in favor of critical multiculturalism as part of emancipatory politics is one way of answering this important question. I prefer this answer because, as pointed out above, it "refuses to position the mere establishment of diversity as its final objective; instead it seeks a diversity that understands the power of difference when it is conceptualized within a larger concern with social justice."[35]

The question concerning what it means to be a human being is also answered by a traditional African aphorism in a special way. The Zulu version runs as follows: *umuntu ngumuntu ngabantu:* a human being is a human being through human beings. Van der Merwe points out that the term *ubuntu* "denotes both a state of being and one of becoming."[36] This entails that it can be interpreted in both a descriptive and a prescriptive manner, that is, it says something about the social nature of being human and it prescribes how we should live. It calls us "to expose ourselves to others, to encounter the difference of their humanness, in order to fully become our own. The meaning would then be: To be human is to affirm one's humanity by recognizing the humanity of others in its infinite variety of content and form." If we take this prescription seriously, then we can view the multicultural set-up in South Africa as a wonderful opportunity to discover our humanness.

Notes

1. J. Comaroff, "Late Twentieth-Century Social Science: A Conversation," in *Transgressing Boundaries: New Directions in the Study of Culture in Africa,* ed. B. Cooper and A. Steyn (Rondebosch, South Africa.: University of Cape Town Press, 1996), 51.

2. K. Malik, *The Meaning of Race: Race, History, and Culture in Western Society* (London: Macmillan, 1996), 170.

3. N. Alexander, "Multiculturalism in the Rainbow Nation: Policy and Practice" (unpublished paper, University of Cape Town, 1998), 6.

4. T. Turner, "Anthropology and Multiculturalism: What Is Anthropology That Multiculturalists Should Be Mindful of It?" *Cultural Anthropology* 8, no. 4 (1993): 411-12.

5. J. L. Kincheloe and S. R. Steinberg, *Changing Multiculturalism* (Buckingham, England: Open University Press, 1997), 3, 12, 15, 20, 22, 26.

6. C. Sypnowich, "Some Disquiet about 'Difference,'" *Praxis International* 13, no. 2 (July 1993): 99-112.

7. J. Degenaar, "The Concept of Politics in Postmodernism," *Politikon* 23, no. 2 (December 1996): 54-71.

8. W. E. Conolly, *Identity/Difference: Democratic Negotiations of Political Paradox* (Ithaca, N.Y.: Cornell University Press, 1991).

9. J. S. Kahn, *Culture, Multiculture, Postculture* (London: SAGE, 1995), 125.

10. M. Walzer, "Modern Tribalism," *Dialogue* 9 (1993): 19.

11. Sypnowich, "Some Disquiet about 'Difference,'" 106.

12. R. Jenkins, *Rethinking Ethnicity: Arguments and Explorations* (London: SAGE, 1997), 29.

13. T. Turner, "Anthropology and Multiculturalism," 413-15.

14. Turner, "Anthropology and Multiculturalism," 426-27.

15. As quoted by Sypnowich, "Some Disquiet about 'Difference,'" 108. Original source of Sypnowich quote: Soyla Benhabib, "The Generalized and the Concrete Other," in *Feminism As Critique,* ed. S. Benhabib and D. Cornell (Oxford: Basil Blackwell, 1987), 93.

16. Sypnowich, "Some Disquiet about 'Difference,'" 109.

17. P. Baker, A. Boraine, and Warren Krabchik, eds., *South Africa in the World Economy in the 1990s* (Cape Town: David Phillip, 1993), 39.

18. As quoted by Turner, "Anthropology and Multiculturalism," 413-14. Original source of Turner quote: Teachers for a Democratic Culture, "Statement of Principles," in *Beyond P.C.: Toward a Politics of Understanding*, ed. Patricia Aufderheide (St. Paul, Minn.: Greywolf Press, 1992).

19. Charles Taylor, "The Politics of Recognition," in *Multiculturalism: Examining the Politics of Recognition* (Princeton: Princeton University Press, 1994), 25-73.

20. Taylor, "The Politics of Recognition," 64.

21. Taylor, "The Politics of Recognition," 67.

22. Charles Taylor, *Philosophical Papers*, vol. 2, *Philosophy and the Human Sciences* (Cambridge: Cambridge University Press, 1985), 125.

23. Taylor, "The Politics of Recognition," 73.

24. A. Gutmann, introduction to *Multiculturalism*, by Taylor, 24.

25. W. Kymlicka, *Multicultural Citizenship: A Liberal Theory of Minority Rights* (Oxford: Clarendon, 1995).

26. Kymlicka, *Multicultural Citizenship,* 26.

27. Kymlicka, *Multicultural Citizenship,* 16-17.

28. Kymlicka, *Multicultural Citizenship,* 194.

29. Kymlicka, *Multicultural Citizenship,* 195.

30. W. L. Van der Merwe, "African Philosophy and Multiculturalism," *South African Journal of Philosophy* 16, no. 3 (August 1997): 73-78.

31. Van der Merwe, "African Philosophy and Multiculturalism," 75.

32. Van der Merwe, "African Philosophy and Multiculturalism," 76.

33. Van der Merwe, "African Philosophy and Multiculturalism," 76.

34. M. Singh, "Identity in the Making," *South African Journal of Philosophy* 16, no. 3 (August 1997): 120-23.

35. Kincheloe and Steinberg, *Changing Multiculturalism*, 26.

36. W. L. Van der Merwe, "Philosophy and the Multi-Cultural Context of (Post) Apartheid South Africa," *Ethical Perspectives* 3, no. 2 (1996): 1-15.

Chapter Ten

Eco-Human Justice and Well-Being

Lizo D. Jafta

Preamble

What progress do people want to make?
They want freedom from the depths of poverty.
They want security, enough to eat, good health, a steady job,
More say in how their lives are run, and not so much oppression.
They want to be treated like human beings.
They want the change for better education.
In a word, what they want is more, and have more,
Because what they really want is to be more.
Yet all the time they go on wanting more,
For most of them, things are getting worse, not better.

—Pope Paul VI[1]

I BEGIN WITH this statement from the pontiff because it summarizes the content of this chapter. Human beings are expansive creatures who do not only want to have more, but who also want to be more because it is natural for them to expand. Economy, humanity, and justice, which this chapter will be dealing with in relation to the South African situation, are all pertinent issues the world over. We have to ask ourselves: What does economy do for people? What does it do to people? If people have to own it, how do they participate in it?

With the inauguration of the government of National Unity in April 1994, a new spirit of nonracialism was introduced in South Africa. While it can be argued that there is, in fact, nothing like nonracialism, it can also be argued that there are no longer any official barriers that impede others from entering zones that were previously enclaves of one race. The question to be seriously asked is: Who now owns the economy?

Political liberation was achieved when a democratic government was put in place in April 1994. We are all proud of this achievement after a long struggle that resulted in the loss of so many lives. But political liberation without

171

economic liberation is a nonstarter. What South Africa needs now is an aggressive economic empowerment program. Some of the previously disadvantaged people of South Africa are now in the high echelons of society while the majority remain where they were before the placement of the democratic government.

Economic empowerment without justice is a recipe for disaster. When people are empowered, there must be surety that this is done with justice and that all the ethnic groups in the country benefit from it. This was not the case before the Mandela government was inaugurated. It was the obvious intention of the apartheid regimes to entrench white power at all costs and to relegate the nonwhites to the background. It was this unjust and racist attitude of the apartheid regimes that provoked the indignation of those who were relegated to the background. Any government that excludes others on the basis of their skin color and gender must be treated with the contempt it deserves. Human beings do not choose to be white or black or brown. They inherit the color of their skin from their forebears.

To rule "justly" and "righteously" is embedded in the Judeo-Christian tradition.[2] Kings of the Old Testament were expected to be just and to fear the Lord. The test of that fear was on the way they treated the poor, the strangers, the widows, and the orphans. There are numerous biblical quotations to prove this point. The early Christian writers were also concerned with the just treatment of the citizens of the Roman Empire. Governments were closely watched as to how they treated their citizens. In his treatise, *Contra Celsum*, Origen wrote in the third century:

> while others fight, Christians also should be fighting as priests and worshippers of God, keeping their right hands pure and by their prayers to God striving for those who fight in a righteous cause and for the emperor who reigns righteously, in order that everything which is opposed and hostile to those who act rightly, may be destroyed.[3]

The key word in Origen's statement quoted above is *righteous*. This word appears a number of times in the Islamic holy book, the Koran, which confirms what has already been said that righteousness is not a prerogative of Christians. Creation, including human beings, is the handiwork of a righteous God. Nature is a book, as St. Augustine reminds us, that reveals its Creator:

> Some people read books in order to find God. Yet there is a great book, the very appearance of created things. Look above you; look below you! Note it; read it! God, whom you wish to find, never wrote that book with ink. Instead, He set before your eyes the things that He had made. Can you ask for a louder voice than that? Why, heaven and earth cry out to you: "God made me."[4]

In light of what I have said in the proceeding paragraphs, I need to return to the theme of this chapter, economic human justice, and ask the following questions: What kind of economic justice can be described as just? How does justice relate to economic development? What can we learn from the global community and from those in history who have significantly influenced society as far as economic development is concerned? How do the rich become richer and the poor become poorer in the world and in South Africa in particular? How can this syndrome be avoided? Some of these questions relate to race, ethnicity, and gender. In a "rainbow" nation like South Africa, it cannot be denied that there are races and ethnicities that have more wealth than others.

It is common knowledge that some political parties in South Africa have been consistently calling not only for the liberation of the country as a whole, but also for the freedom of some ethnicities to have their own homeland within the country. They argue that this has happened somewhere in the global community. Why should it not happen in South Africa, they ask. The Freedom Front is one such party that made that call in the 1994 elections. They have made the same call recently in preparation for the 1999 general elections. The Inkatha Freedom Party (IFP) made a similar call when they emphasized the autonomy of the provinces. It (IFP), of course, was not the only party to talk about provincial autonomy. Some other parties echoed this for other reasons.

The burning questions are: Given the past history of apartheid in South Africa with its emphasis on race discrimination that they euphemistically called "separate development," is it wise at this point in the history of South Africa to emphasize a homeland for any ethnic group? If those, in particular, who worked for the maintenance of apartheid want a homeland, what guarantee do we have that what they want will not develop into another form of apartheid? This is the fear shared with those who totally reject the concept of a homeland for an ethnic group in South Africa. This is exacerbated by the fact that money is still in the hands of those who were protected by the apartheid governments of the past. The poor people of South Africa are still poor. Those who were protected in the past have something to build on that others do not have. To be blunt on this issue, the white community of South Africa was protected by whatever means possible by the apartheid regimes. To grant a homeland to people who had and still have large farms and large sums of money in national and international banks is to create an enclave for the rich while the neighboring community, which was previously deprived by the same government, will be poor because they have nothing to build on.

In my view, there is nothing basically wrong with ethnicity. There are ethnic groups all over the world. South Africa, like many countries of the world, welcomed refugees from other countries, missionaries, and colonizers who ultimately took over the country and destroyed the African kingdoms and grabbed the land and made it theirs. South Africa is now called a rainbow nation. What happened is that those who colonized are now rich and those who were colonized are poor. Correction of this wrong process cannot be effected through ethnic homelands. It can only be done through a real sharing of the resources of the country and by giving priority to those who were previously disadvantaged. Call it by whatever name you want—affirmative action, economic empowerment, redressing the past, restructuring, and so forth, but correction must take place.

Histories of continents and countries are different. Geographies and climates are partly responsible for the differences. If the canton system works in some Western countries, it does not mean that it will work in Africa given the more than eight hundred languages spoken in the continent. Tribal differences in the African continent have been part of the political instability that Africa has experienced. Those tribal differences were exacerbated by colonizers who conveniently played a third force in order to effect a divide-and-rule system. It worked well for the colonizers. They got what they wanted and divided and carved Africa as they wished. Even after colonization was something of the past, neocolonization continued in a number of ways. Tribal divisions in Africa are not solely the causation of Africans. Some of the reasons for the tribal differences were deliberately caused by the Westerners in the process of fostering their power.

Protestant missions, with all their good intentions, further divided Africans into different denominational camps. This is not meant to denigrate the role of Protestantism. Catholics did no better. This is the sad part of the missionary work. What is interesting now is that South Africa is looking for a morality that will help in the rebuilding of the nation, and the search for this morality goes beyond the Christian religion.

Economic Human Justice—A Working Definition

Economic human justice is simply a relationship between economy, humanity, and justice. Economy relates to the wealth and resources of the community—their condition, administration, and distribution. The best economic situation is the one that is a precondition for the advancement of humanity. The worst economic situation is the one that is an obstacle to human development. An advanced, or advancing, country is measured not by the standards of the highest but by those of the lowest. Considering the rate at which the informal settlements are multiplying in South Africa, it becomes difficult to see the country as a developing country. Residents of those informal settlements are neither white nor coloured nor Indian. They are all black Africans.

Professor David Krueger divides justice into three main categories: commutative justice, distributive justice, and productive justice.[5] He defines commutative justice as that form of justice that is basically concerned with fairness in economic exchange. This form of justice, according to Krueger, can be traced back to Greek philosophers like Aristotle. Distributive justice is concerned with fair and equitable distributions of economic goods and services. Productive justice is that form of justice that ensures that the machinery is in place for the production of hard work, effort, skills, and discipline.

I welcome Krueger's categories of justice, and I want to see how they apply in the South African situation. Is there any fairness in economic exchange in South Africa and, if there is, who benefits from it, and how does it affect the poorest of the poor? Can (a democratic) South Africa be proud of its record of distribution of economic goods to all the citizens of the country? Or is this still the privilege of a certain ethnic group? Are the policies of the government assuring a fair distribution of economic goods for the future? The worst that can happen is that a government shares its wealth among its own ethnic group and offers only crumbs to those of other groups. The racist apartheid government had reserved jobs and opportunities for whites at the exclusion of blacks. What must be avoided at all costs is an ethnic-orientated government. What South Africa must work for is an all-inclusive government irrespective of race, religion, and gender. This is what I regard as a just form of government.

Hard work, effort, skill, and discipline are categorized by Krueger as "productive justice." South Africa has a long way to go to put this form of justice in place. Unless people own the economy (fully participate in it); own the government (through proper representation); and, to reiterate the words of Pope John Paul II quoted at the beginning of this chapter, are given the opportunity "to be more," no productive justice will take place. Those blacks who were recruited from the rural areas to work in the diamond and gold mines had no illusion that they were working in foreign territories and were used as cheap labor that would largely benefit a certain ethnic group. No real love of work can take place under such circumstances. No wonder most of them would say *sisayosebenza kwamlungu* (we are going to work in white man's land or we are going to work for the white man).[6]

The Hebrew God revealed himself as the God of justice who requires justice from his people. If there is any word that is foundational in Scripture, it is the word *justice*.

The Problem of Globalization

Those who support the global ideology argue that globalization opens the eyes of the public to the resources of the entire world. They argue that access to these resources can tremendously benefit developing countries. They further argue that with globalization, knowledge has increasingly become mobile; that geographical location and time constraints are no longer major obstacles. At the heart of globalization, they argue, is technological advance and information dissemination. We did not have to go to France to watch the soccer World Cup in 1998. It was technologically brought to us. This also applies to many world events.

Those who are negative toward globalization see it as a new form of economic imperialism—a tendency to use Third World countries as a dumping ground for Western goods. This form of globalization is a system whose ultimate end is to produce consumers and not producers from the Third World. In his editorial address, K. C. Abraham writes:

> Despite national and international legislation, and commercial and political pressure, the problems related to the socio-economic situation in many countries of Asia remain unchanged, and in some case, are even worsening. . . . All across Asia there are instances of several million bonded labourers,

that is, workers under bond to work even for a life time for debts incurred in the past.[7]

What K. C. Abraham is saying about the Asian countries is currently being experienced in South Africa in a number of ways. While the contexts are different, the economic situation is the same.

The decision by South Africa's largest company, the Anglo-American, to move its primary stock exchange listing from Johannesburg to London should be seen in the wider context of a rapidly changing global scene. Anglo-American is one of the world's largest mining companies. The shift of the base from Johannesburg to London can be interpreted in a number of ways. Some argue that it will be more effective, even to the South African community, when it is based in London where the market is more promising than it is in Johannesburg. This argument seems to favor the size and international reputation of the company more than anything else. The other side of the coin, which seems to be overlooked, is that South African employees who worked in this company for so many years may find it difficult to relocate. But the more pressing question is: Why shift to an already economically advanced country anyway? Is this shift the result of crime, corruption, political instability, and fear? If these are the reasons, is shifting a solution? Of course, no one can pontificate for any company anywhere in this world. But we need to seriously address the issue of priorities. We need to ask: Who benefits the most from this shift?

A caption that appeared in the London *Sunday Times* business section on May 3, 1998, reads: "Living Abroad for a Mere 183 Days Can Save You Tax." It was a response to a query raised by a couple who emigrated to the Netherlands. This couple deposited a sum of a hundred thousand rands to a Nedbank before they left and were earning 9.5 to 10 percent interest that was paid monthly. They were exempted from tax because they were now overseas for a period of 180 days. The question is: How many people can afford to invest that amount of money and how many can even afford to live overseas?

In the *Business Times* of October 25, 1998, this story appeared:

> South African Airways (SAA) seals three new alliances ahead of privatization. The race is on among global carrier groupings to secure a stake in the SAA. . . . The interest in acquiring SAA is strong because global alliances are running out of quality partners to join their consortia *as they vie for international domination*[8] (emphasis mine).

The two countries that are extending their influence over South Africa mentioned in this article are Switzerland and Singapore. An alliance had apparently been signed with Lufthansa prior to the Swiss and Singaporean ones. Of great importance is that British Airways and Lufthansa are described as "arch-enemies." Now they each want to dominate the air by expanding their influence on Africa. One does not have to be an expert to know that this was a global game by big Western powers for domination. The bones of contention are influence, power, and international domination. This reminds me of the Berlin

Summit of 1881 when Africa was carved up among the powerful Western countries. *Imperialism* is the term used to describe the Berlin scramble for Africa in 1881.

With the South African Airways sealing three new alliances with the Swiss, Lufhansa, and Singapore airlines, the following questions arise: Who benefits the most from this alliance? Where do the proceeds go? Who gets recognition and at whose expense? The story further states: "although the government has stated that it will initially sell off 49 percent of SAA, only 30 to 35 percent of the carrier will go to the foreign partner or consortium, the rest finding its way to the National Empowerment Fund and staff." Even if these percentages are adhered to, the truth is that this is a game of superpowers in which the little person remains a dwarf while the superpowers become giraffes.

A summary of the implications of globalization on the South African scene can be stated as follows: Television shows in South Africa are dominated by international images and symbols. When European and American domination goes unchallenged, African values, symbols, and images have very little or no room at all. This is intellectual imperialism. This reminds one of apartheid's low-intensity campaign to control the minds of people. South African programs are not dominating overseas, yet overseas programs are dominating in South Africa.

As a result of globalization, governments of the Third World countries find themselves dominated by transnational corporations. It is these corporations that seem to be regulating the lives of people. The ethical issue here is one of ultimate power. Does it lie with the companies or with the government?

As has been noted already, there is international competitiveness. The Anglo-American base shift from Johannesburg to London, which has been mentioned above, must be seen in the light of this international competitiveness. The other example is that of Denel, the arms producer, that is set to form an alliance with two major deals from European companies. This is an attempt by Denel to break into the international market. Denel's interest is in artillery guns.

Every country, of course, needs a defense force. We dare not undermine the importance of the defense force to defend all the citizens of the country. The apartheid regime spent a lot of money defending an unjust system. One would have thought that the present regime would be cautious in spending too much money on defense. The greatest threat to all the citizens of the country at the moment is poverty, unemployment, and corruption. This situation may escalate into gangsterism, more rape incidents, and robbery. This is enemy number one, which will not be eradicated by military force.

The priority of many markets seems to be the maximizing of profits within a short time. The beneficiaries of this profit are not the poor people. The rich are becoming richer and the poor are becoming poorer. While at the moment the unauthorized settlements, euphemistically called squatter camps, are populated by blacks, in the future, this could spread to the other races of South Africa.

An Aggressive Economic and Educational Empowerment

In the light of the economic realism outlined above, South Africa needs an aggressive program of economic empowerment. That program must be more than reformatory. It must be transformatory. This means a revamping of the structures. Pouring new wine into old wineskins does not work. The problem South Africa is facing is that there still is the residue of apartheid. It is a long way from 1948 (when the National Party came into power) to 1994 (when the government of National Unity was put in place). It would be naive to think that structures firmly anchored for fifty years can be turned overnight. It will take years to remove the psychological damage of so many years. The inequality of races entrenched in the minds of all races of this country in euphemistic terms such as "self development is progress," "homelands," and "serving your own people" still remains. Some accepted their superiority while others accepted their inferiority. It requires an aggressive educational program to reverse that mind-set.

Affirmative action is interpreted by some white people as racism in reverse. This is far from the truth. Affirmative action is a temporary measure to redress the deliberately instituted imbalances of the past. Blacks are the majority in South Africa. Economically, they are at the bottom of the ladder. It is only a deliberate, consciously aggressive program that will reverse that order.

South Africa is rated as among the ten developing countries of the Third World. But what is not usually stated or asked is: What population group is responsible for making South Africa one of those ten developing countries? Historically, it has been the white South Africa that has been developing (if by development we mean the acquiring of technological skills and putting those skills into practice). The black section has had little access to those skills. "Own affairs" meant, among other things, unequal educational opportunities, and this was deliberate. Certain skills were, therefore, reserved for a particular group of people favored by the government of the time. Rural areas of South Africa are deplorably underdeveloped. The informal settlements that are mushrooming all over the country are populated by black people. Masses of black people are not properly integrated into the economic system of the country. President Nelson Mandela has admitted that South Africa has two economies—white and black. This is the reality we cannot evade. Economic enterprise revolves around white experience. As the white economy developed in the past, it encroached on and destroyed the black economy. At the end of the colonizing period, more land was in the hands of the whites. In fact 87 percent of the land was occupied and used by whites, and only 13 percent was in the hands of blacks. We need not be experts to see the unfairness of a racist system like this. It was a matter of the survival of the fittest.

Migrant labor was one of apartheid's means to slow down black economic progress. Since the demolition of apartheid, there has been a steady inflow of black professionals from the townships to the suburbs, though the vast majority of urban blacks still live in the townships and commute by trains, taxis, and buses to the industrial areas. Those blacks who commute from the townships to the suburban areas do so for a number of reasons. First, they want to be nearer workplaces. Second, they want better electrical and water facilities. Third, they want better security systems. Township houses are more crowded than houses in the suburbs and the roads are better in the suburbs than in the townships. If this trend is allowed to continue, it will eventually brain drain the townships and deprive them of professional services. The way forward is economic improvement of the townships. This partly means a development of attractive industry in the townships.

Another form of development is needed for the rural areas of South Africa. This is where the majority of South African blacks live, yet this is where the facilities are worse or almost nonexistent in a number of areas. According to Professor Herbert Vilakazi, a 2 percent gross national product is the only contribution of blacks from the rural areas. This is ridiculously low considering the fact that the majority of blacks live in these rural areas. The new South Africa of the next millennium needs to develop what I nickname "Mbekonics"—an aggressive economic program around the new national president Thabo Mbeki. The new president has already spearheaded talks on what he called African renaissance. Many seminars have since been convened by a number of people who were taken up by this phrase, "African renaissance." Nobody knows exactly what it means. It seems to me that whatever the term means, a program earmarked for the development of the rural areas can be initiated as part of the package for the African renaissance. The government of the second millennium in South Africa should develop new economics. At least 50 percent of the national budget should be earmarked for rural development. The South African GNP (Growth National Plan) must be rurally driven.

If justice is to be done, those rural areas from which cheap labor was obtained should be revisited by plowing the economy of the next millennium back into those rural areas. This is not meant to deprive the city of the growth it deserves. This will be a way of consciously and justly paying back for the misuse of human dignity. It will be a way of admitting that cheap labor was, and still is, wrong.

The Truth and Reconciliation Committee that investigated the injustices of the past, and that received so much coverage from the media, is only a start. Proper reconciliation must aim at restoring what was wrongfully taken away from people. As Professor Mosoma stated, it must "restore proper power balance." Cheap labor was theft and robbery. People's labor was stolen with incentives that attracted them to the pastures in which they were denied the basic human rights. At the same time, people were robbed of their traditional farms and were lured into something that seemed promising and yet it destroyed the cherished extended family units. That robbery must be corrected by consciously and deliberately restoring the dignity of the rural areas. The Department of Home Affairs of the postapartheid period must be congratulated for attempts to restore land to its rightful owners. The process is still going on, but it must be more than just restoring the land to its former occupants. This land must be developed by modern technological means in such a way that rural communities find industry at their doorsteps. Implements for cultivating the land must be made available to the rural people at reasonable or subsidized costs.

Environmental Awareness As Part of Rural Development

Environmental issues are the concern of all races. This is one aspect where the principle of the common good applies. While not neglecting the other groups, I want to pay particular attention to the rural areas where the majority of black people live. Environmental awareness can be part of this program to develop rural areas.

The closeness of human beings to the natural phenomena—the soil—particularly with the background of African traditional culture, is very fertile for environmental studies. Soil conservation, particularly in the rural areas where people live mainly on the produce of the soil, would be a meaningful program. Some of the old mission stations have land that they hardly use. It is no use giving land back to people if those people will not make use of it. Agriculture, which raised the level of the economy of the Asian countries, must be made to promote the economy of the rural areas of South Africa.

Many blacks believe in the veneration of ancestors. The soil is important for them because it is the habitat of those ancestors who are believed to address the living in a number of ways, including dreams, visions, and frenzies. Though they are buried in the soil, the ancestors are believed to be everywhere—in the air we breathe, in the rivers, the stones, the trees, and even on the roofs of houses. They are angry when the air is polluted and when the environment where they live is not properly taken care of. This is fertile soil on which to teach environmental issues.

In many African communities, the traditional extended family arrangement still survives. A geographical area belongs to a clan even if families have their own small farms. This extended family arrangement can be positively exploited for the benefit of the economy. Those designated extended family units can, with the consensus of the clan concerned, be developed for different economic purposes. A lively constructive and positive competition that will encourage business and keep rural people occupied can be initiated. This exercise will serve a double purpose: On the one hand, it will encourage proper farming on a small scale and, on the other hand, it will help to keep the environment clean.

The African creation myth in which all human beings are believed to have emerged at the same time, naturally leads to the communitarian lifestyle with an emphasis on extended families. Consequently, the good that one is supposed to do is for the benefit of the community. The other side of the coin is that the evil one does is to the detriment of the community. It was common practice in traditional Africa for an irresponsible person to be corporally punished even by those who were not related to him. Punishment was for the good of the community. For this reason, naughty people would not easily damage property or pollute the environment for fear of punishment.

The call for an African renaissance, which is largely attributed to President Thabo Mbeki, is partly an attempt to revisit and maximize the good aspects of African traditional life. If taken seriously and driven to its logical conclusions, it can be a good resource for teaching environmental and ecological issues. It must not be assumed, however, that African renaissance means baptizing everything African as good and useful. All cultures are dynamic. They inevitably change with time. Among other things, African renaissance means a rediscovery of the closeness of human nature to general nature and the relationship of human beings to other human beings. It means new ways of communicating with natural phenomena in such a way that one generation prepares for the next.

The Asian countries are a good model for rural development. These countries modernized family farms. Agriculture was behind Chinese growth. The ordinary Chinese person became a market. The economy developed from the grassroots. It was people driven. The philosophy behind this was, first, to develop the people and then to enter the world market. The development of the people before they enter the world market is significant for the South African situation. When people are significantly developed, they enter the world market, not crawling on their knees but standing upright on their feet. Entering the world market on one's knees reduces one to a beggar. But entering the market on one's feet makes one a partner.

This discussion can be extended to reconciliation itself. Reconciliation will be cheap if it simply means forgetting the past. Indeed, the wound of apartheid was very deep. The Truth and Reconciliation Committee did a marvelous job in revealing to the world what happened during apartheid. Some of the suspicions that many ardently fought against were confirmed. But the committee left a deep wound that cannot easily heal unless some reparations are made. To reconcile the haves with the have-nots is difficult, more especially so when the gap was deliberately and consciously made by the haves. Even if the have-nots were to forgive and forget, their children, who will materially inherit very little from them, will inherit the unhealed wound and continue to hate when they should be loving.

The problem, as I see it, is that many people in South Africa crossed the bridge into a supposedly new society without confessing the sins of the past. Many people glibly speak of a new democratic society because there are no more racial barriers that hindered free movement and free communication in the past. Those who were previously privileged are crossing the bridge with their possessions. Those who were underprivileged are crossing with their poverty. That poverty is demonstrated in the multiplying squatter camps and in the poor rural settings. It is not enough to use the same facilities, expose ourselves to the same job opportunities, marry across the racial lines, or observe the same labor laws. It is not enough to say South Africans can now vote for the government of their choice, as has been the case since 1994. While South Africans should appreciate all steps taken to ensure inclusivity in secular and religious institutions, the imbalances of the past cannot be eradicated overnight. What has been achieved leaves more to be desired.

The inclusion of nonwhite students and staff in previously white institutions is appreciated as a step in the right direction. No student can now be disallowed from registering in an institution on the basis of the student's skin pigmentation. South African students can now compete with those of other racial groups, but the process will never be complete until the population of the secular society is reflected in the students and faculty.

Human Dignity and Human Resources

In "The Concept of Social Justice," William K. Frankena writes:

> Social justice is the equal treatment of all persons, at least in the long run. This equal treatment must be qualified in the light of certain principles: the recognition of contribution and the desert, the keeping of agreements, non-injury, non-interference, non-impoverishment, protection, and perhaps the provision and improvement of opportunity. This concern is often referred to as respect for intrinsic dignity or value of the human individual.[9]

Frankena seems to take further what John Locke said about human beings, namely that human beings are endowed with life, liberty, and property. These rights, Locke believed, are given to human beings by God. It is self-evident, therefore, that to deprive human beings of these rights is to deprive them of their human beingness. If human dignity is to be maintained in South Africa, at least, the following principles should be observed:

1. Possess a vision of the common good to which we should all aspire. This means a concentration on the common elements of our society and not on the differences. There is much that is common among the different ethnic groups that form our society. There is the human beingness that cuts across all ethnic differences.

2. Appreciate human labor at whatever level it is performed. There is no one race that is responsible for building up the economic system of South Africa. The history of this country tells us that farms, towns, institutions, and so forth are a joint venture of all those who lived and continue to live in them. No one race should speak of "our fatherland" as if they are solely responsible for its growth and development.

3. Keep human beings firmly at the center of business. The end result of business should not be profit but better human beings who live abundant lives. This applies to all human beings. I am aware of the fact that profit is what business people are mostly concerned about. Profit is the cornerstone of capitalism. But capitalism needs a human face that must be the end result of business. People are neither numbers nor percentages. They are not cogs in machines that can be disposed of any time. Human beings of all races have human dignity that is inherent in them.

4. Take the past seriously. There were imbalances in the past that were deliberately and consciously created to empower some while disempowering others. To say, as some do, that the democratic government is now in place and that the previously exclusive institutions and other channels are now open blurs the real situation. Political freedom has not yet produced economic freedom.

As far as human resources are concerned, a new direction has to be taken. It is common practice in South Africa that skilled people from overseas are invited to take up jobs in companies and institutions. Instead, South Africa should produce skilled people from within the country by plowing money into disadvantaged communities and by looking for potential individuals whose skills can be developed. This is a long-term investment on human beings and that will ensure a bright future for the country.

IBM (International Business Machines) has taken a commendable step and indicated a program to address the shortage of skills. The program was directed specifically to new black empowerment initiatives.[10] This is what can be described as investment in human beings for the sake of the common good. A similar program was launched by the South African Telecommunications Regulatory Authority when in May 1998 it made this bold statement:

> Recognizing that the human resources of a nation are its wealth, the committee will be responsible for advising the council on the development of human resources in the telecommunications sector so as to contribute to economic growth and the creation of wealth needed to improve the standard of living in South Africa.[11]

Initiatives like these are highly commendable, especially when the targets are clearly defined and the reasons clearly spelled out. The injustices of the past in South Africa did not affect all of the people of South Africa in the same way. Starting with those who were affected the most is ethically correct. This is not racism in reverse, as some seem to suggest. It is not an exclusion of those who are not targeted by these programs. It is, rather, a recognition of the unjust practices of the past and an attempt to address them squarely. It is, though not categorically stated, an expression of a confession that what happened in the past should not have happened. It is, in fact, an aspect of reconciliation.

Every ethnic group was, to some extent, wounded. Even those who were protected by the apartheid regime were wounded in the process. The whole of South Africa was morally paralyzed. The many deaths that happened in black townships and rural areas morally affected secluded whites living in suburban areas. Whites of good integrity and moral astuteness could not watch and be comfortable when their fellow human beings were daily molested by ruthless apartheid laws. Some of these white feelings were clearly articulated in the Truth and Reconciliation hearings. Some of those who violated human rights did so not because they were convinced that what they did was right, but because they feared their authorities. The point here is simply that when a mishap affects a society, a section of that society may suffer more than others. Prioritizing, then, means adjusting where the adjustment is most needed.

A society without values is like a body without a soul. We need to rediscover the values that bind a society together. While South Africa is a "rainbow country" with different ethnic groups and values that are treasured by each of those groups, there are basic human values that apply to all the ethnic groups. Profit must not supersede human beingness. It must rather be a servant of humanity. Players in the local, provincial, national, and international game must first consider what it means to be a human being before they consider what profits they can make in the contexts where these human beings live.

Conclusion

In this chapter I have tried to tie together economics, humanity, and justice as these apply to the South African situation. It has been argued that political liberation that is not accompanied by economic liberation is a nonstarter. Economic liberation without justice is another nonstarter. There is no way we can speak of a democratic South Africa unless political and economic justice are part of that democracy. Reconciliation without restitution is also a nonstarter. This cannot be done without sacrifice and discipline. This chapter denies cheap reconciliation and opts for a reconciliation that requires all South Africans to reflect on the past and, where necessary, do restitution that leads to a meaningful reconciliation. A program of development and empowerment is suggested, particularly for the rural areas to recompense their exploitation for cheap labor. Built into this program is an attempt to emphasize environmental and ecological studies in the rural areas.

Notes

1. Pope Paul VI, "Populorum Progresio," *Fair Share* 2, no. 3 (June 1998), 7.

2. This, of course, is not a prerogative of only the Judeo-Christian religion. The concept of justice and fairness is basically human and is found in non-Christian traditions. The Greek city-states, for instance, long developed what they considered to be a just system of weights and measures to protect the exploitation of the poor by the rich.

3. Quoted in J. Stevenson, *A New Eusebius: Documents Illustrative of the History of the Church to A.D. 337* (London: SPCK, 1957), 226.

4. Quoted in V. J. Vourke, *Augustine's Quest of Wisdom: Life and Philosophy of the Bishop of Hippo* (Milwaukee: Bruce Publishing, 1947), 123.

5. Professor Krueger has written extensively on business corporations and productive justice, tracing the concept of justice from the Greek city-states to the present. See David Krueger, David Shriver, Donald Nash, ed., *The Business of Corporation and Productive Justice* (Nashville, Tenn.: Abingdon Press, 1997)

6. The practice of recruiting black males into the mines continued for a long time under the exclusive white governments. Because they wanted money, black males tolerated the obvious exploitation and allowed themselves to be used for cheap labor. They knew which race got the most out of that system.

7. K. C. Abraham, Editorial, *Voices from the Third World*, June 1998, 21.

8. *Business Times*, 25 October 1998, 15.

9. W. K. Frankena, "The Concept of Social Justice," in *Ethics* (Engelwood Cliffs, N.J.: Prentice-Hall, 1963), 23.

10. Shortly after the inauguration of the democratic government in 1994, a program called RDP was initiated. That program has since been superseded by another program called GEAR (Growth, Employment, and Reconciliation). Both these government programs were meant to develop the country, particularly those who were negatively affected by the imbalances of the past.

11. The London *Sunday Times*, 29 November 1998, 12.

Chapter Eleven

Truth and Reconciliation: The South African Experience

Pieter Meiring

IT WAS A DAY never to forget: May 31, 1994. Images of newly elected President Nelson Mandela on the steps of the Union Buildings in Pretoria—smiling broadly at the hundreds of thousands of South Africans in the gardens below him, embracing foreign dignitaries, royalty, colleagues from the liberation struggle, his former opponents—were flashed on television screens across the world. Millions, in six continents, saw jet fighters pass by, trailing the colors of the new South African flag. They heard, many for the first time, the national anthem sung in English, Afrikaans, and in different African languages: *Nkosi sikelele i'Afrika*—God Bless Africa!

We have been celebrating too soon, one observer commented in the days that followed. We have jumped from the time of struggle and liberation right across to a time of jubilation and celebration in one gigantic leap. In between there needed to be a time for remembering, even mourning. We had not, he concluded, sufficiently dealt with our past—and it was time that we started doing that. It was impossible simply to close the books, to forgive and forget. "We have to face the past," Archbishop Desmond Tutu was fond of saying, "Because if you don't face the past, it may return!"

How to Deal with the Past

How do we deal with the past? This question was uppermost in the minds also of the delegates at the multiparty conference, which prior to the elections that brought the new South Africa into being, had to struggle with, on the one hand, the plight of the thousands of victims of the apartheid years and, on the other hand, the needs of the many perpetrators who were guilty of gross human rights violations in the past. A simple blanket amnesty would not work—it would have been a total disregard for and dishonoring of the pain and suffering of the victims. On the other end of the scale, Nuremberg-type trials where the victims take the vanquished to court to be convicted and sentenced were also not advisable, especially if reconciliation was the order of the day.

One of the last decisions taken by the multiparty conference was to establish a Truth and Reconciliation Commission. This was not a unique experiment. Between 1974 and 1994 there had been no less than nineteen truth commissions in the world; for example, in Bolivia, Chile, Argentina, San Salvador, Uganda, Chad, Ethiopia, Rwanda, and even in Germany. Some of them were sponsored internationally by the United Nations or by nongovernmental organizations, some were national commissions sponsored by the executive branch, others by the legislative branch of government.

The South African Truth and Reconciliation Commission

In South Africa, the minister of justice of the Government of National Unity, Dullah Omar, announced his intention to establish a Truth and Reconciliation Commission (TRC), immediately after the inauguration of President Mandela in June 1994. In July 1995, the Act on the Promotion of National Unity and Reconciliation was assented to by Parliament. In August 1995, it was signed by the president of the Republic of South Africa.

What were the aims of the TRC? Let me quote from the preamble to the Act:

> Since the Constitution of the RSA provides a historic bridge between the past of a deeply divided society characterized by strife, conflict, untold suffering and injustice, and a future founded on the recognition of human rights, democracy and peaceful co-existence for all South Africans, irrespective of color, race, class, belief, or sex;
>
> And since it is deemed necessary to establish the truth in relation to past events as well as the motives for and circumstances in which gross violations of human rights have occurred, and to make the findings known in order to prevent a repetition of such acts in future;
>
> And since the Constitution states that the pursuit of national unity, the well-being of all South African citizens, and peace, require reconciliation between the people of South Africa and the reconstruction of society;
>
> And since the Constitution states that there is a need for understanding but not for vengeance, a need for reparation but not for retaliation, a need for ubuntu but not for victimization;
>
> And since the Constitution states that in order to advance such reconciliation and reconstruction amnesty shall be granted in respect of acts, omissions, and offences associated with political objectives committed in the course of the conflicts of the past;
>
> . . . therefore a National Truth and Reconciliation Commission will be instituted, with a four-fold agenda:
>
> 1. To establish a[s] complete a picture as possible of the past. The causes, nature, and extent of suffering of human rights violations between 1960 and

1994 have to be established, taking into consideration the following: the circumstances, factors and context of the violations, the perspectives of the victims, as well as the perspectives and motives of the perpetrators.

2. To facilitate the granting of amnesty. After full disclosure of the relevant facts, and if the deed for which amnesty is required complies with the qualifications of the act (specifically the political nature of the act), amnesty may be granted.

3. To establish and to make known the whereabouts of victims, restoring their human and civil dignity, by granting them the opportunity to relate their own accounts of the violations they suffered, and by recommending reparation measures in this respect.

4. To compile a report, as comprehensive as possible, on the activities and findings of the TRC, with recommendations of measures to prevent future violations of human rights in the country.

Three Committees

In December 1996, after lengthy public scrutiny, the seventeen commissioners of the TRC were appointed by the president. They were given the right to co-opt another eleven committee members from the ranks of the different communities, political parties, academic circles, even faith communities, to ensure that the TRC would be as representative as possible of the South African nation. The commissioners and committee members were divided into three committees, each with its own agenda: the Human Rights Violations Committee, the Amnesty Committee, and the Reparation and Rehabilitation Committee. Added to that were two directorates, one for Investigations, the other for Research. Four regional offices—in Cape Town, Johannesburg, Durban, and East London— were established. The TRC officially commenced with its work on February 1, 1996, and closed its doors on July 31, 1998. The final report of the TRC was handed to President Mandela on October 29, 1998.

During the two and a half years of its existence the Human Rights Violations Committee (HRVC) had been hard at work collecting thousands of statements from victims from all parts of South Africa. Many of the victims were invited to submit their statements at public hearings in a number of cities and towns in the different provinces. Media coverage of the hearings was extensive. The press carried daily reports, and night after night the faces of the many victims appeared on the television screens: tearful faces of mothers who had lost their children, men and women who had lost their spouses, bewildered faces of old men and women who had carried their sorrows for many years, proud faces of young comrades who had fought the struggle, high-profile politicians arriving in Mercedes Benzes, simple folk from faraway places who travelled by bus or taxi, farmers who had lost a loved one in a land-mine explosion, innocent passers-by injured when a bomb, hidden in a busy street, exploded.

The definition of "gross human rights violations" in the act was rather restrictive. Not everyone in the country who suffered in one way or another, or were forcefully relocated by apartheid laws, nor those who were humiliated and discriminated against, automatically qualified for statement making. If that were the case, millions would have joined the queue. Victims of gross human rights violations were defined as victims of murder, manslaughter, kidnapping, rape, severe ill treatment, and torture that caused permanent mental or physical harm. Nobody really knew how many of these victims from the different communities, black and white, would come to the fore. By the end, no less than a 140 public hearings had taken place countrywide; 21,400 victims submitted statements; the names of 27,000 victims were officially recorded. To the majority of victims the exercise proved to be worth their while, even though it was difficult to take the stand and to relive the past. Tears flowed freely, but they usually were tears of healing. An old gentleman from Soweto seemed to speak for many when he declared at a Johannesburg hearing: "When my tormentor tortured me at John Vorster Square, he sneered at me: 'Shout your lungs out! Nobody will ever hear you!' Now, at long last, people do hear."

Not everybody reacted positively; there were also those who returned home disappointed and frustrated. But they formed a minority. For thousands of victims it was, indeed, a cathartic experience. I quote from my diary (East London Hearing April 16-19, 1996):

Was everything worth it? I asked myself when, after one of the morning sessions, I walked outside.

What one of the Xhosa women—one of the unknown, practically forgotten witnesses—had to say in the hall just now did not only move the archbishop to tears, but left everyone of us with a lump in the throat. With effort she put her tale on the table: of how she, years ago, sent her fourteen-year-old son to the shop to buy bread. There was unrest in the township and somewhere along the way it must have happened that the boy landed in the cross-fire. For some reason the Security Police arrested the wounded child and subjected him to brutal torture. Two days later, the mother who, panic-stricken, fumbled about to find out what had happened to her son, saw, on her neighbors' television set during the eight o'clock news, the boy being pulled down from a bakkie (open vehicle) by his ankles, how he was being dragged across the tarmac.

It was difficult for the old mother to relate how the police eventually gave her an address where she could find her son. When she arrived there, it was the mortuary. With her own hands she had to prepare her son's body—with the bullet wounds, a gaping wound on the back of his head, the burn marks where he was tortured—for the funeral. One could have heard a pin drop in the hall.

My lunch in my hand, I encountered the woman in the midst of a small group of victims.

"Madam, please tell me," I asked, "you have come such a long way, over so many years, with your story. Yesterday you had to travel such a long distance to come here. All of us saw how difficult it was for you to tell the story of your son in front of all the people. Please tell me: was it worth it?"

The tear marks were still on her cheeks. But when she raised her head and smiled, it was like the dawn breaking:

"Oh yes, Sir, absolutely! It was difficult to talk about all these things. But tonight, for the first time in sixteen years, I think I will be able to sleep through the night. Maybe tonight I will sleep soundly without having nightmares!"

Apart from the victims' hearings, a number of "special event hearings" have been organized to look into specific events: Sharpville 1960, the Soweto uprising of 1976, the Boipatong massacres of the early 1990s, the activities of the so-called Third Force and others. Special interest groups were also invited to hearings: women, youth and children, the media, the health profession, prisoners, conscripts. Political parties from across the board made lengthy submissions at hearings specially organized for them. A special hearing for the Christian churches and the other faith communities in South Africa, to explain their role in the history of the country, was held in East London.

Under Section 29 of the Act, the TRC was mandated to subpoena individuals to appear before the commission if additional information on events, or the involvement of people during these events, was required. In the four regional offices of the TRC these Section 29 hearings became a weekly occurrence. Bit by bit, piece by piece, the TRC tried to build a reliable database of gross violations in the country over the past thirty-four years in the history of South Africa.

When Winnie Midizikela Mandela, the ex-wife of President Mandela, appeared before the nation (November 24-December 24, 1997) to answer questions on no less than eighteen charges, world attention was focussed on the proceedings, as was the case when former president P. W. Botha was subpoenaed. Some of the most shocking revelations resulted from the investigation into the involvement of Dr. Wouter Basson and his colleagues in the former Defence Force's secret chemical and biological weapons program.

The second committee, the Amnesty Committee (AC), had an equally arduous task: to receive applications of perpetrators—from the different sides of the struggle—who needed amnesty. The offer of amnesty was extremely generous—to some critics far too generous—enabling perpetrators of gross violations, on making a full disclosure of the acts under consideration and by persuading the AC of the political and military nature of those acts, to walk out of the amnesty court with a clean slate. No legal actions or civil claims could be brought against a perpetrator once he had received amnesty. The AC consisted of three judges and two lawyers who, together with their legal team, had to trasverse the country to conduct their hearings. The AC had been given very strong powers, having the authority of a court of appeal.

As was the case with the HRVC hearings, nobody really knew how many perpetrators would come to the fore to avail themselves of the amnesty offer.

The AC hearings had a rather slow start, with most of the applications from prisoners serving sentences for a myriad of reasons. Most of them did not really qualify, having been convicted on purely criminal charges. But then, by the middle of 1996, the small stream turned into a river. In the wake of General Johan van der Merwe, the chief of police during the last years of the National Party government, a number of policemen, especially from the ranks of the security police, made their way to the AC. A smaller number of military officers as well as politicians representing many parties followed suit, even though some high-profile politicians and senior military officers, to the disappointment of many, refused to do so.

May I, again, quote from my diary. More than two years after his initial appearance before the Amnesty Committee, General Van der Merwe, sat at his final hearing:

> Johan van der Merwe had aged noticeably. I reminded him that at his first appearance before the TRC, more than two years ago, we had also been standing talking. At that stage everyone had been grateful that he was present, because he had paved the way for many colleagues and subordinates in the Police Force to also come forward.
>
> I had then asked him, just before he was to testify: "Commissioner, what thoughts are going through your head this morning?"
>
> "Well," he had answered, "there are two things, especially, that I am preoccupied with. In the first place, my colleagues queuing behind me and I are unsure where the TRC is taking us, about what the end of it all will be. And, secondly, we are frustrated—no, furious—because the political leaders of the country, the people who earlier on had appointed us and given us orders, who congratulated us and sometimes gave us medals, have now left us in the lurch."
>
> Commissioner Van der Merwe remembered that conversation. With slight amusement, he said, "I still stand by what I said, although I would like to add a third, and fourth, and fifth point today."

The amnesty process had not been without controversy. From the start spokespersons from the side of some victims—notably a number of high-profile victim families, for instance the Biko, Mxenge, and Goniwe families in the Eastern Cape—strongly and publicly opposed the amnesty process. It was, to their way of thinking, morally unacceptable to allow perpetrators of heinous crimes to walk away, scot-free. They should be charged in court and sentenced. Also, the granting of amnesty took away from the victims and their families the possibility of civil suits against their tormentors. Amnesty was costing the victims dearly, they argued.

The first rounds of amnesty hearings were mainly those of perpetrators from the ranks of the previous regime. Day after day the media reported on the criminal acts of police and security police, of people employed by the previous National Party government. A perception among some whites in the country quickly developed that the TRC process was little more than a witch hunt, a one-sided action of blacks (the ANC) against whites with the single purpose to embarrass the previous government. The TRC did its very best to allay these perceptions and fears. The TRC was mandated to work in an evenhanded, unbiased way—and Tutu as well as the Amnesty Committee judges were at pains to point out, time and again, that the TRC indeed operated in that way. Not everybody was persuaded. Ironically, at the very end—exactly one day before the final report was to be tabled—the ANC went to court to request an interdict against the publication of the findings, because the report, in the ANC's opinion, "criminalized" *their* role in the struggle. Perpetrators from the liberation movement, fighting *against* apartheid, operated on a higher moral ground than perpetrators from the previous regime who fought to *uphold* apartheid, and according to the ANC should have been treated with more leniency.

The third committee, called the Reparation and Rehabilitation Committee (RRC), received a number of responsibilities. The first task was to see to it that the necessary support systems were put into place to help the victims who appeared at the hearings, as well as their families, through the often traumatic process of reliving and dealing with the past. This service was, after some debate, also extended to perpetrators who applied for amnesty and their families.

A second task was to assess the harm suffered by the victims and their families and to make proper recommendations to government on reparation and rehabilitation. In order to do this the RRC had to keep proper record of the personal circumstances of the victims and their families, carefully listing their most urgent needs. Five categories of needs quickly manifested themselves: medical, emotional, educational, material, and "symbolic" needs—the latter referring to such symbolic acts as erecting tombstones, reburials, expunging of criminal records, erecting memorials and monuments, special ceremonies of reconciliation, and the like.

The RRC worked hard, preparing its proposals, lobbying the different provincial and national government departments to make available special services for the victims on an urgent as well as a long term basis. The TRC felt strongly about it: The victims of gross human rights violations had a legal and a moral right to proper reparation. If the amnesty process seems to indicate that the TRC process is a "perpetrator-friendly" process, the reparation proposals were to show that the process was indeed also, and primarily, "victim friendly." The very generous offer of total indemnity made to perpetrators was to be counterbalanced by proper reparation for the victims. Taking into account the needs of victims, five categories of reparation proposals were decided upon: urgent interim reparation for victims who were old, sick, or in dire need; individual reparation grants (ranging from R17,000 to R21,000 per person, annually, for six years); the improvement of community services; symbolic reparation; and institutional reparation.

Success?

The Truth and Reconciliation process was expensive, not only in terms of money, but especially in terms of manpower and time. Did it succeed in its task?

José Zalaquett (who headed the Chilean Truth Commission) had great expectations for the truth and reconciliation process in our country. In one of his documents, Zalaquett, however, made the interesting remark based on the collective wisdom of the nineteen similar commissions held worldwide over the past decades that three clear prerequisites for success had manifested: In the first place, the nation has to accept ownership for the process. Second, government must show political will not only to appoint and provide the commission with an infrastructure, but also to implement the proposals made by the commission at the end of its course. Third, according to Zalaquett, the process must stop! Just as a patient undergoing a critical operation should not stay in the theater too long, a truth commission should know when to call it a day.

It is not difficult to determine whether the last two prerequisites have been met. Whether the government, which set the process in motion at the beginning of 1996 with the support of all the political parties and maintained the infrastructure, will ultimately also be prepared to execute all the proposals—especially those that deal with the reparation and compensation of victims—will be determined within the following year or two. And regarding the conclusion of the process, well, this *has* finally taken place! Not as soon as everyone wanted—instead of eighteen months it became thirty—but eventually the end did come. With the appointment of extra judges on the panel and doubling its hearings, the Amnesty Committee should have its final addendum report tabled by July 1999.

But to assess the first prerequisite, that the nation should make the process its own, is quite another matter. Historians would be the first to warn that it is far too early to make a proper assessment of this. Only in ten or twenty years—possibly only a generation or two later—will it finally be clear whether the TRC achieved its goals. But, albeit preliminary or tentative, a few remarks can still be made on the way in which the victims and the perpetrators, as well as the wider community, owned the process.

For the 21,400 victims and their families, who submitted their stories in writing or told them in public, it was generally a healing experience. Not everyone experienced it positively; there were also those who returned home disappointed and frustrated. But for the great majority it was a cathartic experience, even though it was difficult to take the stand, to relive the past. The tears that flowed freely were usually tears of healing. The aged Xhosa woman who in East London told the terrible story of her fourteen-year-old child's being tortured and killed, spoke on behalf of many others: "Oh, yes, Sir, it was worth the trouble!"

A nagging worry, however, remains: What about the other victims, the large number of men and women who did *not* come forward? Some, also from the white community, stayed away because of political reasons or because they did not trust the process; others, like many in the war-torn KwaZulu-Natal, for fear of intimidation and retaliation. Then there were also the millions who probably wanted to come forward, but the narrow definition that the act ascribed to gross human rights violations—murder, culpable homicide, kidnapping, rape, serious torture resulting in physical and psychological damage—effectively disqualified them. Millions of South Africans were, however, humiliated and persecuted over the past decade, arrested for petty apartheid offenses and dragged to prison. A total of 3.5 million were forcefully removed from their homes and "transferred" to other parts of the country. These people probably have just as much bottled-up frustration and pain, just as many questions and an equally great need for a process of healing and catharsis. What is to be done for them? Do they not also have the right to be heard?

For the more than seven thousand amnesty applicants, the process meant just as much, especially for those who were granted amnesty. Initially most of the applications came from behind bars, from criminals who did not really qualify but wanted to put their case to the TRC as a last resort. When General Johan van der Merwe and his police colleagues eventually reported to the Amnesty Committee, the initially small stream became a river. The fact that relatively few politicians and Defence Force officers from the former dispensation came forward was reason for great concern. When the TRC closed its doors, it was reported that the final number of amnesty applications had grown to 7,124. Of them, approximately two-thirds, 4,696, had already been dealt with—the majority without the need for protracted public hearings. In cases where public hearings took place, seventy-five applicants had already been granted amnesty, while sixty-one applications had been turned down. Of the applications being handled, 54 percent came from the ANC, 20 percent from the side of previous government and its security forces, 12 percent from the Pan-Africanist Congress (PAC), 9 percent from the Inkatha Freedom Party (IFP), and 5 percent from the far-right wing.

A great concern was the fact that the Amnesty Committee—because of the unexpected large number of applications and the lengthy and reasonably tedious legal procedure required by law—could not finish its work on time. When the final report was tabled, some twelve hundred amnesty applications were still outstanding, and all of them required public hearings.

Three Concerns

Three concerns, however, remain if the nation truly has to take ownership of the truth and reconciliation process.

The Need to Acknowledge and Record the Past Is Still with Us

"Why don't we just close the books and get on with life?" many asked during the TRC years. The answer, of course, was: "Yes, the time has to come when we should be able to put our past behind us. But you can only close a book, once you have opened it properly." The pain of the past, the history of what had happened to our anguished society, needed to be acknowledged and recorded. On an individual level, the experiences of men and women and children—many of them half forgotten by history—needed to be remembered. There were those who were invited to speak, and those who were challenged to listen.

The process, however, has to continue. Thousands of victims who, because of the strict definition of the act, did not come to the fore, still have to speak. "Africa is a place of story telling," Ellen Kutzwayo once wrote. "We need more stories, never mind how painful the exercise might be. This is how we will learn to love one another. Stories help us to understand, to forgive and to see things through someone else's eyes."

The question remains: Can we handle the truth? How do we react to the harrowing disclosures made by the victims and the perpetrators? These have long since ceased to be academic questions. In the past years, with the daily items in the papers and the nightly reports on television, we have learned how fragile our society is. At the inauguration of the TRC, President Mandela said: "Looking at the guilt and the suffering of the past, one cannot but conclude: In a certain sense all of us are victims of apartheid, all of us are victims of our past." The truth of that statement, we have come to experience, time and time again.

The truth, as far as was humanly possible, had come out. The victims needed it. It was the first step in the direction of reparation and rehabilitation. José Zalaquett commented on his experience in Latin America: "We owe the truth to the victims and their families," he emphasized, "the truth is at least as important as justice." The nation, too, needed to hear the truth—as far as the TRC was able to present it. The TRC was not a perfect commission, and the report not a perfect report. Future generations will, no doubt, be able to point out the deficiencies. What the commission, however, achieved, in the words of Michael Ignatief was "to curtail the number of lies that up till now had free reign in society." The fact that the TRC's report was in the end criticized from all sides, that all political parties—the National Party as well as the ANC—felt their toes had been trodden on, in a peculiar way, emphasized its impartiality.

Speaking the truth, however, is one thing; acknowledging the truth is quite another. Many South Africans, who in the past sided with the previous regime, mostly English- and Afrikaans-speaking whites, were thrown into a deep existential crisis by the TRC revelations. Many reacted similarly to people who undergo a deep traumatic experience—terminal illness, the death of a spouse or a child, the breakup of a marriage—moving from one stage to the other: from outright denial, to anger, to a position of bargaining, to a deep depression, to eventual acceptance and peace.

It was at this stage that a person's faith, the support given to him or her by the churches, became of utmost importance, guiding people along the way, helping them to deal with their anxieties and fears to the point where they, too, experienced the fact that the truth eventually does set one free.

The Need for Forgiveness and Reconciliation Is Still with Us

The name of the commission I am reporting on was the Truth *and Reconciliation* Commission. Uncovering the past, learning about the different contexts within which people operated, trying to understand the motives of all the role-players in the drama, provided for only one leg of the TRC. The other leg was the leg of reconciliation, for in the long run, after the walls of history have been brought down, we need to face one another: perpetrator and victim, white and black, young and old.

Forgiveness and reconciliation, we learned, can never by obtained in a cheap and superficial way. True to say, there were the cynics (realists, they would call themselves!) who warned against high expectations, who contended that if only you can keep people out of each other's hair, if you can teach people just to tolerate one another, you had to be content.

Others did have high hopes. The majority of South Africans profess to be Christians, confessing that we are able to forgive and to reconcile and accept one another as Christ has accepted us. The churches were challenged to keep alive the belief that "in Christ there is a new creation, the old has passed away, the new has come. . . .This is from God who through Christ reconciled us to Himself—and gave us the ministry of reconciliation" (2 Cor 5: 17-18). Drawing from the deepest sources of their beliefs, members of other faith communities— Jewish, Muslim, Hindu, Buddhist—in a similar way encouraged their fellow believers to reach out, and to work for reconciliation in the country.

During the last months of the TRC's life, serious attention was given to the process of reconciliation. Workshops were held countrywide where all the stakeholders in the process—from state departments and civil society, from churches and religious organizations, from NGOs (non-governmental organizations) and universities—were asked to help us think through the process. Many questions needed answers: What, exactly, did we mean by reconciliation? What was attainable? How does one handle the necessary prerequisites of reconciliation: justice, reparation, and restitution? Who were the instruments of reconciliation? Who would carry the flame once the TRC's life comes to an end?

We all recognized that it was a costly and time-consuming process. Reconciliation could not be "organized," could not be switched "on" and "off." Microwave reconciliation does not last. Sometimes, however, heaven smiled on us, so that even in the hectic program of the TRC, heartwarming instances of reconciliation did occur. "It never ceases to astonish me," Archbishop Tutu often says, "the magnanimity of many victims who suffered the most heinous of violations, who reach out to embrace their tormentors with joy, willing to forgive and wanting to reconcile."

A last quote from my diary (Port Elizabeth, April 21, 1997):

"One can see God's influence in what is happening tonight," Mcibisi Xundu, pastor and committee member of the TRC said. Looking solemnly at Eric Taylor, former security police officer, who applied for amnesty for his part in the killing of the 'Cradock Four.' "It is God who has led you to take this step towards reconciliation. . ."

A few weeks earlier a young Dutch Reformed Church pastor Charl Coetzee had approached me with a request. One of his parishoners, Eric Taylor, wanted to meet the Goniwe family. He was applying for amnesty for the murder of a well known ANC activist, Matthew Goniwe and his three colleagues.

A meeting was eventually arranged in Coetzee's church on a Monday night. Mrs. Goniwe, a strong critic of the TRC process, refused to come, but the rest of the family—as well as the families of the other members of the Cradock Four—travelled from Cradock to Port Elizabeth for the occasion. Suspicion and anger were in the air, Coetzee reported. The families of the victims had many questions, needed many answers. Taylor answered the best he could. At the end of the evening he turned to the Goniwe family, and to their colleagues: "I came to ask you to forgive me, if the Lord can give you the strength to do that. . ."

The response was moving. One after the other, the family members came to the fore to shake Eric Taylor's hand, and to assure him of their willingness to accept his apology, to forgive him for what he had done. Many a cheek was wet with tears.

The son of Mathew Goniwe walked up to the ex-policeman. His right arm was in plaster, but with his left arm he embraced Eric Taylor. "It is true," he said. "You murdered our father. But we forgive you!"

When Charl Coetzee reported to me on the meeting, I immediately phoned Desmond Tutu in Cape Town.

"I have heard the news," he commented. "Mrs Goniwe told me this morning that, the next time, she would be there!"

When I, after a few minutes wanted to end the conversation, to replace the phone on the hook, Tutu called to me (in Afrikaans):

"Oh, no, old chap, not so quick! First, we are going to pray."

I will never forget his prayer over the telephone line, he in Cape Town and I in Johannesburg:

"O Lord, we thank You for being the God of Surprises—for surprising us every day. . . for the miracles of reconciliation in our country, time and time again!"

The Need to Create a New Moral Order in South Africa Is Still with Us

How do we learn the lessons of the past? How do we build a new South Africa without repeating the errors of the society we come from? The TRC was tasked by the act to provide, to the best of its ability, answers to these questions. This the commission could never attempt on its own. Creating a new moral order, realizing the fond dream of "a rainbow nation," still needs all the willpower, all the wisdom, all the effort, of every single member of society.

South Africa has recently adopted its new constitution, founded on the highest principles of human dignity and human rights. But what is on paper needs to be put into practice.

As we step out of the wreckage of the past, South Africa is still in many respects a spiritual wasteland, a reality painfully expressed by the appalling crime rate, the breakdown of family structures, a growing disrespect for the dignity of the human person. We are a nation in need of healing in every sense of the word.

But there is hope. Desmond Tutu, at the end of the process, after guiding South Africa on its via dolorosa, concluded: "We have been wounded but we are being healed. It is possible even with our past of suffering, anguish, alienation, and violence to become one people, reconciled, healed, caring, compassionate, and ready to share as we put our past behind us to stride into the glorious future God holds before us as the Rainbow People of God."

"I Accept the Report As It Is"

It was, once again, a day never to forget: Thursday, October 29, 1998. Just after twelve o'clock Desmond Tutu rose to present the official report of the TRC to President Mandela, at a ceremony in Pretoria. Millions of South Africans as well as overseas viewers, again glued to their TV screens, saw the archbishop, smiling broadly, pretending to stagger under the the of the five heavy volumes.

He had every reason to! Not only did the TRC staff work for months to finalize the report—it was nearly not handed in on that day. A few days earlier the National Party sought an interdict to prohibit certain information on the role of former president F. W. de Klerk to be published. And then the final blow: the evening before the report was to be presented to President Mandela, the ANC, too, went to the Cape High Court to stop the report from being published. It criminalized their role in the struggle, the ANC protested.

Early the next morning, the judge gave his ruling: The presentation may proceed.

> "Not everybody will be happy with the report," Tutu remarked at the ceremony. "Many have already started to discredit it in advance. But even should they succeed, what will they achieve? It will change nothing of the facts. . . "

> "I accept the report as it is, with its deficiencies as the TRC's contribution to reconciliation and nationbuilding," Mandela answered. He added: "Let us approach the future together. Finally free, we can accept our calling with responsibility. But to build a better future, we need everybody's hands—your hands as well as mine."

As if to say "Amen" to that, the choir from Soweto sang—even more beautifully than on that remarkable day four-and-a-half years earlier, when at the Union Buildings in Pretoria, the process was started—*Nkosi Sikele i'Afrika*, God Bless Africa!

Index

abolitionism, 27-30. *See also* church; movement.
Abraham, K. C. *See* globalization.
Act on the Promotion of National Unity and Reconciliation, 188
affirmative action, 91, 149, 150, 173, 178
African National Congress (ANC): and authoritarian rule, 95; banned, 106; founders of, 59; and Bantu Holomisa, 92; and the Kairos Document, 113; and the liberation movement, 81; and Winnie Mandela, 92; and the National Party, 85; and religious organizations, 90, 92; and the sunset-clause, 112; and the Truth and Reconciliation Commission, 193, 199. *See also* government.
Africanization, 105
Afrikaners: alienated, 32; and Christian principles, 133; cultural struggle of, 130; independent state for, 146; and industrialization, 22; and land rights, 30; and nationalism, 29, 33, 38, 42; and self-government, 24; and the University, 134
agonism, 159, 160
agriculture: prosperous, 25; in South Africa, 22, 24; in the United States, 20, 21. *See also* environment.

American Holocaust, the, 22. *See also* indigenous.
amnesty: and the Amnesty Committee (AC), 189, 191-93, 195; blanket, 187
Anglo-Boer War, 32, 42, 59
antagonism, 159, 160
antiapartheid: advent of, 63; and Babel, 107-8, 109; campaign against, 89, 90; critique of, 110; and the Defiance Campaign, 66; defined as false faith, 107; degenerated, 115-16, 117; dehumanizing system of, 107; demolition of, 178-79; and Jaap Durand, 108, 110; ecclesiastical, 116; and English-speaking churches, 38, 41; formal rejection of, 47; guilt of, 48-49; heretical theology of, 110, 116, 117; origins of, 49; policy, 63; philosophical justification for, 129; political system of, 123, 136; and power, 172; racist, 175; not racism per se, 114-15; reality of, 33; regime of, 91; residue of, 178; resolutions, 48; root of, 108; and South African churches, 71-73; sinful, 110; and M. Singh, 168-69; as *status confessionis*, 67, 110, 116; Stoker's philosophy of, 130-32; struggle against, 67; system of, 116; theological

About the Contributors

M. Elaine Botha is professor of philosophy and academic vice-president at Redeemer College, Ancaster, Ontario, and adjunct faculty member at the Institute for Christian Studies, Toronto, Canada.

H. Russel Botman is professor of practical theology and missiology in the Faculty of Theology, University of Stellenbosch.

G. Daan Cloete is professor in New Testament studies in the department of religion and theology at the University of the Western Cape, Bellville. He also served as the dean of the faculty of religion and theology, and as acting rector of the university.

Johan Degenaar is professor of philosophy, emeritus, at the University of Stellenbosch.

John W. De Gruchy is the Robert Selby Taylor Professor of Christian Studies at the University of Cape Town.

Lourens M. du Plessis is director of the Research Unit for Legal and Constitutional Interpretation at the University of Stellenbosch.

Lizo D. Jafta is head of the department of church history at the University of South Africa, Pretoria.

Tracy Kuperus is assistant professor of political studies at Gordon College, Wenham, Massachusetts.

Pieter Meiring is head of the department of science of religion and missiology at the Faculty of Theology at the University of Pretoria. He is also a regular columnist in the Afrikaans daily newspaper *Die Beeld.* He also served as a member of the Truth and Reconciliation Commission.

R. Drew Smith is scholar-in-residence and director of the public influences of African-American Churches Project, Leadership Center, Morehouse College, Atlanta, Georgia.

Desmond Tutu is archbishop emeritus of the diocese of Cape Town, South Africa, and currently the Robert W. Woodruff Visiting Professor of Theology at Emory University in Georgia. He was the 1984 winner of the Nobel Peace Prize and chairman of the Truth and Reconciliation Commission.

William E. Van Vugt is professor of history at Calvin College, Grand Rapids, Michigan.

DATE DUE

AUG 1 1 2005

MAR 2 0 2006

MAY 1 7 2006

APR 2 0 2007

HIGHSMITH #45230